W9-CWV-725

Seeking Growth under Financial Volatility

Seeking Growth under Financial Volatility

Edited by Ricardo Ffrench-Davis

338.98
S451

© Economic Commission for Latin America and the Caribbean 2006

All rights reserved. No reproduction, copy or transmission of this publication may be made without written permission.

No paragraph of this publication may be reproduced, copied or transmitted save with written permission or in accordance with the provisions of the Copyright, Designs and Patents Act 1988, or under the terms of any licence permitting limited copying issued by the Copyright Licensing Agency, 90 Tottenham Court Road, London W1T 4LP.

Any person who does any unauthorized act in relation to this publication may be liable to criminal prosecution and civil claims for damages.

The authors have asserted their rights to be identified as the authors of this work in accordance with the Copyright, Designs and Patents Act 1988.

First published 2006 by
PALGRAVE MACMILLAN
Houndmills, Basingstoke, Hampshire RG21 6XS and
175 Fifth Avenue, New York, N. Y. 10010
Companies and representatives throughout the world

PALGRAVE MACMILLAN is the global academic imprint of the Palgrave Macmillan division of St. Martin's Press, LLC and of Palgrave Macmillan Ltd. Macmillan® is a registered trademark in the United States, United Kingdom and other countries. Palgrave is a registered trademark in the European Union and other countries.

ISBN-13: 978–1–4039–96350 hardback
ISBN-10: 1–4039–96350 hardback

This book is printed on paper suitable for recycling and made from fully managed and sustained forest sources.

A catalogue record for this book is available from the British Library.

Library of Congress Cataloging-in-Publication Data

Seeking growth under financial volatility / edited by Ricardo Ffrench-Davis.
    p. cm.
  Includes bibliographical references and index.
  ISBN 1–4039–9635–0 (cloth)
    1. Economic development–Case studies. 2. Latin America–Economic policy. 3. Developing countries–Economic policy. 4. Comparative economics. I. Ffrench-Davis, Ricardo.
  HD82.S396 2005
  338.98–dc22   2005050154

10   9   8   7   6   5   4   3   2   1
15   14   13   12   11   10   09   08   07   06

Printed and bound in Great Britain by
Antony Rowe Ltd, Chippenham and Eastbourne

Contents

University Libraries
Carnegie Mellon University
Pittsburgh, PA 15213-3890

List of Tables

List of Figures

List of Contributors

Ricardo Ffrench-Davis, Principal Regional Adviser of ECLAC and Professor of Economics, University of Chile, Santiago de Chile; former Director of Research, Central Bank of Chile, and Director of CIEPLAN.

Stephen Gelb, Executive Director, The EDGE Institute, and Visiting Professor in Development Studies, University of the Witwatersrand, Johannesburg, South Africa.

Zainal-Abidin Mahani, Professor, University of Malaysia, Kuala Lumpur, Malaysia.

José Antonio Ocampo, Under-Secretary General for Economic and Social Affairs of the United Nations, New York; and former Executive Secretary of ECLAC and Minister of Finance of Colombia.

Kwanho Shin, Professor, Korea University, Seoul, Republic of Korea.

Leonardo Villar, member of the Board of the Central Bank of Colombia and Professor of Economics, University of Los Andes, Bogotá, Colombia; former Technical Vice-Minister of Finance of Colombia.

Yunjong Wang, Vice President, Economic Research Office, SK Research Institute for SUPEX Management, Seoul, Republic of Korea.

Roberto Zahler, President of Zahler & Co, Santiago de Chile; former President of the Central Bank of Chile, 1991 to 1996.

Foreword

by José Luis Machinea

This volume deals with macroeconomic issues and their relation to economic growth. It belongs to a line of research developed by ECLAC during recent years on the globalization of financial volatility, macroeconomic management, and growth.

This line of research has been encouraged by the frustrating GDP growth of Latin American economies since the 1980s. Even disregarding the so-called lost decade resulting from the debt crisis, in the subsequent period 1990–2004 growth averaged a disappointing 2.6% per year. One policy area associated to that outcome has been a short-legged macroeconomic environment, detrimental for both capital and labor performance. It has been dominated by highly unstable aggregate demand and misaligned exchange rates, frequently far away from trend levels. These imply an "unfriendly" environment for investment decisions, commonly with "wrong" prices for an efficient resource allocation. Our purpose in this volume is to analyze policy measures that contribute to avoid costly mistakes and to recover economic growth. We build on the reforms already made, making *reforms to the reforms* when necessary. We seek to achieve a *macroeconomics-for-growth*, or *real macroeconomics*.

This new book is the result of a research project coordinated by ECLAC, supported by the Ford Foundation, on *Management of Volatility, Financial Globalization and Growth in EEs*, studying the gestation and bust of the Asian crises and the contagion experienced by Latin America. Additionally, the country cases of Korea and Malaysia in East Asia under the Asian crisis, and of South Africa in the post-apartheid period were analyzed. These three countries exhibit features that make them especially relevant.

Capital flows have been at the core of the financial crises, macro-instability and, in general, the poor growth performance of EEs in recent times. The demand for "accountability" has grown recently, activated by the fact that, in the last seven-year period (1998–2004), the Latin American economies (LACs) grew only 1.7% per year on average and per capita GDP stagnated.[1] The growth performance of South Africa is also dismal, though the causes are more complex than in Latin America. The six main East Asian countries performed somewhat better over that period, with a 3.3% average GDP increase, where the Republic of Korea and Malaysia stand out as two dynamic outliers. This average is, however, well below the 7 or 8% rates of their previous historical performance. In both regions, real macroeconomic instability – in terms of aggregate demand, interest rates and exchange rates – has been present in an outstanding fashion. In fact, in these recent crises sharp gaps between actual and potential GDP and outlier exchange and interest rates have been recorded. Actual total factor productivity has contracted and the supply of physical and human capital has been discouraged. Several EEs have stepped down to lower growth paths; from Argentina, to Korea, to Malaysia or Chile.

Firms and labor, as well as tax proceeds, have been hit by real macroeconomic instability. Extreme macroinstability has been associated with strong swings in aggregate demand. For instance, all across-the-board changes in Latin American economic activity have been led by fluctuations in aggregate demand; the sharper swings in GDP have been endogenous to those changes in aggregate demand, all of which have been driven by capital surges. The recessive adjustments in East Asia in 1997–98 were also led by reversals of capital flows, which followed the voluminous previous inflows.

Of course, out-surges are not the only relevant variable; there are other international variables and many country specific, economic and political, variables playing around. However, for the Latin American region as a whole, capital account cycles have been notably strong compared to any combination of other domestic or external variables. The sudden stops in capital flows have been located mainly in flows other than greenfield foreign direct investment (FDI), and have largely been associated with the behavior of the private sector, rather than the fiscal accounts. We show that the private sector response has been, frequently, misled by a procyclical bias in macroeconomic policies.

We are convinced that the present volume is a significant contribution to this crucial concern of ECLAC: to develop a market economy capable to growth in a sustained way, in which both productivity and

[1] We include, in these averages, estimates for 2004 that was a year of recovery, the best since 1997 for the majority of LACs; South Africa and East Asian economies also exhibited significant recovery in 2004.

the welfare of people expand persistently, and are distributed in a growingly more equitable fashion. That is why we are highly indebted with the authors of the chapters of this volume and, particularly, with Ricardo Ffrench-Davis, the coordinator of this project.

José Luis Machinea
Executive Secretary
ECLAC

Preface

by Ricardo Ffrench-Davis

Development is a complex process, and few countries have been successful in a sustained fashion. An efficient combination of macro and meso or micro policies is required; just missing one significant ingredient can lead to failure. Domestic efforts are crucial, but also the external environment is most relevant. Our main concern is the effect on growth and equity, the two crucial joint objectives of economic policy. The aim is to develop a growing, better functioning economy, in which both the productivity and the well-being of people will increase. How do capital stock, capital formation and labor markets react to changes in capital flows and the macroeconomic environment? How does overall productivity evolve and how is it distributed among people? How can alternative macroeconomic approaches contribute to build equity into the economic system and thus achieve growth with equity? What are the key variables behind the time span of adjustment and how different markets respond? Some of these concerns are addressed in this book.

This policy-oriented research follows a solid line of work of ECLAC on macroeconomics, capital flows and the nexus with growth. Two related institutional books, published in recent years by ECLAC, are: (i) *Growth with Stability*, a contribution to the 2002 Monterrey International Conference on Financing for Development, and (ii) *Globalization and Development*, which was the central issue of the twenty-ninth session of ECLAC, held in Brasilia in 2002. A number of specific projects have dealt with these issues. Three of them are:

(i) *Capital Flows and Investment Performance* (published by OECD/ECLAC in 1998), a research conducted jointly with the OECD Development Centre, that examined the behavior of capital formation in Latin America in response to the capital surges of the 1990s.

xiii

(ii) *Financial Crises in "Successful" Emerging Economies*, supported by the Ford Foundation and published by the Brookings Institution Press in 2001, studied the emergence of financial crises in four "successful" emerging economies (EEs). The analysis focused on two Latin American (Chile and Mexico), and two Asian countries (Republic of Korea and Taiwan Province of China).

(iii) *From Capital Surges to Drought* (a Palgrave/WIDER publication, 2003), which was the output of a joint project of ECLAC with the World Institute for Development Economics Research (WIDER) of the United Nations University. This research focused mainly on the analysis of agents supplying external funding since the Asian crises.[1]

This new book is the result of a research project coordinated by ECLAC and supported by the Ford Foundation on *Management of Volatility, Financial Globalization and Growth in Emerging Economies*, studying the gestation and bust of the Asian crises, the contagion experienced by Latin America, and policy responses. Additionally, the macroeconomic experiences of Korea and Malaysia in the East Asian crisis, and of South Africa in the post-apartheid period were analyzed. All three countries exhibit features that make them especially relevant.

We chose to focus on emerging economies and issues that can provide relevant lessons for Latin American countries. We have selected six papers of the ECLAC project for this volume. One paper deals with the links between macroeconomic and meso or microeconomic policies, and the nexus between long-term and short-term effects, in the search for a better macroeconomics for productive development. Several LACs have been performing ambitious reforms of their pension systems. There are numerous studies of the reforms in themselves, on fiscal implications and impact on domestic capital markets. However, research on the macroeconomic implications of the regulation of investments of pension funds, particularly overseas, is notably scarce. Another paper focuses in this issue, first in general analytical terms, and then takes the paradigmatic case of Chile, country with a deep pension reform that is a quarter of a century old.

Some countries made innovative macroeconomic reforms by introducing market-based prudential regulations of capital inflows. Two

---

[1] Among other issues, it examined bank lending criteria, multinational banks, prudential supervision experiences, derivative markets, the behavior of risk-rating agencies, and explored some domestic counter-cyclical policies in EEs.

such cases are illustrated by Colombia and Chile in the 1990s; one paper makes a comparative analysis of these two LACs. We selected three non-LAC emerging economies: Korea, Malaysia and South Africa. One paper compares the outstanding differences as well as similarities in the approaches adopted, by Korea and Malaysia, after the explosion of the East Asian crisis; both countries, after a period of orthodox recessive adjustment, applied sharp positive macroeconomic shocks. Another paper focuses on South Africa, that followed an approach rather in line with the Washington Consensus in a few years before the end of apartheid and strengthened that approach afterwards, particularly in relation to macroeconomic and trade policies.

The introductory chapter, by the project coordinator, discusses four issues relevant for macroeconomic balance and growth in emerging economies. First, it examines the potential contribution of capital flows to economic convergence between EEs and developed nations, and compares it with the actual growth outcome. Latin America is found to have diverged, not only during the "lost decade" of the 1980s, but as well during the subsequent decade and a half. Second, channels linking financial crises with slack growth are set out; how countries hit by crisis tend to move to a lower growth path; the intensity of the downward adjustment depends on how deep is the penetration into *vulnerability zones* during the "good" or boom years: intensity of exchange rate appreciation, short-term shares of external liabilities, currency mismatches are examples of sources of vulnerability (real macroeconomic imbalances, in our terminology). Third, it analyzes the reasons why, during capital surges, financial capital continue to flow into EEs that display mounting vulnerabilities; the leading procyclical role of short-termist agents, both domestic and international, is emphasized. Fourth, two alternative definitions of macroeconomic balances are discussed. The prevailing "neo-liberal" or "orthodox" definition based on purely financial macroeconomic balances (principally, low inflation and balanced fiscal budgets), is contrasted with an alternative approach based on comprehensive balances, that explicitly include an economic activity close to the production frontier (potential GDP), "right" exchange rates and sustainable external balances; that is, "macroeconomic balances of the real economy". A fiscal approach based on structural balances is a new significant facilitator for achieving those real balances. The research confirms that the adoption of a reformed macroeconomic approach is one crucial ingredient for correcting the severe "growth frustrations" experienced by many EEs.

Chapter II, by José Antonio Ocampo (Under-Secretary General for Economic and Social Affairs of the United Nations and former Executive Secretary of ECLAC), tackles the issue of Latin America's frustratingly low economic growth, notwithstanding the deep market reforms implemented during the 1990s. The new development strategy – including across-the-board trade and financial liberalization – was effective in reducing inflation, bringing budget deficits under control, generating export dynamism, attracting FDI and increasing productivity in leading firms and sectors. Nonetheless, economic growth has been frustratingly low and volatile, with frequent balance-of-payments disequilibria or crises, and persistently depressed domestic savings and investment. Overall productivity performance has been poor, largely because of a significant underutilization of physical capital and labor. Increasing productive and labor market dualism has become one of the most outstanding effects of the reform process, where the expansion of a segment of "world class" firms coexists with rising unemployment and labor market informality. This paper examines the growth record of the reform period in the light of both macroeconomic and sectoral (mesoeconomic) performance, and discusses the links of macro and meso policies with growth performance. Ocampo offers a "structuralist" interpretation and puts forward policy proposals.

One outstanding feature of structural changes has been the reform of pension systems. In chapter III, Roberto Zahler (President of the Central Bank of Chile from 1991 to 1996 and international consultant), focuses in the macroeconomic implications of private pension funds and their role in the transmission of external shocks.

Most analyses of pension fund portfolio diversification take as given the macroeconomic context in which they are inserted, and focus on the microeconomic conditions under which returns are maximized and/or risk minimized. The analysis of the macroeconomic implications of pension funds is usually limited to their long-term impact, specifically on savings. Zahler explores some of the short-run macroeconomic implications in EEs, based on the Chilean experience, where a reformed fully-funded system has been in place for over two decades. The analysis suggests that the size of the Chilean pension funds and the degree of concentration of that industry imply that they can have strong effects on the foreign exchange and domestic financial markets, thus altering the macroeconomic environment. This could feedback on less employment and/or lower wages, consequently affecting overall welfare, the labor market and the future benefits of workers as pensioners. In particular, he argues that the costly macroeconomic adjustment of 1998–99 was aggravated by the Chilean pension funds pro-cyclical behavior of their investments abroad. The chapter concludes that the signilicant weight achieved by institutional investors is such that, in emerging economies, public regulations governing their portfolio decisions should consider not only microeconomic matters, but also issues of real macroeconomic stability and growth.

Chapter IV, by Ffrench-Davis (Principal Regional Adviser of ECLAC and Professor of Economics, University of Chile) and Leonardo Villar (member of the Board of the Central Bank of Colombia and Professor of Economics, Universidad de los Andes), presents a comparative analysis of the macroeconomic policies of Chile and Colombia during the 1990s; in particular, it considers their exchange rate regimes, capital account regulations, and the genesis and management of financial crises. In 1995, when contagion from the tequila crisis was spreading through Latin America, both countries were exempt from contagion and recorded high rates of economic growth. Many analysts attribute this positive performance to their having undertaken a comprehensive set of prudential measures to avoid excessive exposure to short-term capital flows and pressures toward excessive real appreciation. In fact, both countries were using a market-based reserve requirement on short-term inflows, crawling-bands, and other instruments for reducing domestic vulnerability to capital flows. Despite the fact that short-term debt represented only a small share of foreign debt in both countries, after the Asian crisis vulnerability to international shocks was rather significant. In both nations, real interest rates rose sharply in 1998 and GDP growth was negative in 1999; outflows associated to short-term external debt were small, while outflows by domestic residents, via institutional investors, were very sizable, as also documented in the chapter by Zahler, and had significant recessive effects on economic activity. The similarities between Chile and Colombia, however, do not go much further. During the 1990s, average GDP growth rates were very high in Chile and posted fiscal surpluses and high private savings, while in Colombia average GDP growth was below historical levels, and there was an increasing fiscal deficit and falling domestic savings.

Chapter V reviews the post-crisis macroeconomic adjustment and the impact of policy responses on the real economies of Korea and Malaysia. In both countries, the gestation of the crisis was rather similar to that of LACs, notwithstanding that their fundamentals – rates of GDP growth, of capital formation and of domestic savings – were notably superior. Both economies opened their capital accounts in a situation of plentiful international supply of funding. Given their evident sound economic fundamentals, these countries attracted huge inflows with outcomes rather similar to those of LACs in the same circumstances: real exchange rate appreciation, external balance deficits, rising short-term foreign liabilities, increasing price/earnings ratios in stock markets. Both countries suffered under the Asian financial crisis, with GDP drops of 7% in 1997. Initially, both applied restrictive policies, subsequently their policy responses were quite different in several respects. Korea sought liquidity assistance from the IMF, which obliged it to implement a structural adjustment program, while Malaysia was able to recover policy independence in the process of crisis resolution. Korea and Malaysia adopted diametrically contrasting policies on capital flows in response to the crisis. Korea drastically liberalized its capital account (however, keeping some restrictions on capital outflows by residents) with a floating exchange rate regime (although with a huge accumulation of reserves during recovery), while Malaysia imposed stringent capital controls and returned to a fixed (but devalued) exchange rate. However, both countries, to face recession in 1998, made a swift change toward a sharp expansionary macroeconomic policy stance, based on vigorous expansive fiscal and monetary policies. This contributed to an economic recovery, in 1999, notably faster and stronger than in other EEs. The positive role of counter-cyclical macroeconomic policies in post-crisis recovery raises the question of whether the initially tight monetary and fiscal policy was kept for too long and, therefore, deepened the crisis in Korea and Malaysia. The experiences of these two economies, and their management of the aftermath of the crisis appear to be extremely relevant for LACs.

Chapter VI examines macroeconomic policy and performance in South Africa since the transition from apartheid to democracy in April 1994, which opened the way for re-integration into the global economy. After a decade of democracy, annual growth averaged 2.7%, official unemployment was over 28% and there had been little reduction in the high inequality inherited. It is argued that the poor performance in the real economy has been linked with the policy emphasis on purely financial stability, in particular lowering the fiscal deficit to below 3%, and using interest rates to lower the inflation rate to the target range of 3–6%, with little regard to the cyclical changes of aggregate demand and macro prices. The paper outlines how the political economy of the transition to democracy produced this policy stance and the process of external liberalization that guided it. It then traces the evolution of fiscal, monetary and exchange rate policies over the decade, and shows that notwithstanding their "success" in achieving domestic financial objectives (low inflation and fiscal discipline), instability was simply transferred to the external account, in the form of three foreign exchange crises and to the real economy via unstable aggregate demand and macro-prices. With productive investment further reduced by low confidence and savings depressed by rising consumption propensities – both linked to the transition – the prospects for sustained growth remain poor.

We appreciate the active participation of authors and invited specialists at two international seminars, conducted in 2002 and 2003, at ECLAC headquarters in Santiago. We acknowledge the valuable support of the Ford Foundation and the intellectual encouragement from Manuel Montes. As usual, ECLAC provided a stimulating environment for a most fruitful discussion. Heriberto Tapia gave highly professional support in revising the analytical and empirical content of drafts of all chapters. Lenka Arriagada and Marcela Osses were exceptionally efficient in the preparation of the final typescript. Naturally, all the opinions set forth here are the sole responsibility of the respective authors.

Ricardo Ffrench-Davis
ECLAC

I
Macroeconomics-for-Growth under Financial Globalization: Four Strategic Issues for Emerging Economies

*Ricardo Ffrench-Davis**

Introduction

Latin America has exhibited contrasting features in its economic performance in the last decade and a half of market-based reforms. There has been good progress in achieving low inflation, improved fiscal balances, and high export growth. However, in parallel, low average GDP growth, low productive investment, and high volatility of economic activity associated with changes in capital flows are outstanding features of the performance of Latin American economies (LACs) since the early 1990s. Here we examine their relation to the sort of macroeconomic policies that were implemented. Success in achieving low inflation and moderate fiscal balances has not been accompanied by an effective demand close to potential GDP nor by interest and exchange rates providing sustainable signals for efficient resource allocation. The macroeconomic environment, in general, has been providing an *unfriendly* framework and *wrong* macro-prices for productive development.

In this chapter we document these features and offer policy proposals, particularly contributing to build into the market a macroeconomic environment prone for growth.

* The author did benefit from a stimulating discussion in two international seminars of this project, organized at ECLAC's Headquarters in 2002 and 2003, and valuable comments received at seminars at the OECD and the 2004 Congress of the Latin American Studies Association (LASA). I appreciate the comments of several colleagues at ECLAC and the research support and comments of Heriberto Tapia.

The incidence of capital flows on domestic economic activity has been an outstanding feature of LACs during the past quarter century. In the last ten years, East Asian economies joined the club. Actually, in recent decades, the association of flows with economic growth has been heterogeneous, and apparently has been worsening: on frequent occasions, capital surges have not been accompanied by vigorous capital formation and sustainable GDP growth. This fact highlights the central role played by the mechanism by which externally generated boom-bust cycles in capital markets are transmitted to the different host markets, and the vulnerabilities and hysteresis effects they may generate. This implies that an essential objective of macroeconomic policies is to reap the benefits from external savings, but reducing the intensity of capital account cycles and their negative economic and social effects on LACs, and more generally on emerging economies (EEs).

Capital account cycles are associated to the twin phenomena of volatility and contagion, both in the expansive phases and in the contractive episodes. Significant shifts in expectations, usually reinforced by subsequent risk-rating changes, lead to sharp procyclical adjustments in the availability of financing, maturities and spreads. The most damaging, as argued below, are the medium-term fluctuations rather than very short-term volatility: several years of abundant financing (i.e. 1991–94 and mid-1995 to 1997), followed by several years of dryness (most of 1998–2004).

In section 1, the arguments in favor of a generalized capital account opening by developing economies are analyzed. It is conventionally argued that capital inflows are a significant source for economic convergence for developing economies. We focus on what actually has happened with economic convergence and capital surges to EEs since the 1990s (first issue). In section 2, the implications of bust episodes are discussed. It is argued that all recessions leave significant lasting economic and social costs (second issue). Even the better-behaved recoveries usually end in a GDP plateau notoriously below the pre-crisis plateau. In section 3, it is analyzed why, repeatedly, crises are built, principally, in boom periods (third issue). The role of short-termist agents and *processes* of persistent positive shifts of the supply of funding during the boom stage are emphasized. In section 4, a contrast is presented between the "orthodox" view of purely financial macroeconomic balances (limited principally to low inflation and balanced fiscal budgets), and an alternative approach concerned with comprehensive balances, that also includes employment, economic activity persistently close to potential GDP, and sustainable external balances, that is, "macroeconomic balances of the real economy" (fourth issue).

1. Capital inflows for economic development convergence

Flows of funds from capital-rich to capital-scarce countries, and catching-up in technological and managing innovation, are two crucial ingredients for a successful process of international convergence of living standards; to simplify matters, we use as a measure of convergence per capita GDP levels (see Table I.1, below).

a) Benefits from flows

i. Flows from capital-rich to capital-scarce economies

Mobilization of external savings is the most classic, and certainly the strongest, argument in favor of capital flows to LDCs. At the aggregate level, capital movements from developed to developing countries are assumed to improve the efficiency of world resource allocation, because real returns on marginal investment in capital-rich countries are expected to be systematically lower than those in capital-scarce countries. Consequently, flows to LDCs can benefit both supplier and

Table I.1   Per capita GDP growth in selected economies, 1971–2004

	(annual averages, percentages)		
	1971–80	**1981–89**	**1990–2004**
Korea	5.7	7.3	4.9
Malaysia	5.4	2.8	3.9
East Asia (6)	5.2	4.4	3.7
Argentina	1.2	–2.4	1.3
Brazil	6.1	0.1	0.4
Chile	0.9	1.1	3.7
Colombia	3.0	1.5	0.8
Mexico	3.4	–0.8	1.4
Latin America (19)	3.3	–0.7	0.9
South Africa	1.4	–0.8	–0.3
United States	2.2	2.5	1.8
World	1.9	1.4	1.1

Source: Based on figures from ADB, ECLAC, IMF and the World Bank. East Asia includes Indonesia, Korea, Malaysia, Philippines, Taiwan and Thailand. Latin America includes 19 countries.

4 Seeking Growth under Financial Volatility

demander economies.[1] Indeed, net inflows of external savings can supplement domestic savings, raise productive investment and boost growth. In turn, expansion of aggregate income can further increase domestic savings and investment, thereby creating a virtuous circle in which there is sustained economic expansion, eventual elimination of net foreign debt, and transformation of the country into a capital exporter; it is the so-called virtuous debt cycle (ECLAC, 1995, ch. X), that contributes to the convergence of levels of economic development. LDCs more likely to receive private capital inflows are the EEs. Actually, they concentrate the overwhelming majority of private flows to LDCs.

Although obviously highly stylized, this traditional framework has some powerful implications. First, capital inflows should consistently be directed to augment aggregate investment, and not be diverted to consumption; that is, the crowding-out of national savings should be avoided.[2] Second, an aggressive domestic savings effort is called for: from the outset of a debt cycle, the marginal savings rate must attain a level much higher than the average rates of domestic savings as well as of investment; thus, it would eventually give way to a savings surplus. Initially, matching interest and profits remittances; subsequently, for the repayment of capital. Third, there must be efficient absorptive capacity in the domestic market; that is, investment must be allocated efficiently (requiring the supply of the other ingredients of the production function – whether domestic or imported, for instance via FDI – and a real macroeconomic environment suitable for productive investment). Fourth, the country must invest intensively in tradable goods and services in order to generate a trade surplus large enough to transform domestic savings into foreign currency, to service external liabilities. Fifth, creditors must be willing to provide stable and predictable flows of finance on reasonable terms.

[1] Recent literature argues that marginal returns to capital can be equalized without equalizing marginal productivities. Gourinchas and Jeanne (2004, section IV) assert that this "would imply that the capital flows that need to be preserved are FDI, and not necessarily credit flows", as a way "to import productivity". This approach inserts in recent literature that underscores the weight of factor quantity on GDP growth. On the contrary, the fact that GDP per capita is strongly associated with the stock of capital per worker supports the view that the speed of capital formation is a significant determinant of GDP growth. In 2000, the capital intensity per worker of the US and the Latin American economies, was US$111,000 and US$16,000, respectively, in constant prices of 1995 (see Ffrench-Davis and Tapia, 2004; Ros, 2000, ch. 1).

[2] This implies that domestic savings increase, at least, in the amount that the rent of foreign capital rises.

These conditions may not all be complied with in practice: countries may experience a significant crowding-out of domestic savings by foreign savings; investments may not always be efficient or channeled sufficiently into tradables, and creditor behavior may differ from the desired pattern. Indeed, as convincing as the traditional argument for the transfer of international savings to relatively poorer countries is, the above problems and ensuing payments crises have often caused this valuable developmental mechanism to fail its target.[3]

ii. Flows compensating shocks

A second contribution of capital mobility is that it can help to balance transitory differences between output and expenditure, or to spread out over time the adjustment to permanent changes in relative prices; thus, it allows stabilizing consumption and investment, generating a stabilizing intertemporal adjustment. However, this counter-cyclical behavior not always does evolve smoothly in practice. Usually, it is not easy to ascertain whether a downturn in the external sector is transitory and, if so, for how long. This uncertainty, coupled with imperfections in international capital markets (especially informational asymmetries, enforcement obstacles, and contagion of changes of suppliers mood; see section 3, and Stiglitz, 2000), represent obstacles to the arrival of matching amounts of external finance at those times when they are required.

Given the smallness of EEs markets, *vis-à-vis* international financial markets, a stabilizing behavior is potentially feasible. However, that has happened systematically only during periods of generalized abundant supply. For instance, in 1991–97 (except early 1995 for Latin America), the specific agent affected by a falling export price could borrow rather easily. On the contrary, in other cases, of moderate or weak supply, a worsening of the terms of trade has led to sharper dryness or to a consolidation of an already existing binding external restriction, as in 1998–2003; the outcome tends to be a private capital account contributing to a destabilizing intertemporal adjustment.[4] In

---

[3] See the research presented in Ffrench-Davis and Reisen (1998), particularly, that of Uthoff and Titelman (1998).
[4] It is interesting to recall that it was public (multilateral and bilateral) supply of funds, which behaved counter-cyclically in the 1980s and 1990s (see ECLAC, 2002a, ch. 4). Prasad, Rogoff, *et al.* (2003, section I.c and table 4), conclude that "procyclical access to international capital markets appears to have had a perverse effect on the relative volatility of consumption for financially integrated developing economies". Kindleberger (1978) and Eichengreen (2003, ch. 2) provide interesting historical analysis of financial cycles.

these circumstances, financial markets, systematically, have pressed EEs authorities to face the negative external shocks with a procyclical recessive policy.

When this second role of international capital mobility is played procyclically, the costs of adjustment for developing countries can be enormous. That is because in the face of negative external shocks (and easily exhaustible domestic international reserves), any shortfall in capital inflows will require immediate cutbacks in domestic expenditure to restore the external balance. As discussed in section 2, even when actual GDP is below potential GDP, output will almost certainly fall because of the natural rigidities standing in the way of resource reallocation, and a perverse hysteresis comes into action because there also tends to be an over-proportional cutback in investment (see section 4). The crisis-affected economy will be unable to return to the previous growth path; actually, it would be facing multiple equilibria.

iii. Flows diversifying risk

Third, if analytically finance is treated analogously to goods, social benefits could be perceived in a multi-way international exchange in financial assets, since capital mobility would allow individuals to satisfy their risk preferences more fully through greater asset diversification; this is a micro-benefit. This argument has been widely-used for justifying a full opening of the capital account of developed and developing countries alike, particularly including the opening to outflows of domestic funds.[5]

There are several ways to diversify risk or insure against diverse types of risk. For instance, by trade diversification and stabilization funds (including international reserves policy) to face exports and imports instability as a prudential macroeconomic policy. At the micro-level, with sectoral and geographical diversification by the firm, and by producers of goods and services operating with derivative markets (see Dodd, 2003). But, a quite different matter is a capital account opening to diversify the financial assets and equity stock portfolio of residents.

---

[5] It is relevant that Korea and Malaysia – the two fastest recovering EEs after the Asian crisis – kept restrictions on outflows by residents as a countercyclical macroeconomic device (Mahani, Shin and Wang, 2005). Zahler (2005) discusses the macroeconomic implications of outflows from domestic institutional investors, illustrated with the case of Chilean private pension funds.

It is evident that free trade in goods, as well as flows of greenfield FDI, and free trade in financial assets are not identical (Díaz-Alejandro, 1985; Devlin, 1989; Bhagwati, 1998). The former transaction tends to be complete and instantaneous, whereas trade in financial instruments is inherently incomplete and of uncertain value, since it is based on a promise to pay in the future. In a world of uncertainty, incomplete insurance markets, informational costs and contagious changes of mood, *ex ante* and *ex post* valuations of financial assets may be radically different. The gap in time between a financial transaction and payment for it, generates externalities in market transactions that can magnify and multiply errors in subjective valuations, to the point where finally the market corrections may be abrupt, overshooting and destabilizing (Stiglitz, 1998); that would imply a macroeconomic cost. Thus, some form of regulation of trade in financial assets may not only make specific markets function more efficiently, but improve the overall performance of the economy through the enhancement of macroeconomic stability and better long-term investment performance.

From the point of view of growth convergence, this third argument is not too relevant for enhancing development. First, for a given country, financial opening for the implementation of financial risk diversification implies liberalizing outflows by residents. Most, probably, it would tend to encourage net outflows from – the more incomplete, smaller, less liquid and less deep – developing or emerging markets, rather than the opposite. Evidently, that may diversify risk for domestic financial investors and agents (most probably does not contribute to diversity risk on returns to domestic producers), but probably reduces savings available domestically and financing for productive investment.

Second, there are some interesting analytical pieces in the literature supporting this third argument. For instance, Obstfeld (1994) develops a model based on the hypothesis that global financial integration implies a portfolio shift from low-risk-low-returns capital to high-risk-high-returns capital. He concludes that that shift could contribute to "enormous welfare gains" (Obstfeld, 1998, p. 10). There are three comments I would like to pose in this respect: (i) the assertion about the size of the effects – even more than the sign – reveals an *a priori* belief or desire; (ii) there is an overlapping of the risk diversification argument with that of flows from capital-rich to capital-scarce markets in response to differential returns; there is need to identify what is truly different in the pure financial risk diversification argument;[6] (iii) actually, what do we observe? That cross-border flows tend to move into better-known and non-high risk assets; a look at stocks (for instance, ADRs or GDRs) and bonds of EEs transacted internationally, documents it sharply: they usually correspond to large, mature, and better graded domestic firms. In particular, the same happens with financial investment abroad of EEs residents. The exception, covering a broader set of assets, is in the case of the bubbles, in which investors actually do not reveal an appetite-for-risk, but rather an assumption away of risk during the contagion of over-optimism. In brief, there is no well-documented connection of risk diversification with the sources of domestic productivity increases.

Third, international financial diversification has presently being given evident priority in policy-making; for instance, when eliminating capital gains taxes on cross-border operations and in the encouragement to financial investment in offshore markets. But, the fact is that both activities are quite isolated from the sources of systemic competitivity and productive development. That sort of priority tends to concentrate energy of economic agents in purely financial activities; this implies a *neo-rent-seeking* attitude: to make profits at the expense of other agents, instead of profit derived from increased productivity. The problem is not one of all or nothing, but of a rebalance in favor of "productivism" and longer-term horizons.

iv. Capital account opening and macroeconomic discipline

This is the newest argument in favor of capital account liberalization. It states that the dependency from inflows can make a significant contribution to deter political authorities from following irresponsible and populist macroeconomic policies. It is argued that, consequently, fully opening the capital account would encourage "sound macroeconomic fundamentals". This is partly true for *domestic* sources of instability, i.e., large fiscal deficits, permissive monetary policy and arbitrary exchange-rate overvaluation. However, actually, we have observed that lax demand policies or exchange-rate overvaluation has tended to be encouraged by financial markets during booms (in periods of over-optimism

---

[6] Other relevant argument is the obvious positive role fulfilled by financial intermediaries in relaxing liquidity constraints and in reducing search costs for small- and medium-sized agents (SMEs), which is crucial for economic growth and equity. It is domestic intermediaries who concentrate that role overwhelmingly. Access abroad of SMEs is notably limited.

of financial agents), whereas excessive punishment during crises has tended to force authorities to adopt overly contractionary policies ("irrational overkill").[7]

In fact, the opening of the capital account may lead EEs to import external financial instability, with capital inflows engendering a worsening in macroeconomic fundamentals. Thus, although this market discipline can serve as a check to *domestic* sources of instability – not necessarily very efficient, given the whims of opinions and expectations characteristic of financial markets – it certainly becomes a *source* of externally generated instability. Not only the market may perceive inaccurately that some domestic policies are inadequate, indeed, it may induce deviations of those variables from sustainable levels: it is the market itself which, during the booms, has generated incentives for EEs to enter *vulnerability zones* (see section 3).

One additional, most worrisome, implication is that legitimate national political authorities may lose the capacity to pursue the policy proposals for which they were elected. To this issue we turn at the end of this chapter.

b) Actual growth performance

In the post-war II period, global GDP growth has recorded high per capita rates. The average for the whole world in the last half-century is similar to the rates achieved by Great Britain and United States when they conquered, in that sequence, the role of more powerful economy in the world (see Maddison, 2001). The speed of world growth has shown a declining trend in recent decades, with GDP per capita rising 1.9% in the 1970s, 1.4% in the 1980s, and 1.1% in 1990–2004 (table I.1). Of course, there are many other intervening variables in the evolution of GDP, but in this latter period there are two outstanding new factors.[8] One is the technological revolution taking place in recent years, evidently a positive contributing factor for increasing productivity and, we assume, generating higher growth; the other is the more

---

[7] This source of market discipline can also pose obstacles to necessary social reform (for instance, to higher taxes to finance efficient human capital investment) or to the ability to capture economic rents from natural resources that would otherwise be forgone.

[8] In the case of Latin America there has been a significant financial and trade liberalization and massive privatizations, with much broader room for private markets. Analysis of reforms and outcomes are presented in Kuczynsky and Williamson (2003); Stallings and Peres (2000); Ffrench-Davis (2005). See certain similarities with the South African reforms after Apartheid in Gelb (2005.)

intensive increase in domestic and international financial activism. This is a good candidate to explain, at least partly, the slower growth due to the deviation of resources and efforts from productivity enhancement ("productivism") and toward neo-rent seeking ("financierism"), with a procyclical bias. Efficiency, in any human activity, requires a sound balance between different activities, objectives, voices, time horizons, etc. That balance must be recovered.

Here we will focus on growth trends in EEs during the latter period. Given the four arguments discussed above in favor of capital account opening, we want to document whether there has been growth convergence during this recent period of broad liberalization of capital accounts and other structural reforms in EEs.[9] Table I.1 shows that, in the 1970s, both East Asia and Latin America (notably Brazil) converged with the United States and progressed faster than the world economy. In the next two decades, East Asia continued to converge, though more mildly: it converged even in the most recent period (1990–2004), notwithstanding its 1998 recession. Latin America, on the contrary, has diverged since the 1980s (ECLAC, 2002b; IDB, 2004; Ocampo, 2005). In the period of deep free market reforms, significant liberalization of trade and high capital inflows, in 1990–97 (with a brief downturn in 1995), a significant share of foreign savings was not directed to capital formation (GKF), and of the fraction allocated to GKF a significant share was invested in the production of non-tradables.[10] Consequently, it generated severe vulnerabilities for the following period of supply drought (since 1998). Overall, annual growth per capita in 1990–2004 was merely 0.9% in Latin America, as compared to 1.1% in the world as a whole, and 1.8 % in the United States.

It is interesting that, within Latin America, there was a convergence in the adoption of neo-liberal reforms, but there was an increased divergence in economic growth of the region with respect to the USA and the world average. Table I.1 shows that one exception in Latin

---

[9] An excellent, comprehensive re-interpretation of recent growth experiences is developed in Rodrik (2003); an earlier analysis is in Barro and Sala-i-Martin (1995). Prasad, Rogoff, *et al.* (2003) present an interesting survey on the effects of financial globalization on LDCs growth.

[10] Two simple, straight-forward relations: (i) in 1990–97, net capital inflows increased more, in comparison to the 1980s, than GKF (even after changes in domestic savings are controlled by terms of trade); (ii) exports increased less than imports, and the standard way of measuring "tradables" usually exhibits a falling share in GDP, despite the significant rise in the export ratio (see Ffrench-Davis, 2005, ch. IV).

American growth performance was the case of Chile, whose average growth per capita doubled that of the USA in 1990–2004 (3.7% versus 1.8%). Those years enclose two different subperiods; it is most relevant that a significant welfare convergence was achieved only in 1990–97 (with 5.3% per capita growth), period in which Chile searched quite actively for real macroeconomic balances, including the regulation of short-term and liquid capital inflows, active exchange rate and monetary policies, a significant fiscal surplus during boom periods and a copper stabilization fund by the Treasury. The set of policies initiated in 1990, with the return to democracy, represented a *reform to the reforms* conducted in the 1970s (Ffrench-Davis, 2002, ch. 10).[11]

2. Recessions, recovery and elusive growth

A dominant feature of the "new generation" of business cycles in EEs are the sharp fluctuations in domestic private spending and balance sheets, associated to boom-bust cycles in external financing. The rise of external financing contains a significant exogenous or push origin (Calvo, 1998); but actual inflows tend to produce policy changes, which introduce pull or endogenous factors. We interpret that the former effect prevails when a growing deficit on current account and appreciating exchange rates coexist with an accumulation of international reserves. That happened in most LACs in 1990–94 and 1996–97, and in East Asia in 1992–96.

External shocks, both positive and negative, are multiplied domestically if the exchange rate, fiscal and monetary policies stance are procyclical, as it is actually expected to be by financial market agents and even by multilateral financial agencies As a consequence of a procyclical behavior, during the capital surges we have observed that EEs have, frequently, penetrated in *vulnerability zones*, during *adjustment processes* including some combination of (i) rising external liabilities, with a large liquid or short-term share (IMF, 1998; Rodrik and Velasco, 2000), (ii) large current account external deficits, (iii) appreciated exchange rates, (iv) currency and maturity mismatches, (v) high price/earnings ratios of domestic financial assets, and (vi) high prices of real estate.

---

[11] Outstanding features of trade, financial and macroeconomic reforms of the 1990s in LACs were rather similar to those of Chile in the 1970s, sharing what I have shown to be severe mistakes, prone to financial crisis and "unfriendly" with productive investment (see Ffrench-Davis, 2002, on Chile; and 2005, chs. I and III, on Latin America).

Bust in EEs, usually has come after a boom in capital inflows, which have been generating all these destabilizing market signals (Ffrench-Davis and Ocampo, 2001).

The longer and deeper the economy's penetration into those *vulnerability zones*, the more severe the *financierist trap* in which authorities could get caught, and the lower the probability of leaving it without undergoing a crisis and long-lasting economic and social costs. The absence or weakness of policies moderating the boom – putting breaks during overheating – [12] endangers the feasibility of adopting a strong reactivating policy under a recessive environment after the bust.

Bust has been led by a sudden stop of inflows and a sudden rise of outflows: Latin America in August 1982; Mexico in December 1994 and East Asia in 1997; or a somewhat more gradual change brought in by the Asian contagion[13] toward Latin America in 1998–99. All have implied a shift from liquidity to dryness in domestic financial and currency markets.

In this sort of crises, a downward adjustment on aggregate demand takes place after the drying of supply. The negative financial shock underlying the Asian crisis was compounded by a concomitant worsening of the terms of trade; evidently, there were no spontaneous capital flows compensating the swings of the terms of trade. Usually, there has been an "automatic" component in the domestic adjustment, associated to a significant lost of reserves, complemented to different degrees, with policy-increased interest rates, depreciation and fiscal contraction. Naturally, the drop in domestic demand (or of its rate of growth) tends to correct the external deficit, and consequently that source of the demand for foreign currency. In all sharp processes, then follows a drop in GDP (growth), what tends to make necessary a subsequent additional fall in aggregate demand. Obviously, the larger the cumulative drop in GDP, the heavier the economic and social costs of adjustment and the foregone welfare. A positive feature, nonetheless, is that the resulting output gap (potential GDP minus actual GDP) provides room for a subsequent recovery.

---

[12] A feature of the gestation of modern financial crises is that "overheating" has taken place, frequently, with falling inflation rates, led by exchange rate appreciation and rising external deficits. A notorious case is that of Argentina in 1996–2001 with a negative average inflation in that period.

[13] We use a definition which includes the contagion of optimism among financial agents during the capital surge, as well as a contagion of pessimism with the bust.

Indeed in all moderately or well-managed economies, a recovery follows usually the fall in activity. We stress that most of the drop in GDP does not imply, necessarily, a destroyal of capacity but a transitory underutilization, an *output gap*. That is a *recessive gap*. In a perfectly flexible economy, with an efficient combination of demand-reducing and switching policies there would be no output loss associated to the downward adjustment of aggregate demand. The actual huge GDP losses with respect to the previous growth trend, in all the cases we have observed, clearly signal that the universe we are dealing with is not too flexible *vis-à-vis* sharp recessive shocks, and that policies are not efficient or have become less efficient with the loss of effective tools.

Even in the outstanding cases of fast recovery – the so-called v-shaped recoveries – significant costs have been observed. Generally, countries, which have undergone severe crises, display evidence that they are pushed into a lower GDP path: in brief, an economy that exhibited a 7% growth trend and suffers a 7% drop, tends to experience a 14% output gap; consequently, a 7% recovery, in the year after recession, tends to leave a 14% gap. Figure I.1 depicts the cases of Korea and Malaysia, that exhibit the better-behaved recoveries among EEs. Before the crisis, both were in a growth trend in the order of 7% per year, considered sustainable by most observers. Even these two outstanding economies, after 1998, remain notoriously below the previous trend.[14] Financial crises are extremely costly, stressing the importance of crises-avoiding reforms and policies.

There are three particularly relevant medium-term effects on GDP. One is a sharp reduction of productive investment that occurs during the crisis, which naturally deteriorates the future path of potential GDP; for instance, the already mediocre investment ratios in LACs fell 1.5 points between the averages of 1992–99 and 2000–2003, reaching a ratio even lower than in the lost decade of the 1980s (see section 4).

Second, the worsening of balance sheets (Krugman, 1999), as shown by the experience of EEs, indicates that restoring a viable financial system takes several years, generating adverse effects throughout the period in which it is rebuilt; frequently, also, the Treasury or the Central Bank have diverted funds to support banks or debtor firms. Third, a growing body of evidence documents that boom-bust cycles have ratchet effects on social variables (Rodrik, 2001; World Bank, 2003). The deterioration of the labor market (open unemployment, a

---

[14] In econometric terms, this implies the existence of a unit root in real GDP.

A. Korea (billion won, 1995 prices)

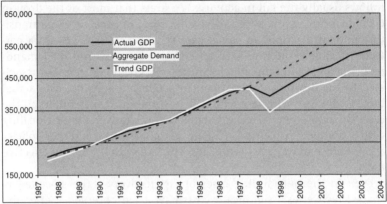

B. Malaysia (million Ringgit, 1987 prices)

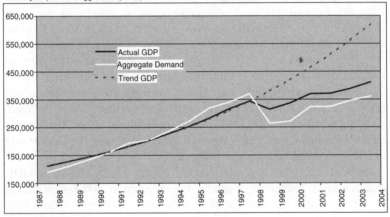

Figure I.1   GDP and aggregate demand in Korea and Malaysia, 1987–2003
Source: Author's calculations based on ADB data.

worsening in the quality of jobs or in real wages, and rise in informality) is generally very rapid, whereas the recovery is slow and incomplete. This is reflected in the long-lasting worsening of real wages in Mexico after the tequila crisis (Frenkel and Ros, 2004); one crucial variable behind this outcome, that leaves negative "structural" changes in the labor market, is that labor supply keeps rising, while capital formation experiences a sharp drop and the average rate of use of the stock of capital is reduced.

These three problems signal policy priorities during the crisis: sustaining public investment, encouraging private investment; contributing to reschedule liabilities, and assisting in solving currency and maturity mismatches; reinforcing a social network that uses the opportunity to improve the productivity of temporarily underutilized factors, and the need to reform the approach to macroeconomic policies (see section 4).

3. Why private non-FDI flows to EEs are procyclical and tend to destabilize macroeconomic balances

Most recent macroeconomic crises in East Asia and Latin America have shown a close association with strong swings of private capital flows. An outstanding feature is that currency and financial crises have been suffered by EEs that usually were considered to be highly "successful" by IFIs and financial agents; actually, they were awarded with growingly improving grades from international risk rating agencies (Ffrench-Davis and Ocampo, 2001; Frenkel, 2004; Reisen, 2003; Williamson, 2003b); accordingly, EEs were rewarded with falling spreads, in parallel with accumulating rising stocks of external liabilities (see figure I.2 below).

The sharp increase of international financial flows since the early 1990s was notably more diversified than in the 1970s. But the outcome is potentially more unstable, in as much as the trend has been a shift from mid-term bank credit, which was the predominant source of financing in the 1970s, to a set of equity portfolio flows, liquid bonds, medium- and short-term bank financing; short-term time deposits; acquisitions of domestic firms by foreign investors. Thus, paradoxically, since the 1990s there has tended to be a *diversification toward highly reversible sources of funding*; they tend to share the spreads of over-optimism and over-pessimism. The reversibility of flows is not observed during the expansive-boom stage of the cycles, but its pervasiveness, for real macroeconomic stability, explodes abruptly with the negative change of mood of markets.[15] Notwithstanding the rising share of FDI along the past decade, the capital account still included a significant proportion of volatile flows, as well as inflows unlinked

---

[15] The accelerated growth of derivatives markets contributed to soften "micro-instability" but has tended to increase "macro-instability" and to reduce transparency. See an analysis of the channels by which stability and instability are transmitted in Dodd (2003).

with the direct generation of additional productive capacity such as mounting mergers and acquisitions.[16]

That change in the composition of supply – associated to technological innovation, institutional and policy changes in developed economies, led by US authorities and powerful lobbying forces (Bhagwati, 2004; Pfaff, 2000) – was accompanied by a fast opening in the capital accounts of EEs, particularly in East Asia and Latin America; this opening was implemented in a period of abundant supply. The fact is that both regions moved into *vulnerability zones* (we repeat the signals: some combination of large external liabilities, with a high short-term or liquid share; currency and maturity mismatches; a significant external deficit; an appreciated exchange-rate; high price/earnings ratios in the stock market, plus low domestic investment ratios in LACs). In parallel, as discussed below, agents specialized in microeconomic aspects of finance, placed in the short-term or liquid segments of capital markets, acquire a dominant voice in the generation of macroeconomic expectations.

There is an extremely relevant and interesting literature on the causes of financial instability: the asymmetries of information between creditors and debtors, and the lack of adequate internalization of the negative externalities that each agent generates (through growing vulnerability), that underlie the cycles of abundance and shortage of external financing (Krugman, 2000; Stiglitz, 2002; Harberger, 1985). Beyond those issues, as stressed by Ocampo (2003), finance deals with the future, and evidently concrete "information" about the future is unavailable. Consequently, the tendency to equate opinions and expectations with "information" contribute to herd behavior and multiple equilibria. Actually, we have observed a notorious contagion, first of over-optimism, and then of over-pessimism in many of the financial crises experienced by EEs in the last three decades.

However, over and above these facts, there are two additional features of the creditor side that are crucially important. One feature is the particular *nature of the leading agents* acting on the supply side (Ffrench-Davis, 2003). There are natural asymmetries in the behavior and objectives of different economic agents. The agents predominant in the

---

[16] It must be recalled that about one-half of FDI inflows into Latin America in 1995–2002 corresponded to acquisitions and mergers (UNCTAD, 2003). Prasad, Rogoff, *et al.* (2003, table 1 and figure 3) report data on volatility of total inward FDI, bank loans and portfolio investment. They confirm the conclusion from other abundant research that FDI is less volatile.

financial markets are specialized in short-term liquid investment, operate within short-term horizons, and naturally are highly sensitive to changes in variables that affect returns in the short-run.[17] The second feature is the gradual spread of information, among prospective agents, on investment opportunities in EEs. In fact, agents from different segments of the financial market become gradually drawn into new international markets as they take notice of the profitable opportunities offered by emerging economies previously unknown to them. This explains, from the supply-side, why the surges of flows to emerging economies – in 1977–81 and 1991–97 – have been *processes* that went on for several years rather than one-shot changes in supply. In this sense, it is relevant for policy design to make a distinction between two different types of volatility of capital flows, short-term ups-and-downs, and the medium-term instability, which leads several variables – like the stock market, real estate prices and the exchange rate – to move persistently in a given direction, providing "wrong certainties" to the market and encouraging capital flows, *seeking economic rents* rather than differences in real productivity. Private capital flows, led by midterm volatility (or reversibility) of expectations, usually have a strong and costly procyclical bias.

On the domestic side, high rates of return were potentially to be gained by creditors from capital surges directed to EEs. At the time of their financial opening, in the 1980s and early 1990s (see Morley, Machado and Pettinato, 1999), Latin American economies were experiencing recession, depressed stock and real estate markets, as well as high real interest rates and initially undervalued domestic currencies. Indeed, by 1990, prices of real estate and equity stocks were extremely depressed in Latin America, and the domestic price of the dollar was comparatively very high (see ECLAC, 1995; Ffrench-Davis and Ocampo, 2001).

In the case of East Asia, when they opened their capital accounts during the 1990s, the international supply of funding was already booming. As compared to LACs, they were growing notably fast,

---

[17] Persaud (2003), argues that modern risk-management by investing institutions (such as funds and banks), based on value-at-risk measured daily, works procyclically in the boom and bust. Procyclicality is reinforced by a trend toward homogenization of creditor agents. A complementary argument by Calvo and Mendoza (2000) examines how globalization may promote contagion by discouraging the gathering of information and by strengthening incentives for imitating market portfolio.

with high savings and investment ratios. However, equity stock was also cheap as compared to capital-rich countries (exhibited low price/earnings ratios), and liquid external liabilities were extremely low. Naturally, as discussed in section 1, the rate of return tends to be higher in the productive sectors of capital-scarce EEs than in mature markets that are capital-rich. Then, there is potentially space for very profitable capital flows from suppliers in the latter to the former markets. The expected adjustments in any emerging economy moving from a closed to an open capital account, in those conditions, should tend to be similar to those recorded in LACs. The outcome in both emerging regions, for instance, was a spectacular rise in stock prices, multiplying in average the price index by four in 1990–94 and (after a drop with the tequila crisis) by two in 1995–97 in LACs, and by two in East Asia in 1992–94 (see Ffrench-Davis, 2003, table 2.1).

During the boom is when the degrees of freedom to choose policies are broader. The increased supply of external financing in the 1990s generated a process of exchange-rate appreciation in most LACs, as well as, more moderately, in East Asia; the expectations of continued, persistent, appreciation encouraged additional inflows from dealers operating with maturity horizons located within the expected appreciation of the domestic currency.[18] For allocative efficiency and for export-oriented development strategies, a macro-price – as significant as the exchange rate –[19] led by capital flows conducted by short-termist agents reveals a severe policy inconsistency. The increase in aggregate demand, pushed up by inflows and appreciation, and a rising share of the domestic demand for tradables, augments "artificially" the absorptive capacity and the demand for foreign savings. Thus, as said, the exogenous change – opened by the transformations recorded in international capital markets – was converted into an endogenous process, leading to domestic vulnerability given the potential reversibility of flows.

[18] For short-termist agents the actual and expected profitability were increased with the appreciation process. That same process, if perceived as persistent, would tend to discourage investment in the production of tradables intensive in domestic inputs. Therefore, it is most relevant, because of its policy implications, what happens with the behavior of exchange rates during the expansive or boom stage. It is then when external imbalances and currency and maturity mismatches are, inadvertently, being generated.
[19] Since the allocative role of the exchange rate was notably enhanced with trade reforms, its instability became more damaging for allocative efficiency. See ECLAC (1995, chs. III and IV); Velasco (2000); Williamson (2003a).

In brief, the interaction between the two sets of factors – *the nature of agents and a process of adjustment* – explains the dynamics of capital flows over time: why suppliers keep pouring-in funds while real macro-economic fundamentals worsen. When creditors *discover* an emerging market, their initial exposure is low or non-existent.

Then they generate a series of consecutive flows, which result in rapidly increasing stocks of financial assets in the EE; actually, too rapid and/or large for an efficient absorption; frequently, the absorption is artificially increased by exchange rate appreciation, and a rising real aggregate demand with an enlarged external deficit as a consequence.

The creditor's sensitivity to negative news, at some point, is likely to, suddenly, increase remarkably when the country has reached *vulnerability zones*; then, the creditors take notice of (i) the rising level of the stock of assets held in a country (or region), (ii) the degree of dependence of the debtor market on additional flows, which is associated with the magnitude of the current account deficit, (iii) the extent of appreciation, (iv) the need of refinancing of maturing liabilities, and (v) the amount of liquid liabilities likely to flow out in face of a crisis. Therefore, it should not be surprising that, after penetrating deeply in those vulnerability zones, the sensitivity to adverse political or economic news and the probability of reversal of expectations grows steeply (Calvo, 1998; Rodrik, 1998).

The accumulation of stocks of assets abroad by financial suppliers, until well advanced that boom stage of the cycle, and, then, a subsequent sudden reversal of flows, can *both* be considered to be *rational* responses on the part of individual agents with short-term horizons. This is because it is of little concern to this sort of investors whether (long-term) fundamentals are being improved or worsened while they continue to bring inflows. What is relevant to these investors is that the crucial indicators from their point of view – prices of real estate, bonds and stock, and exchange-rates – can continue providing them with profits in the near term and, obviously, that liquid markets allow them, if needed, to reverse decisions timely; thus, they will continue to supply net inflows until expectations of an imminent near reversal build up.

Indeed, for the most influential financial operators, the more relevant variables are not related to the long-term fundamentals but to short-term profitability. This explains why they may suddenly display a radical change of opinion about the economic situation of a country whose fundamentals, other than liquidity in foreign currency, remain rather unchanged during a shift from *over-optimism* to *over-pessimism*.

Naturally, the opposite process tends to take place when the debtor markets have adjusted downward "sufficiently". Then, the inverse process makes its appearance and can be sustained for some years, like in 1991–94 or 1995–97, or short-lived like in late 1999 and 2000. It is relevant for equity and average growth that the upward process usually tends to be more gradual or slower than the downward adjustment, which tends to be abrupt.

It is no coincidence that, in all three significant surges of the last quarter century, loan spreads underwent, in a *process*, a continued decline, notwithstanding that the stock of liabilities was rising sharply: spreads fell for 5–6 years in the 1970s; over 4 years before the tequila crisis, and over a couple of years after that crisis. Figure I.2 depicts the evolution of EMBI for LACs, exhibiting a persistent improvement between the first quarter of 1995 and the third quarter of 1997.

This behavior of spreads has implied, during the expansive side of the cycle, a downward sloping locus, drawing a sort of a medium-run supply curve, a highly destabilizing feature indeed. During all three expansive processes there has been an evident contagion of over-optimism among creditors and, rather than appetite for risk, there prevails

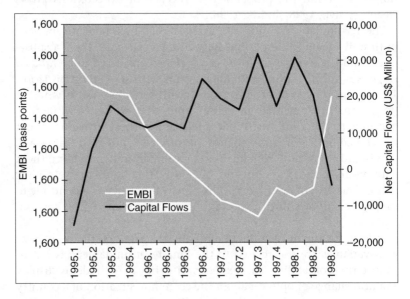

Figure I.2   Country risk and capital flows to Latin America, 1995–98
Source: Bloomberg and IMF.

an underestimation or assuming away of risk. In this respect, it is interesting to recall the evident parallel, in the 1990s, between spreads of Mexico (today praised as then a well-behaved reformer) and Argentina (today qualified as a non-reformer in that decade) (see Ffrench-Davis, 2003, figure 2.2). Apparently, creditors did not perceive any significant difference between these two economies until 1998.

With respect to debtors, in periods of over-optimism, most debtors do not borrow thinking of default and expecting to be rescued or to benefit from a moratoria. Contrariwise, expectations of high yields tend to prevail: borrowers are also victims of the syndrome of financial euphoria during the boom periods (Kindleberger, 1978).

In conclusion, economic agents specialized in the allocation of financial funding (I will call it *microfinance*, as opposed to macrofinance), who may be highly efficient in their field but operate with short-horizons "by training and by reward", have come to play the leading role in determining macroeconomic conditions and policy design in EEs. It implies that a "financierist" approach becomes predominant rather than a "productivist" approach. Growth with equity requires improving the rewards for productivity enhancement rather than *financial rent-seeking* searching for capital gains. There is need to rebalance priorities and voices.

4. A macroeconomics-for-growth

There is a broad consensus that macroeconomic "fundamentals" are a most relevant variable. However, there still is wide misunderstanding about what constitutes "sound fundamentals", and how to achieve and sustain them.

a) A two-pillar macroeconomics

The approach that has been in fashion in the mainstream world and IFIs, even up to today, emphasizes macroeconomic balances of two pillars: low inflation and fiscal balances, with a clear omission of the overall macroeconomic environment for producers, which includes other most influential variables such as aggregate demand and exchange rates. We call it financial macroeconomic balances.[20]

---

[20] See analyses on shortcomings in the macroeconomic policies implemented in the 1990s in Latin America, in Williamson (2003a) and Ffrench-Davis (2005, ch. 2). As said, Prasad, Rogoff, *et al.* (2003), document the procyclical behavior of financial flows and some of its implications.

This approach evidently includes other ingredients, but assumes, that the hard, relevant, proof is in fulfilling those two pillars. This interpretation implies that success in achieving those two pillars leads to productive development in a liberalized economy, or that it becomes sufficient with the addition of microeconomic reforms. This approach is well illustrated, for example, by Stanley Fischer (1993), that after mentioning several intervening variables, concludes that "the evidence reviewed and presented in this paper supports the conventional view that a stable macroeconomic environment, meaning a reasonably low rate of inflation and a small budget deficit, is conducive for sustained economic growth". Additionally, a frequent assertion in the more recent conventional literature is that an open capital account imposes macroeconomic discipline to EEs.[21] Indeed, this approach assumes, sometimes explicitly or frequently implicitly, that full opening of the capital account would contribute to balance the external sector and automatically generate an aggregate demand consistent with productive capacity. It is well documented that that is not the usual experience in the frequent cases of external, positive and negative, financial shocks experienced by EEs (Ffrench-Davis and Ocampo, 2001).

As shown, LACs were successful in the 1990s in reducing inflation to one-digit figures, and balancing their fiscal budgets (fiscal deficits averaged, of course, with diversity among countries, less than 0.5% of GDP in 1995–97). In fact, several LACs fulfilled the main requirements of neo-liberal macroeconomic balances. However, economic activity was notably unstable, as depicted in figure I.3; in the period covered, overall changes in GDP were led by ups-and-downs in aggregate demand, and these responded mostly to shifts in net capital flows; for instance, monetary adjustments were associated to changes in international reserves rather than to changes in domestic credit by the Central Bank (both are sources of high-power money).

The behavior of aggregate demand, at levels consistent with potential GDP, is a crucial part of a third pillar of real macroeconomic balances, which has frequently failed in neo-liberal experiences. As well, are well-aligned macroprices, like interest and exchange rates. Frequently, these prices and aggregate demand were out-of-equilibria, as reflected in

---

[21] A recent working paper of the IMF (Tytell and Wei, 2004) examines the "discipline effect" of financial globalization on macroeconomic balances, focusing on the two pillars in fashion – low inflation and fiscal balances – disregarding the other components of a comprehensive set of real macroeconomic balances.

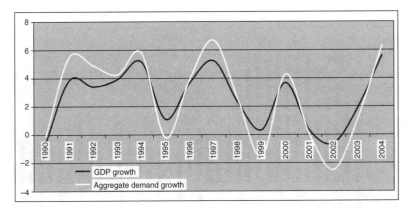

Figure I.3 Latin America: GDP and aggregate demand, 1990–2004 (annual growth rates, %)
Source: ECLAC data. Includes 19 countries. Preliminary figures for 2004.

economies working either below potential GDP or at full capacity with a large external deficit. They tend to miss the intermediate area where, precisely, mid-term equilibrium values are usually found.

East Asia fulfilled for decades real macroeconomic balances: low inflation, fiscal responsibility, together with sustainable exchange rates and external balances, and moderate interest rates (with a mild financial repression). In the 1990s, East Asia continued to fulfill the two conventional pillars – low inflation and fiscal surpluses – but lost the third pillar, of sustainable macrobalances for the real economy. Therefore, most EEs were implementing a financial or two-pillar macroeconomics at the outset of the Asian crises, with the euphoric support of specialists in *microfinance*. A *financierist* approach had become binding.

b) Imbalanced financierism and macroeconomic instability

"Financierism" tends to lead, unsurprisingly, to unsustainable macroeconomic imbalances, with an effective demand that deviates sharply from the production frontier and with "wrong" or outlier macroprices and ratios. In figure I.3, we observe a notorious mid-term instability of GDP growth for the total of Latin America; obviously, that of individual countries tends to be even more unstable. The data show that changes in GDP have been led by ups-and-downs in aggregate demand. Given that fiscal balances have characterized East Asia, and that LACs

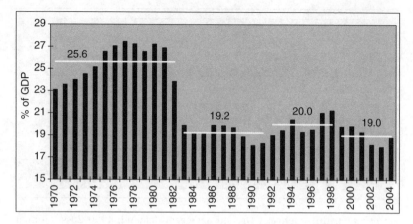

Figure I.4 Latin America: Gross fixed capital formation, 1970–2004 (% of GDP, scaled to 1995 prices)
Source: ECLAC data for 19 countries. Preliminary figures for 2004.

reduced their deficits during the 1990s capital surges, it is evident that increases in aggregate demand were intensive in private expenditure, an outcome strongly associated to the evolution of net capital inflows (Marfán, 2005). Actually, capital tended to flow from private sources to private users.

The resulting real macroeconomic instability in EEs, in this era of globalization, provides an undermined environment for productive investment. That is one strong force behind the poor achievement of LACs investment ratios in the 1990s, when they averaged 20% of GDP; they surpassed by merely one percentage point the 1980s average (19%), but remained about six points below that in the 1970s; with the contagion of the Asian crisis, in the present decade the investment ratio experienced a drop even below the level exhibited in the 1980s (see figure I.4).

c) The role of output gaps and capital formation

A significant, well-documented, variable underlining the drop in productive investment is the output gap between actual and potential GDP (Agosin, 1998; Schmidt-Hebbel, Servén and Solimano, 1996). The gap reflects the underutilized installed capacity in firms and other components of the stock of physical capital, falling employment and reduced actual total factor productivity (Ffrench-Davis, 2005, ch. 3).

Profits tend to decrease while the mood of lenders becomes somber.[22] A notorious effect of these recessive situations, usually, has been a sharp reduction in investment ratios; for instance, a drop of fixed capital formation in 1995, of 13% in Argentina and 30% in Mexico; in 1998 fell 21% in Korea and 43% in Malaysia; in 1999 it declined 18% in Chile, and between 1998 and 2002, the drop recorded 56% in Argentina and 11% in all Latin America.

With the various episodes of economic recovery, investment ratios usually increased from their previous depressed levels (in 1985, 1990, 1995) as shown by Figure I.4. However, there tended to persist a significant (although gradually reduced) output gap. Experience indicates that strong increases in investment are associated to a macroeconomic environment that is able to place effective demand at a level consistent with potential output, with right exchange and interest rates, and that situation is expected by private investors to be sustainable. Chile was the outstanding case to fulfill those conditions, and to exhibit a noticeable increase in the investment ratio in 1991–98 (see Agosin, 1998; Ffrench-Davis and Villar, 2005).

Two additional forces have strengthened the negative incidence of output gaps on domestic private investment. One is a change in the relative composition of FDI from greenfield investment to acquisitions (UNCTAD, 2003), stimulated by depressed prices of domestic assets and depreciated currencies; it is likely that many of these acquisitions would not have taken place under real macroeconomic equilibrium. The second is a negative response of public investment. In particular, expenditure in infrastructure. As documented by Easterly and Servén (2003), most LACs "witnessed a retrenchment of the public sector from infrastructure provision and an opening up to private participation". In most LACs, "private participation did not fully offset the public sector retrenchment".

The reported drop in investment ratios is a significant variable explaining why GDP growth was 5.6% in the 1970s, and averaged merely 2.6% in the fifteen years between 1990 and 2004.

It is policy relevant to disaggregate GDP into two components. One component of GDP are exports of goods and services,[23] whose demand

---

[22] The gap naturally differs among sectors, destinations, and type of firms. Where the gap is expected to persist, producers naturally will tend to postpone or cancel investment plans. In recessions, additionally, the financial sector restraints its lending activity, particularly to producers of non-tradables.

[23] The relevant figures are the value-added to GDP by exports; that is, gross exports of goods and services minus their imported inputs.

Table I.2   Growth of GDP per components, 1990–2003

	(annual averages, percentages)		
A. East Asia (6)	Total GDP	Exported GDP	Non-exported GDP
1990–1997	7.1	10.9	5.7
1998–2003	2.9	7.6	0.6
1990–2003	5.3	9.5	3.5
B. Latin America (19)	Total GDP	Exported GDP	Non-exported GDP
1990–1997	3.2	8.3	2.4
1998–2003	1.2	5.4	0.3
1990–2003	2.4	7.1	1.5
C. Chile	Total GDP	Exported GDP	Non-exported GDP
1990–1997	7.6	10.5	6.9
1998–2003	2.6	5.7	1.7
1990–2003	5.5	8.4	4.6
D. Korea	Total GDP	Exported GDP	Non-exported GDP
1990–1997	7.2	13.9	5.4
1998–2003	4.0	11.9	0.1
1990–2003	5.8	13.0	3.1

Source: Author's calculations based on national account data in constant prices from ADB and ECLAC. "Exported GDP" is an estimate of the value-added in exports of goods and services; naturally, it covers only part of "exportables".
East Asia includes Indonesia, Korea, Malaysia, Philippines, Taiwan and Thailand. Latin America includes 19 countries.

is more closely associated with the external macroeconomic environment (and trade policies); the other is the rest of GDP – or non-exports – whose demand depends more intensively on the domestic macroeconomic environment. Actually, in the transit from boom to recession, the major share of changes in GDP growth rates has been located in non-exports performance, as can be estimated from table I.2.

Given that in both regions the *value-added* by exports average less than half of GDP (about one-third in EA and one-fifth in LACs), a vigorous overall economic growth requires a significant growth of non-exports output. For instance, in Chile and in the average of the six East Asian countries, in the dynamic years 1990–97, non-exports rose about 6% per year (see Table I.2.A and I.2.C), while during recessive years (1998–2003) they were nearly stagnant in average. Figures for Chile are rather similar to those of East Asia for 1990–97 and for 1998–03. Non-exports rose 6.9% in the former period and 1.7% in the latter. Over 80% of the drop in GDP growth, from 7.6% to 2.6%, was explained by the recessive impact on non-exports. It can be expected that, in these situations, the large majority of GDP growth slow-down be explained by a rise in the actual/potential output gap in non-exports.

d) Toward comprehensive real macroeconomic balances

A comprehensive definition of macroeconomic fundamentals should include – alongside low inflation and a sound fiscal balance – sustainable external deficits and low net liquid external liabilities, reduced currency and maturities mismatches, sustained public investment in human capital, high and efficient investment in physical capital, non-outlier real exchange rate, a crowding-in of domestic savings, and strong prudential regulation, supervision and transparency of the financial system. It is true that it looks like too many requirements; that is why sustained development is exceptional: few nations achieve it.

In boom periods, authorities should accumulate resources in stabilization funds, improve fiscal balances, increase international reserves, prepay external debt, avoid exchange rate appreciation, and regulate capital inflows. In recessive periods, it should imply, for instance, (i) continued implementation of a structural fiscal balance (recognizing that during recession tax proceeds are abnormally low and that, in those circumstances, public expenditure should not follow taxes in their descending runaway, and vice versa during the boom!), and (ii) a strong encouragement to effective demand,[24] with effective switching policies when domestic activity is clearly below productive capacity (see Ffrench-Davis, 2005, ch. 2).

A severe obstacle to a counter-cyclical policy has been the policy in fashion of full, across-the-board, opening of the capital account during booms. The predominant role exerted, during the recessive periods, by the policy recipe of IFIs and financial agents to pursue restrictive monetary and fiscal policies has tended to prolong the depressed economic activity in several EEs, and to generate a significant output gap.

Indeed, a macroeconomics for growth requires effective and efficient domestic policies. Certainly, the degrees of freedom in an increasingly (but also incompletely and unequally) globalized economy are more

---

[24] Both Korea and Malaysia offer clear cases of fiscal and monetary encouragement to aggregate demand, plus a significant devaluation, to recover economic activity after their respective 1998 recessions (Mahani, Shin and Wang, 2005).

limited than before, but there is still space to choose among a wide variety of alternative paths to *make* globalization, and effectively capturing net benefit with it. The cases of passive economic approaches, like Chile before the debt crisis of 1982, Mexico in the first half of the 1990s and Argentina during the 1990s, have proved to be extremely costly for EEs, because of their high propensity to external crises.

On the other hand, we find that prudential domestic policies, such as the selective capital controls established in Chile and Colombia in the 1990s (see ch. IV, in this volume), can reduce the external vulnerability and allow for counter-cyclical exchange rate and monetary policies. Furthermore, even once a crisis has taken place, domestic policies are also crucial to minimize its negative effects and accelerate economic recovery. Korea and Malaysia, two countries that performed comparative quite well after their severe crises, followed different policy approaches but both developed active and consistent counter-cyclical macroeconomic policies (see Mahani, Wang and Shin, 2005), in contrast with most EEs, particularly in Latin America; their respective GDP evolution attest to it.

e) Financial globalization and governance

There is a growing duality, worrisome for democracy, in the constituencies taken into account by authorities in EEs. The increasing complexity and globalization of the economic system is raising the distance between decision-makers and financial agents *vis-à-vis* the domestic agents (workers, firms and tax proceeds) bearing the consequences. As discussed above, an outcome of the specific road taken by globalization has been that experts in financial intermediation – a microeconomic training – have become determinant, in too many cases, for the evolution of the domestic macroeconomic balances and their volatility.

The integration of capital markets has remarkable implications on governance, room for domestic policies, and on the constituencies to which national governments respond. In fact, many leaders in emerging countries are living a *"dual constituency syndrome"* (Pietrobelli and Zamagni, 2000; Stiglitz, 2001): on the one hand, political authorities are elected by their countries' voters, and promise to implement a platform designed before their election, but on the other hand they also seek, after being democratically elected, the support of those who "vote" for their financial investments (not necessarily productive investments or may be at their expense). Recent cycles in financial markets have revealed a significant contradiction between the two, in a negative-sum game, with large output gaps and discouraged capital formation.

In summary, what is "irrational", and evidently inefficient from the perspective of resource allocation and total factor productivity, is that the decisions of authorities, which should obviously be taken with a long-term horizon, seeking sustainable growth with equity, become entrapped with the lobbying and policy recipes of microfinance experts, what leads to "irrational exuberance" (to use Greenspan's expression). Thus, in the next cycle, economic authorities should undertake the responsibility of making macro-fundamentals prevail (sustainable external deficit; moderate stock of external liabilities, with a low liquid share; reasonable matching of terms and currencies; crowding-in of domestic savings; limited real exchange rate appreciation; effective demand consistent with the production frontier), in order to achieve macroeconomic balances that are both sustainable and functional for long-term growth. That requires them to avoid entering *vulnerability zones* during economic booms-cum-capital surges. When placed inside those zones, a much needed counter-cyclical policy becomes impossible during the period of dryness or without a recessive traumatic adjustment as experienced by Argentina.

References

Agosin, M. (1998), "Capital inflows and investment performance: Chile in the 1990s", in Ffrench-Davis and Reisen (1998).

Barro, R. and X. Sala-i-Martin (1995), *Economic Growth*, McGraw-Hill, New York.

Bhagwati, J. (2004), *In Defense of Globalization*, Oxford University Press, New York.

—— (1998), "The capital myth: The difference between trade in widgets and dollars", *Foreign Affairs*, May–June.

Calvo, G. (1998), "Varieties of capital-market crises", in G. Calvo and M. King (eds.), *The Debt Burden and its Consequences for Monetary Policy*, Macmillan, London.

—— and E. Mendoza (2000), "Rational contagion and the globalization of securities markets", *Journal of International Economics*, 51.

Devlin, R. (1989), *Debt and Crisis in Latin America: The Supply Side of the Story*, Princeton, University Press, Princeton.

Díaz-Alejandro, C. F. (1985), "Goodbye financial repression, hello financial crash", *Journal of Development Economics*, Vol. 19, No. 1/2, September–October.

Dodd, R. (2003), "Derivatives, the shape of international capital flows and the virtues of prudential regulation", in Ffrench-Davis and Griffith-Jones (2003).

Easterly, W. and L. Servén (2003), (eds.), *The Limits of Stabilization*, Stanford University Press, Palo Alto, California.

ECLAC (2002a), *Growth with Stability: Financing for Development in the New International Context*, ECLAC Books, No. 67, Santiago.

—— (2002b), *Globalization and Development*, United Nations, Santiago; an abridged version, edited by J. A. Ocampo and J. Martín, Stanford University Press, 2003.

—— (1995), *Policies to Improve Linkages with the Global Economy*, United Nations, Santiago (Fondo de Cultura Económica, second edition, Santiago, 1998).

Eichengreen, B. (2003), *Capital Flows and Crises*, The MIT Press, Cambridge Mass.

Ffrench-Davis, R. (2005), *Reforming Latin America's Economies: After Market Fundamentalism*, Palgrave Macmillan, London.

—— (2003), "Financial crises and national policy issues: An overview", in Ffrench-Davis and Griffith-Jones (2003).

—— (2002), *Economic Reforms in Chile: from Dictatorship to Democracy*, University of Michigan Press, Ann Arbor.

—— and S. Griffith-Jones (2003), *From Capital Surges to Drought*, Palgrave Macmillan/WIDER, London.

—— and J. A. Ocampo (2001), "The globalization of financial volatility", in R. Ffrench-Davis (ed.), *Financial Crises in "Successful" Emerging Economies*, Brookings Institution, Washington, DC.

—— and H. Reisen (1998), (eds.), *Capital Flows and Investment Performance: Lessons from Latin America*, ECLAC/OECD Development Centre, Paris.

—— and H. Tapia (2004), "Macroeconomic policies for emerging economies, in an era of globalization", in J. Stiglitz, R. Ffrench-Davis and D. Nayyar (eds.), *Macroeconomic Policies*, Oxford University Press, London and New York, forthcoming.

—— and L. Villar (2005), "Real macroeconomic stability and the capital account in Chile and Colombia", in this volume.

Fischer, S. (1993), "The role of macroeconomic factors in growth", *Journal of Monetary Economics*, Vol. 32, No. 3.

Frenkel, R. (2004), "From the boom in capital inflows to financial traps", prepared for the Capital Account Liberalization Task Force, IPD, Columbia University. (http://www.gsb.columbia.edu/ipd/pub/Frenkel5_3_04.pdf)

—— and J. Ros (2004), "Macroeconomic policies and the labor market in Argentina and Mexico", ECLAC project on *Management of Volatility, Financial Globalization and Growth in Emerging Economies*.

Gelb, S. (2005), "Macroeconomics in post-apartheid South Africa: Real growth versus financial stability", in this volume.

Gourinchas, P. O. and O. Jeanne (2004), "The elusive gains from international financial integration", *Working Paper No. 04/74*, Research Department, International Monetary Fund, Washington DC, May.

Harberger, A. (1985), "Observations on the Chilean economy, 1973–83", *Economic Development and Cultural Change*, 33, April.

IDB (2004), *Good Jobs Wanted: Labor Markets in Latin America*, chapter 4, Inter-American Development Bank (IDB), Washington DC.

IMF (1998), *World Economic Outlook, 1998. Financial Crises: Characteristics and Indicators of Vulnerability*, Chapter VII, International Monetary Fund (IMF), Washington, DC, May.

Kindleberger, Ch. (1978), *Manias, Panics and Crashes: A History of Financial Crisis*, Basic Books, New York.

Krugman, Paul (2000), "Crises: The price of globalization?", Federal Reserve Bank of Kansas City, *Symposium on Global Economic Integration: Opportunities and Challenges*, Jackson Hole, Wyoming.

—— (1999), "Balance sheets, the transfer problem, and financial crises", in P. Izard, A. Razin and A. Rose (eds.), *International Finance and Financial Crises*, Kluwer Academic Publishers, Dordrecht, The Netherlands.

Kuczynski, P. and J. Williamson (2003), (eds.), *After the Washington Consensus*, Institute for International Economics, Washington, DC.

Mahani, Z., K. Shin and Y. Wang (2005), "Macroeconomic adjustment and the real economy in Korea and Malaysia since 1997", in this volume.

Maddison, A. (2001) *The World Economy: A Millennial Perspective*, OECD Development Centre, Paris.

Marfán, M. (2005), "Fiscal policy efficacy and private deficits: A macroeconomic approach", in J. A. Ocampo (ed.), *Rethinking Development Challenges*, Stanford University Press, Palo Alto, California.

Morley S., R. Machado and S. Pettinato (1999), "Indexes of structural reform in Latin America", ECLAC, Santiago.

Obstfeld, M. (1998), "The global capital market: Benefactor or menace?", *Journal of Economic Perspectives*, Vol. 12 (Fall).

—— (1994), "Risk-taking, global diversification and growth", *American Economic Review*, Vol. 84.

Ocampo, J. A. (2005), "Overcoming Latin America's growth frustrations: The macro and mesoeconomic links", in this volume.

—— (2003), "Capital account and counter-cyclical prudential regulations in developing countries", in Ffrench-Davis and Griffith-Jones (2003).

——, S. Zamagni, R. Ffrench-Davis and C. Pietrobelli (2000), (eds.), *Financial Globalization and the Emerging Economies*, ECLAC/Jacques Maritain Institute, Santiago.

Persaud, A. (2003), "Liquidity black holes", in Ffrench-Davis and Griffith-Jones (2003).

Pfaff, W. (2000), "A challenge to globalization theory", in Ocampo, *et al.* (2000).

Pietrobelli, C. and S. Zamagni (2000), "The emerging economies in the global financial market: Some concluding remarks", in Ocampo, *et al.* (2000).

Prasad, E., K. Rogoff, S. Wei, and M. Kose (2003), "Effects of financial globalization on developing countries: Some empirical evidence", *IMF Occasional Paper*, No. 220, September.

Reisen, H. (2003), "Ratings since the Asian crisis", in Ffrench-Davis and Griffith-Jones (2003).

Rodrik, D. (2003), "Growth strategies", *NBER Working Paper*, 10050, October.

—— (2001), "Why is there so much economic insecurity in Latin America?", *CEPAL Review*, No. 73, Santiago, April.

—— (1998), "Who needs capital account convertibility?", in P. Kenen (ed.), *Should the IMF Pursue Capital Account Convertibility?*, Princeton Essays in International Finance, No. 207.

—— and A. Velasco (2000), "Short-term capital flows", *Annual World Bank Conference on Development Economics 1999*, The World Bank, Washington, DC.

Ros, J. (2000), *Development Theory and Economics of Growth*, The University of Michigan Press, Ann Arbor.

Schmidt-Hebbel, K., L. Servén and A. Solimano (1996), "Savings and invest-ment: Paradigms, puzzles, policies", *World Bank Research Observer*, Vol. 11.1, Washington, DC.

Stallings, B. and W. Peres (2000), *Growth, Employment and Equity: the Impact of the Economic Reforms in Latin America and the Caribbean*, The Brookings Institute, Washington, DC; and Economic Commission for Latin America and the Caribbean (ECLAC)/Fondo de Cultura Económica, Santiago.

Stiglitz, J. (2002), "Information and the Change in the Paradigm in Economics", *American Economic Review*, June.

—— (2001), "More instruments and broader goals: Moving toward the Post-Washington Consensus", in H. Chang (ed.), *The Rebel Within*, Wimbledon Publishing Company, London. Originally presented as the 1998 WIDER Annual Lecture, Helsinki, January.

—— (2000), "Capital market liberalization, economic growth and instability", *World Development*, Vol. 28, No. 6, June.

—— (1998), "The role of the financial system in development", in World Bank Conference on Development in Latin America and the Caribbean, San Salvador, June.

Tytell, I. and S. Wei (2004), "Does financial globalization induce better macro-economic policies?", *Working Paper* WP/04/84, International Monetary Fund, Washington DC.

UNCTAD (2003), *Foreign Investment Report 2003*, United Nations, Geneva.

Uthoff, A. and D. Titelman (1998), "The relation between foreign and national savings under financial liberalization", in Ffrench-Davis and Reisen (1998).

Williamson, J. (2003a), "Overview: An agenda for restarting growth and reform", in Kuczynski and Williamson (2003).

—— (2003b), "Proposals for curbing the boom-bust cycle in the supply of capital to emerging markets", in Ffrench-Davis and Griffith-Jones (2003).

World Bank (2003), *Inequality in Latin America and the Caribbean: Breaking with History?*, chapter 8, World Bank, Washington DC.

Zahler, R. (2005), "Macroeconomic stability and investment allocation by domestic pension funds in emerging economies: The case of Chile", in this volume.

II
Overcoming Latin America's Growth Frustrations: The Macro and Mesoeconomic Links

José Antonio Ocampo *

Whereas the moderate rates of economic growth of 1990–97 generated positive evaluations of Latin America's reform efforts (see Edwards, 1995; IDB, 1997; and World Bank, 1997), the return to very slow rates of growth in 1998–2003 (a phenomenon that ECLAC characterized in 2002 as a new "lost half-decade") brought an extensive reevaluation of these early assessments (ECLAC, 2003a; Kuczynski and Williamson, 2003). The new development strategy has been effective in generating export dynamism, attracting foreign direct investment (FDI) and increasing productivity in leading firms and sectors. In most countries, inflation trends and budget deficits have been effectively brought under control, and confidence in the macroeconomic authorities has increased. Nonetheless, economic growth has been frustratingly low and volatile, and domestic savings and investment have remained depressed. Overall productivity performance has been poor, largely as a result of the growing underutilization of both physical capital and labor. Increasing production and labor market dualism has become one of the most distinctive effects of the reform process, with the expansion of "world class" firms (many of them subsidiaries of multinationals) coinciding with increasing unemployment and labor market informality.

   This paper evaluates the poor growth record of the reform period in the light of both macroeconomic and sectoral (mesoeconomic) performance. Section 1 looks at macroeconomic performance and the links between growth and liberalization. Section 2 considers sectoral and

* The valuable comments received at two international seminars organized at ECLAC are acknowledged.

structural performance. Section 3 suggests a structuralist interpretation of this evidence.

1. Macroeconomic performance

The most salient economic advance in the 1990s was the increasing confidence in the region's macroeconomic authorities generated by improvements in fiscal conditions and reductions in inflation rates. On average, central-government budget deficits declined significantly in the second half of the 1980s, remained in an average range of between 1% and 2% of GDP through most of the 1990s, but have increased to levels of around 3% since 1999. Progress in this area has been uneven across the region, as reflected in the fiscal crises that some countries have experienced in recent years, and the high public-sector debt ratios that continue to characterize several countries. Progress in the fight against inflation has been more uniform and long-lasting. Average inflation in Latin America fell steadily up to 2001, when it reached single digits in most countries. Setbacks in 2002, when average inflation increased for the first time in a decade, were concentrated in a few countries, and were followed by a renewed reduction in 2003.

Nonetheless, the expectation that advances in the fiscal area and control of inflation would be reflected in access to stable external capital flows, high investment rates and strong economic growth did not materialize. Renewed access to international capital markets was evident in the early 1990s. As figure II.1 indicates, there was a sharp turn from negative to positive net resource transfers in the early 1990s. Financial flows played the key role in the early part of this reversal, but it was replaced by FDI since the mid-1990s. The Asian crisis generated a return to large negative resource transfers through financial flows, indeed in magnitudes similar to those of the 1980s. FDI served as a compensatory factor up to 2001, but its sharp fall in 2002–2003 generated large negative overall net resource transfers for the first time in more than a decade.

Although renewed growth had characterized a handful of Latin American economies in the second half of the 1980s, broad-based growth only took off in the early 1990s and was closely associated to renewed capital flows. Capital flows facilitated structural reforms and exchange-rate-based stabilization policies and, in turn, the boom in external financing was facilitated by reforms (through more liberal capital account regulations and privatization, which induced larger FDI flows, among other channels). However, the broad-based deceleration

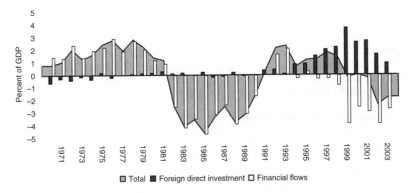

Figure II.1 Net resource transfers, 1970–2003 (% of GDP)
Source: ECLAC, on the basis of IMF data.

in growth that took place in 1995 and, particularly, in 1998–2003 indicates the prominent role of capital flows – especially of *financial flows* – as determinants of swings in economic growth. Thus, although trade and domestic factors also played a role, fluctuations in the capital account became the major single determinant of the Latin American business cycle.

Overall, long-term growth has been frustratingly low. Between 1990 and 2003 as a whole, the average growth rate, of only 2.6% a year or 0.9% per capita, was less than half the level experienced by Latin America between 1950 and 1980, namely 5.5% per year or 2.7% per capita (table II.1). The demographic transition adversely affected per capita trends in the earlier period of State-led (or import substitution) industrialization, while the opposite was true in the 1990s, when the region benefited from a "demographic bonus". This is reflected in the fact that the labor force grew in the 1990s at rates quite similar to those that characterized the period 1950–1980. Indeed, as table II.1 indicates, GDP per active worker slowed down more sharply than GDP per capita, a fact that is consistent with other measures of productivity performance presented below (see section 3).

Macroeconomic policy management has been partly responsible for the sensitivity of economic growth to capital flows, for some features of the restructuring of the production sectors and for the propensity to domestic financial crises. Indeed, a particular feature of the reform period has been the building up of *automatic destabilizers* (Stiglitz, 2003), associated in particular with *private* rather than public-sector deficits and balance sheets. This has generated tensions between

Table II.1   Latin America's growth and volatility, 1950–2003 (%)

	1950–1980	1980–2003	1990–2003
Average GDP growth			
Weighted average	5.5	2.0	2.6
Simple average	4.8	2.0	2.9
Large and median countries	5.2	2.0	2.7
Small countries	4.5	2.1	3.0
Average GDP per capita growth			
Weighted average	2.7	0.1	0.9
Simple average	2.1	0.0	0.9
Large and median countries	2.4	0.1	1.0
Small countries	1.8	–0.1	0.8
Average GDP per worker growth			
Weighted average	2.7	–0.7	0.0
Simple average	2.4	–0.9	0.0
Large and median countries	2.7	–0.9	0.0
Small countries	2.2	–0.9	–0.1
GDP growth volatility			
Weighted average	1.4	2.2	1.9
Simple average	3.8	4.1	3.3
Large and median countries	3.4	4.6	3.9
Small countries	4.2	3.8	2.9
ICOR			
Simple average a/	3.8	9.5	6.8

Source: ECLAC.
Large and median countries: Argentina, Brazil, Chile, Colombia, Ecuador, Mexico, Peru, Venezuela.
a/ Excluding Venezuela.

macroeconomic policies and reform objectives. In particular, the strong bias in favor of currency appreciation that characterized the periods marked by an abundance of external financing was partly responsible for the adjustment problems faced by tradable sectors in several countries, as well as for the speculative attacks and the increased risks of domestic financial crises that arose when there was a sudden stop in capital flows. Also, the tendency to adopt procyclical fiscal and, particularly, monetary and credit policies – which foster lending booms and drops in interest rates during periods of expansion, as well as marked monetary contraction and high interest rates during crises – has been an underlying cause of unstable economic growth and national financial crises. About half of the Latin American countries experienced domestic financial crises during the 1990s, absorbing considerable fiscal and quasi-fiscal resources, and affecting the functioning of financial systems, sometimes for extended periods of time (ECLAC, 2002b; 2003a, chapter 3; Ffrench-Davis, 2003; Ocampo, 2003b).

Dependence on external financing was also associated with a *structural* deterioration in the trade balance/growth trade-off (see below) and a high degree of sensitivity in the trade balance to economic activity. The tendency to substitute foreign for domestic saving, which characterizes periods of intense capital inflows, played a similar role. More broadly, domestic savings remained depressed in the 1990s, making investment highly dependent on external savings at the margin. Investment rates experienced a partial recovery – particularly if the simple rather than the weighted average is considered, indicating that smaller countries did better in this regard – but this was cut short by the interruption of capital flows since the Asian crisis (see figure II.2). Beyond that, however, the investment-growth link has deteriorated, as reflected in the high incremental capital-output ratios that have characterized the reform period (see table II.1 again). This issue has not been extensively analyzed, and may reflect the fact that volatile growth leads to a high average rate of underutilization of production capacity, reducing the productivity of investment (Ffrench-Davis, 2005), as well as the significant destruction of capital generated by the reform effort and, in some cases, the high capital intensity of some of the leading sectors induced by structural reforms. As we will see below, these results also call into question the assumed link between reforms, the investment climate and investment efficiency.

This mixed record indicates that macroeconomic policies should be based on a broad definition of stability, that recognizes that there is no single correlation between its alternative definitions and that significant trade-offs may be involved. Cross-country evidence indicates, indeed, that all forms of macroeconomic instability – high inflation, as well as real instability and the frequency of domestic financial crises – have adverse effects on growth (Loayza, *et al.*, 2002).

Two lessons of the recent historical period are particularly important in this regard. The first is that *real* instability is very costly. A narrow view of inflation targeting may thus be as damaging as past macroeconomic practices that underestimated the costs of inflation. Recessions entail a significant loss of resources that may have long-run effects: firms may sustain irreparable losses in terms of both tangible and intangible assets (tacit technological and organizational knowledge, commercial contacts, the social capital accumulated in the firm, its goodwill, etc.); the human capital of the unemployed or the underemployed may be permanently lost; and children may leave school and

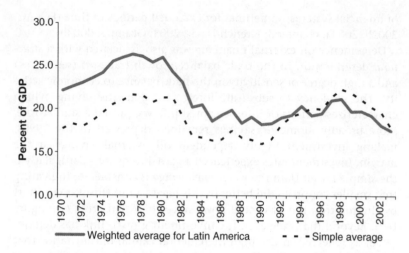

Figure II.2   Fixed investment as a percentage of GDP, 1970–2003 (estimated at 1995 prices)
Source: ECLAC.

never return. The uncertainty associated with variability in growth rates may consequently have stronger effects on capital accumulation than moderate inflation. Indeed, it encourages "defensive" microeconomic strategies (i.e., those aimed at protecting the existing corporate assets of firms that find themselves in an unfriendly environment) rather than the "offensive" strategies that lead to high investment rates and rapid technical change.

The second lesson is that private deficits are just as costly as public sector ones. Moreover, risky private sector balance sheets may be as damaging as flow imbalances. In financially liberalized economies, both may interact in non-linear ways with capital account shocks. The lack of strong prudential regulation and supervision typical of the early phases of financial liberalization is part, but certainly not the whole of the story. Boom-bust cycles are an inherent aspect of financial markets. Private spending booms and risky balance sheets tend to accumulate during periods of financial euphoria and are the basis for crises once exceptional conditions normalize. During such bouts of euphoria, economic agents tend to underestimate the intertemporal inconsistency that may be involved in existing spending and financial strategies. When crises lead to a financial meltdown, the associated costs are extremely high. Asset losses may wipe out years of capital accumulation. The socialization of losses may be the only way to avoid a systemic crisis, but this will affect future fiscal (or quasi-fiscal) performance. Restoring confidence in the financial system takes time, and the financial sector itself becomes risk-averse, a feature that undermines its ability to perform its primary economic functions.

These two lessons are basically interconnected, due to the prominent role played by financial swings as a determinant of the Latin American business cycle. An essential task of macroeconomic policy is thus to manage them with appropriate countercyclical tools, based on the combination of three policy packages, whose relative importance will vary depending on the structural characteristics and the macroeconomic policy tradition of each country. The first is consistent and flexible macroeconomic – fiscal, monetary and exchange-rate – policies aimed at preventing public or private agents from accumulating excessive levels of debt and at forestalling imbalances in key macroeconomic prices (exchange and interest rates) and in the prices of fixed and financial assets. The second is a system of strict prudential regulation and supervision with a clear counter-cyclical orientation. This means that prudential regulation and supervision should be tightened during periods of financial euphoria to counter the mounting risks incurred by financial intermediaries. The third element is a liability policy aimed at ensuring that appropriate maturity profiles are maintained with respect to domestic and external public and private commitments. Preventive capital account regulations (i.e., those applied during periods of euphoria to avoid excessive borrowing) can play a role, both as a liability policy – encouraging longer-term flows – and as an instrument that provides additional degrees of freedom for the adoption of counter-cyclical monetary policies (Ocampo, 2003a and 2003b; Ffrench-Davis, 2003).

Managing counter-cyclical macroeconomic policies is no easy task, as financial markets generate strong incentives for developing countries to overspend during periods of financial euphoria and to overadjust during crises. Moreover, globalization places objective limits on national autonomy and exacts a high cost for any loss of credibility when national policy instruments are poorly administered. For this reason, it may be necessary for counter-cyclical macroeconomic policy to be supported by institutions and policy instruments that help to provide credibility, including fiscal stabilization funds and independent central banks. It also means that an essential role of international financial institutions, from the point of view of developing countries, is to counteract the procyclical effects of financial markets. This can be achieved by smoothing out boom-bust cycles at the source through adequate regulation and by providing developing countries with additional degrees of freedom to adopt counter-cyclical policies (e.g., adequate surveillance and incentives to avoid the build-up of risky macroeconomic and financial conditions during periods of financial euphoria, together with mechanisms to smooth out adjustments in the event of abrupt interruptions in private capital flows).[1]

In any case, it must be clear that sharp financial cycles, procyclical policies and the resulting macroeconomic volatility are part, but certainly not the whole explanation for the poor growth record of Latin America during the reform period. This fact is highlighted in figure II.3. There is, indeed, a strong negative association between macroeconomic volatility (as measured by the standard deviation of the GDP growth rate) and growth, but this link is associated with the poor growth record of economies with very high GDP volatility (Argentina, Uruguay and Venezuela). The rest have lower volatility but still a poor average growth record.

Is it the extent of economic liberalization (structural reform, in the current terminology) what explains these outcomes? This issue has been explored in the recent literature with no conclusive results. The mere comparison of the recent growth record with that achieved during the age of the State-led industrialization contradicts the view that there is a strong association between economic liberalization and growth. Indeed, it is symptomatic of the weakness of this association that even supporters of economic liberalization now regard the State-led industrialization period as a "golden age", and the growth rates achieved during that period as a goal for future Latin American performance.[2] On the other hand, the evidence presented above on weak investment performance and high incremental capital-output ratios calls into question any simple association between economic liberalization and improved investment climate and efficiency.

Evidence from ECLAC research indicates that links between reforms and growth have been, at best, weak: some reforms had positive effects on growth but others had negative effects, and these impacts balance out to a statistically insignificant overall net effect. Furthermore, even

---

[1] The negative relationship between volatility and GDP growth and the causality from the former to the latter have been widely documented. See, for example, Fatás (2002) and Ramey and Ramey (1995). Hnatkovska and Loayza (2003) highlight, in addition, that this effect has become considerably larger in the last two decades.

[2] See Kuczynski and Williamson (2003), pp. 305 and 29, respectively.

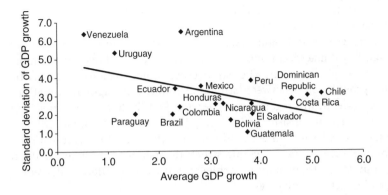

Figure II.3 Volatility and growth, 1990–2003
Source: ECLAC.

if their long-term effect were neutral or positive, their short-term impact was clearly negative (Escaith and Morley, 2001; Stallings and Peres, 2000).[3] These results are consistent with those of Lora and Panizza (2002) when compared with the earlier evidence presented in Lora and Barrera (1998). Whereas the earlier paper estimated strong effects of reforms on growth, the latter only calculated weak temporary effects.

Although the World Bank has also claimed, based on recent research (Loayza, *et al.*, 2002), that reforms had significant effects on long-term growth, they measure the effects of some long-term *characteristics* rather than *reforms*. Particularly, the results of the evidence that they present indicate strong long-term effects of human capital accumulation and infrastructure on economic growth. They also show somewhat weaker effects of effective trade openness and financial depth, but do *not* estimate those of trade and domestic financial *reforms*.

Indeed, there is a significant confusion in the debate derived from the tendency to mix *structural reforms* aimed at reducing the public sector's role in the economy and liberalizing markets with *macroeconomic stabilization policies*, as well as the tendency to confuse structural *characteristics* with structural *reforms* aimed at liberalization. Some aggressive reformers introduced liberalization together with major stabilization packages (e.g., Chile in the mid-1970s, Bolivia in the mid-1980s, and Argentina and Peru in the early 1990s), but this pattern was

[3] See also the sensitivity analysis of Correa (2002).

far from universal. The difference is substantial, as macroeconomic balances can be achieved with large differences in the degree of economic liberalization and, conversely, liberalized economies can maintain significant macroeconomic imbalances, as we saw above. Furthermore, there is evidence that, whereas macroeconomic balances are essential for growth, links between structural reforms and growth are at best weak (see, in this regard, Rodríguez and Rodrik, 2001). The latter statement is not inconsistent with recognizing the fact that some structural characteristics may affect economic growth – e.g., the accumulation of human capital, improved infrastructure, openness and financial depth – but all of them may be achieved with quite different degrees of public-sector involvement.

2. Integration into the world economy and restructuring of the production sectors

Weak growth performance cannot be attributed to the lack of success of economic liberalization in achieving one of their most direct objectives: increased integration into the world economy. Indeed, from 1990 to 2000, the region posted the fastest growth of export volumes in its history (close to 9% per year), much higher than the rate achieved by world trade as a whole; the 2001–02 world slowdown obviously interrupted this process. The strong growth of Mexican exports explains much of this strength over the 1990s, but the poor Brazilian export record in that period also brought the Latin American average down. Most other countries experienced healthy real export growth over the 1990s, close to 8% a year on average. Although variable in terms of the strategies followed by multinationals in different countries, FDI also boomed through the 1990s, as figure II.1 indicates.

According to recent ECLAC analysis, integration into the world economy followed two basic patterns of specialization, which approximately obey a regional "North-South" divide (ECLAC, 2002a; Mortimore and Peres, 2001). The "Northern" pattern is characterized by manufacturing exports with a high content of imported inputs (in its extreme form, *maquila* exports), mainly geared towards the United States market, and attracts FDI associated with the development of internationally integrated production systems. This pattern goes hand in hand with traditional agricultural exports and agricultural export diversification in Central America, as well as the growth of tourism in Mexico and the Caribbean. The "Southern" pattern is characterized by the combination of extra-regional exports of commodities and natural-resource-intensive manufactures (many of which are also capital-intensive) and diversified intra-regional trade, and mainly attracts FDI associated with the search for natural resources or access to domestic markets (in services, as well as large domestic and subregional markets). In the case of Brazil, this is mixed with some technology-intensive manufactures and services, and in Brazil and a number of other countries, with labor-intensive manufacturing exports. This implies that Mexico and some Central American and Caribbean countries have been participating to a greater extent in the more dynamic world markets for manufactures, whereas South America has focused on the less dynamic commodity markets. Nonetheless, a more detailed breakdown indicates that most Latin American countries specialize in goods that are not playing a dynamic role in world trade – i.e., even manufacturing exporters concentrate in non-dynamic segments of world trade (ECLAC, 2002a and 2002c). There is also a third pattern of specialization, which is found in Panama and some small economies in the Caribbean Basin, in which service exports (financial, tourism and transport services) predominate.

The contrast between the dynamic internationalization of the Latin American economies and the weak GDP performance is not inconsistent with a strong cross-sectional correlation between export and GDP growth in Latin America, as figure II.4.A indicates. So, higher export growth has led to faster GDP growth in individual countries, but the export-growth link has weakened for all of them. This evidence may be interpreted as a sign of the weakening of the links between international trade, FDI and domestic production (and, thus, GDP) and, as a consequence, it is contrary to the evidence much discussed in the literature of the 1970s and 1980s on the positive externalities of deeper integration into international markets. Indeed, it points out to a reduction in the domestic production and technological linkages of export sectors, which increasingly outsource in international markets, together with the simultaneous destruction of the production linkages generated by previous import-substitution sectors unable to reconvert into export activities, or able to do so only through increased imports of intermediate goods and services. Outsourcing by multinational firms, even in non-tradable sectors (e.g., services), has further contributed to the weakening of their domestic linkages.

Thus, in a significant sense, many internationalized sectors have an increasing "enclave" component: they participate actively in international transactions but much less in the generation of domestic value added. Indeed, in this sense, the natural-resource-intensive sectors of

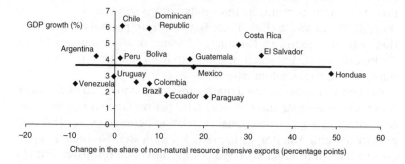

Figure II.4   Specialization patterns, exports and GDP growth, 1990–2000
A   Exports and GDP growth
B   Change in the share of non-natural resource intensive exports and GDP growth
Source: ECLAC.

the "Southern" pattern of specialization may provide more opportunities for the formation of domestic production and technological linkages than the assembly activities characteristic of the "Northern" pattern (see ECLAC, 2003b, ch. III; World Bank, 2002).

A particular way in which these transformations have affected macroeconomic aggregates has been the deterioration in the growth/trade deficit trade-off.[4] The trade deficit tended to widen in 1991–97, reaching levels comparable to those of the 1970s, but at

[4] See a similar analysis in UNCTAD (1999), which shows that this deterioration has occurred throughout the developing world, except in China and some other Asian economies.

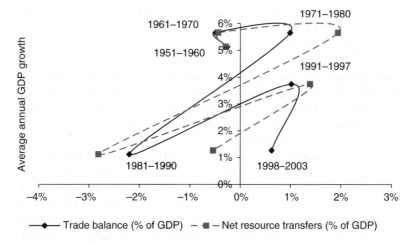

Figure II.5 Trade balance/growth trade-off
Source: ECLAC.

growth rates that were two percentage points below those registered in that decade (see figure II.5). This was the joint effect of *structural* changes in production activities brought about by economic liberalization – including weaker domestic linkages of internationalized sectors – and the short-term *macroeconomic* policy bias towards real currency appreciation generated by booming capital inflows. Heavy dependence on volatile external financing was, in this regard, an effect but also a cause of this deterioration. Interestingly, this worsening of the growth/trade deficit trade-off is even worse if the point of reference is the 1950s and 1960s, when rapid growth was consistent with small trade surpluses. This process worsened further during the 1998–2003 slowdown, when the trade deficit remained stubbornly high despite very slow economic growth.

A paradoxical effect of policies aimed at deeper integration into the world economy was the relative dynamism of tradable vs. non-tradable sectors in many countries (ECLAC, 2003a, chs. 4 and 5; Stallings and Peres, 2000; Katz, 2001). Non-tradables, such as transport, communications, energy and financial services, as well as construction, were indeed dynamic, particularly during the expansionary phases of the regional business cycle. Among tradable sectors, manufacturing generally suffered the most in comparison with its own historical record prior to the debt crisis. This was especially true in the more traditional, labor-intensive industries (apparel, footwear and leather manufactures, furniture, etc.), with the exception of those industries associated with in-bond assembly (*maquila*) activities. The manufacturing sectors that performed better include *maquila* activities, the automobile industry (which is favored, in Mexico, by access to the United States market and, in South America, by special protection mechanisms provided by current integration arrangements), some natural-resource-processing industries, and certain activities geared towards the domestic market during periods of booming demand (such as construction materials, beverages and food processing).

The mix between the growth of tradable and non-tradable sectors was diverse across the region through the 1990s and did not follow the Northern-Southern divide that characterized trade specialization patterns. The association between specialization patterns and the relative dynamism of manufacturing was, on the other hand, quite strong (ECLAC, 2003a). Economies specializing in manufacturing exports were characterized by the rapid relative growth of manufacturing production, while the opposite was the typical pattern in economies that specialized in natural-resource-intensive exports. Employment trends – and, particularly, employment in manufacturing – were also more positive under the Northern pattern (ECLAC, 2002a, ch. 10; Stallings and Weller, 2001).

It must be emphasized that, contrary to the literature on the "natural resource curse" and to the significant evidence of long-term and medium-term deterioration of the terms of trade of primary commodities over the past two decades (Ocampo and Parra, 2003), neither export nor overall GDP growth has been associated with particular specialization patterns (figure II.4.B). Chile is the outstanding example of a country specializing in natural-resource-intensive exports that has experienced rapid export and GDP growth in the 1990s. Ecuador and Venezuela are opposite cases. Mexico has extracted relatively slow GDP growth out of its outstanding export growth and diversification. In this regard, Costa Rica and El Salvador, and particularly the Dominican Republic, have done better. As was indicated, the high import content of manufacturing exports and the tendency to specialize in the technologically simpler tasks within internationally integrated production systems may, indeed, result in natural-resource-intensive exports generating more domestic value added and linkages than manufacturing exports.

Slow GDP growth was associated with poor productivity performance, but the causal links involved must be carefully drawn. Particularly, the neo-classical link used in most of the literature, which assumes that GDP is determined by productivity growth, cannot be assumed to be the appropriate one. Even in some of the manufacturing sectors where productivity rose, the gap with the industrialized economies actually widened in the 1990s. Indeed, in many countries and manufacturing activities, the productivity gap in relation to the United States narrowed more quickly during the 1970s and 1980s than during the 1990s, reflecting in part the slower pace of technological change in United States manufacturing during those previous decades. At the subsectoral level, the closing of the technology gap had more to do with the pace of economic growth in a particular sector and country than with patterns of technological catch-up induced by the reform process (Katz, 2001).

In general, productivity trends reflect a large discrepancy between the positive evolution of this variable in a group of successful firms and sectors and a poor performance at the aggregate level. Growth in total factor productivity (TFP) slowed down relative to its pre-debt crisis pace (see table II.2, and Hofman, 2001). Furthermore, an analysis of the joint effects of productivity and trade elasticities indicates that the reduction in the technological gap *vis-à-vis* the world frontier was not enough to compensate the extraordinary increase in the (gross) income elasticity of the demand for imports, with the consequent deterioration of the trade multiplier (the ratio of the technological gap to the elasticity for imports), thus generating overall adverse effects on growth (Cimoli and Correa, 2005). The slowdown was sharper for labor productivity, as the estimates of productivity of the labor force in table II.1 indicate. Rising unemployment and, particularly, underemployment, largely due to poor overall economic growth, drove aggregate labor productivity. More broadly, overall productivity performance reflects the fact that labor, capital, technological capacity and, sometimes, land that were displaced from sectors and firms undergoing restructuring were not adequately reallocated to dynamic sectors.

These patterns of productivity performance bring to light one of the main features of the restructuring of the production processes that characterized the region during the reform period: the increased diversity of production sectors and agents within each economy – i.e. increasing dualism (or "structural heterogeneity", using traditional ECLAC terminology). This indicates that the expectations that rising productivity in internationalized sectors would spread throughout the economy, thereby leading to rapid overall economic growth, turned out to be quite optimistic. Productivity *did* increase in dynamic firms and sectors, and external competition, FDI and privatization played an

Table II.2   **Total factor productivity, 1950–2002 (annual rates of change)**

	1950–1980	1980–1990	1990–1997	1997–2002	1990–2002
Argentina					
TFP	1.2	–2.2	4.6	–4.5	0.7
DATFP	0.6	–2.9	3.9	–5.2	0.0
Bolivia					
TFP	1.6	–1.9	1.3	–0.2	0.7
DATFP	0.5	–2.9	0.2	–1.5	–0.5
Brazil					
TFP	2.6	–1.5	0.0	–0.3	–0.1
DATFP	1.4	–2.2	–0.8	–1.4	–1.0
Colombia					
TFP	2.4	0.6	1.6	–1.2	0.4
DATFP	1.4	–0.8	0.6	–1.7	–0.4
Costa Rica					
TFP	2.3	–1.1	1.2	1.0	1.1
DATFP	1.3	–2.0	0.1	–0.2	0.0
Chile					
TFP	1.6	0.5	4.6	–0.5	2.4
DATFP	0.9	–0.6	3.8	–1.1	1.7
Ecuador					
TFP	3.0	–1.6	0.8	–1.8	–0.3
DATFP	1.9	–2.6	0.0	–2.5	–1.0
Mexico					
TFP	1.9	–1.4	–0.2	–0.5	–0.3
DATFP	0.5	–1.9	–0.7	–1.7	–1.1
Peru					
TFP	1.8	–3.7	2.9	–1.0	1.2
DATFP	0.9	–4.7	2.5	–1.4	0.9
Venezuela					
TFP	1.9	–1.4	2.2	–2.2	0.3
DATFP	0.5	–2.7	1.4	–2.7	–0.3
Latin America					
Simple average					
TFP	2.0	–1.4	1.9	–1.1	0.6
DATFP	1.0	–2.3	1.1	–1.9	–0.2
Weighted average (2001 GDP at 1995 prices)					
TFP	2.1	–1.4	1.1	–1.1	0.2
DATFP	1.0	–2.2	0.4	–2.0	–0.6

Source: Hofman (2001) and data provided by this author.
DATFP: Doubly augmented total factor productivity.

important role in that process. However, contrary to the expectations of reformers, positive productivity shocks did *not* spread out, but rather led to greater dispersion in relative productivity levels within these economies.

3. A structuralist (and, particularly, Schumpeterian-Hirschminate) interpretation of restructuring of the production sectors underway

As the evidence presented above indicates, understanding why growth has been so frustrating in Latin America in the post-reform period requires a look at both macroeconomic and structural dynamics. In this section, we will concentrate on the latter, drawing upon historical variants of structuralism in economic thinking, broadly defined. This view emphasizes the close connections among structural dynamics, investment and economic growth. According to this view, economic growth is not a linear process, in which "representative firms" grow or new representative firms respond to the "investment climate" generated by macroeconomic conditions and structural reforms. It is a more dynamic process in which some sectors and firms grow and move ahead while others fall behind, thereby completely transforming economic structures. This process involves a repetitive phenomenon of "creative destruction", to use Schumpeter's metaphor (1962, ch. VIII). Not all sectors have the same ability to inject dynamism into the economy, to "propagate technical progress", according to the concept advanced by Prebisch (1951). The complementarities (externalities) between enterprises and production sectors, along with their macroeconomic and distributive effects, can produce sudden jumps in the growth process or can block it (Rosenstein-Rodan, 1943; Taylor, 1991; Ros, 2000) and, in so doing, generate successive phases of disequilibria, according to Hirschman's (1958) classic view. Under- or unutilized resources are essential to guarantee this dynamics and, thus, economies are not assumed to operate under full employment of resources. Since technical know-how and knowledge in general are not available in fully specified blueprints, the growth path of firms entails an intensive process of adaptation and learning, closely linked to production experience, that largely determines the accumulation of technical, commercial and organizational know-how, following an evolutionary path.

The central theme of this literature is that the dynamics of the production structures is the basic determinant of changes in the momentum of economic growth. This dynamics obviously interacts with a stable macroeconomic environment, broadly defined (see section 1), generating positive feedbacks that result in "virtuous" circles of rapid economic growth, but may also lead to the opposite outcome, if either dynamic restructuring or macroeconomic stability are absent. A facilitating institutional environment, and an adequate supply of human capital, long-term capital, and infrastructure, also play an essential role in this process, but only as "framework conditions" rather than that of active determinants of the growth momentum (Ocampo, 2005). The ability to constantly generate new dynamic activities is, in this view, the essence of successful development. In this sense, in the context provided by a facilitating macroeconomic and institutional environment, growth is essentially a *mesoeconomic* process, as its essential determinant, structural dynamics, is a mesoeconomic phenomenon that summarizes the joint evolution of the sectoral composition of production, intra- and inter-sectoral linkages, market structures, the functioning of factor markets and the institutions that support all of them. Dynamic microeconomic changes are the necessary building blocks, but it is the *system-wide* processes that matter.

In this regard, the dynamics of production structures may be visualized as the interaction between two basic forces, namely (i) *innovations* (the Schumpeterial link), broadly understood as new activities and new ways of doing previous activities, and the *learning and diffusion processes* that characterize both the full materialization of their potentialities and their spread through the economic system; and (ii) the *complementarities, linkages or networks* (the Hirschminite link) among firms and production activities, and the *institutions* required for their consolidation, whose maturation is also subject to learning. As noticed, the elastic supply of factors of production is an essential condition for these dynamic processes to unfold their full effects (see Ros, 2000). International factor mobility can also contribute to this result.

These different mechanisms provide complementary functions: innovations are the basic engine of change; their diffusion and the creation of production linkages are the mechanisms by which they generate system-wide effects; learning and diffusion of innovations and the development of complementarities generate dynamic economies of scale, which is an essential ingredient of rising productivity; and the last factor determines the elasticity required of the system for the former to operate as the driving force of economic growth.

Innovation includes the "creation" of enterprises, production activities and sectors, but also the "destruction" of others. The particular mix between "creation" and "destruction" is critical. The term coined by Schumpeter (1962), "creative destruction", indicates that there tends to be net creation. This is, of course, essential for growth, but is not necessarily the expected result in any specific location at a certain point in time. There may be cases in which there is in fact little destruction, or its opposite, large-scale destruction of previous economic activities, or a mixed negative case, "destructive creation".

A common feature of most forms of innovation is that they involve the creation of knowledge or, more explicitly, of the capacity to apply it to production. They thus stress the role of knowledge as a source of market power. Following this approach, success in economic development can be seen as the ability to create enterprises that are capable of learning and appropriating knowledge and, in the long run, of generating new knowledge (Amsden, 2001).

In industrial countries, the major incentive to innovate is provided by the extraordinary profits that can be earned by the pioneering firms that introduce technical, commercial, or organizational changes, or which open new markets or find new sources of raw materials. This incentive is necessary to offset the uncertainties and risks involved in the innovators' decisions, as well as the higher costs in which they incur, due to the costs of developing the new know-how, the incomplete nature of the knowledge they initially have and the absence of the complementarities that are characteristic of well-developed activities. In developing countries, innovations are primary associated to the spread of new products, technologies, organizational or commercial strategies previously created in the industrial centers. These represent the "moving targets" which generate the windows of opportunity open to developing countries (Pérez, 2001). The extraordinary profits of innovators are generally absent and, indeed, production usually involves entry into mature activities with thinner or, indeed, thin profit margins. Thus, *entry costs* are not associated to the development of new know-how, but to the process of acquiring, mastering and adapting it, as well as those associated to generating information about and creating a reputation in new markets and, particularly, exploiting opportunities to reduce costs to successfully break into established marketing channels. Entry costs may turn out to be prohibitive for new firms; in this case, possibilities open to developing countries will be limited to attracting multinationals willing to shift the location of production.

All these processes require investment and learning. Innovations are, indeed, intrinsically tied to investment, as they require physical investments, as well as investments in intangibles, particularly in technological learning and the design of marketing strategies. Moreover, to the extent that innovative activities are the fastest growing of any economy, they have high investment requirements. These facts, together with the falling investment needs that characterize established activities, imply that overall capital formation is directly dependent on the relative weight of innovative activities and on their capital intensity. High investment is thus associated to a high rate of innovation and structural change.

On the other hand, innovations involve learning. Technical know-how must indeed go through a learning and maturing process that is closely linked to the production experience. More generally, to reduce the technology gaps that characterize the international economic hierarchy – to "leapfrog" in a precise sense of the term – an encompassing research and development strategy, and an accompanying educational strategy, would be necessary. The essential insights on learning dynamics have been provided by the "evolutionary" theories of technical change.[5] These theories emphasize the fact that technology is to a large extent tacit in nature – i.e., that "blueprints" cannot be completely spelled out. This implies that technology is incompletely available and imperfectly tradable, and that proficiency in its use cannot be detached from production experience – and thus has a strong "learning by doing" component.

Given existing dualism – producers who are at very different stages in the organization of production and technology, and who have varying degrees of access to information and to factor markets – developing countries will always have a considerable mass of underemployment or informality. There may also be significant endogenous elements in investment and domestic savings. Moreover, while developing countries lag behind in the areas of production, technology, and institutional development, there is always the possibility of proactively speeding up the learning of technology and the development of institutions. In such circumstances, the predominance of creative over destructive forces generates virtuous circles of rapid growth; this is reflected in the absorption of an increasing number of workers in dynamic activities, the existence of significant investment opportunities, induced creation of savings, and accelerated learning of technology and institutional development. At the same time, the predominance of destructive forces has the opposite effect, giving rise to a vicious circle that leads to increased structural heterogeneity as surplus manpower is absorbed in less productive activities; the reduction of investment incentives; the destruction of saving capacity, and the loss of

[5] See, in particular, Nelson and Winter (1982); Nelson (1996); Dosi, *et al.* (1988); with respect to developing countries, see Katz (1987); Lall (1990); Katz and Kosacoff (2000).

production experience, all of which further accentuates the lag in technology and the weakening of institutions.

At the aggregate level, these processes give rise to changes in productivity – labor or total factor productivity – depending on whether dualism increases or decreases and on the performance of this variable at the microeconomic level. The fact that some economic agents are approaching the technological frontier thanks to the incentives generated by a competitive environment or to their own learning effort does *not* necessarily mean that aggregate productivity will show the same degree of progress. The process itself may cause productive resources to be under- or unemployed (thus increasing dualism), and this has a negative effect on aggregate productivity.

Over the last few decades, positive and negative external forces have generated the creation as well as the destruction of production activities. The technology revolution associated with information science and communications, the resulting disintegration of production chains in the industrialized countries that has caused assembly activities to be exported to developing countries, and the growing demand for services in international tourism are among the positive factors. The weakness of many raw materials markets and the accompanying deterioration of world real commodity prices is one of the negative factors. However, the changes associated with the structural reform process have played an equally or even more decisive role.

The impact of these processes has been varied. On the positive side, they have led to a number of "innovations" as companies strive to become more competitive; equipment and inputs have become cheaper as a result of tariff reductions; companies have an incentive to enter external markets; sources of raw materials have opened up; and new market structures have been established in privatized sectors, often bringing windfall profits because of the low prices at which these assets were sold (i.e., with considerable implicit subsidies to buyers) and the inadequacy of regulatory mechanisms. At the same time, many destructive forces have hit the economies. Some branches disappeared as they could not compete with imports, producers of internationally tradable goods and services suffered as internal funds (undistributed profits) became scarce owing to the reduction of protection and real exchange rate appreciation, and technological capabilities that had been built up during the previous stage were lost as laboratories (of privatized public enterprises) and technology development centres were dismantled. These situations were reinforced by the macroeconomic instability that has prevailed over the last two decades.

The formation of internationally integrated production systems gave rise to significant changes in complementarities, as so-called "value chains" disintegrated, and production processes that had previously been carried out in one location are now carried out in many different places. As information and communications systems have improved, some factors, such as location near suppliers of inputs, became less important, but others, especially access to financial, infrastructure and other services, became more important. In any case, the fact that the trend towards specialization has increased rather than decreased is an indication of the fact that complementarities and the related phenomena of spatial agglomeration of certain activities still play an important role.

The weakening of many public and private institutions, which had been established to support the development of production sectors during the previous stage, further contributed to this process. With the rejection of public intervention in production, very little effort was made to establish new institutions to replace them. Nevertheless, networks were created to promote exports and establish free trade zones, tourism was actively promoted, regulatory mechanisms in the mining sector were improved, and some governments encouraged the development of production clusters, especially at the local level. These developments serve as foundations upon which countries can build new strategies for the future.

As the evidence presented in section 2 indicates, the tendency to underestimate the role of policies aimed at supporting production was not "neutral" from the standpoint of the development of production sectors, economic growth, and their social linkages. This view is also reflected in the abundant literature claiming that there is no strict relationship between "incentive neutrality" and the rates of technological change and economic growth.[6] Thus, it is essential that production development strategies and policies be resumed in order to ensure progress towards a dynamic economy. As regards structural change, the fundamental objective is to facilitate and instill momentum into production activities by encouraging innovation, developing the complementarities needed for them to mature, including institutional support; as a counterpart, activities that tend to be displaced need to be restructured in an orderly fashion, so as to facilitate the transfer of resources to new sectors.

---

[6] See, for example, the studies mentioned in Helleiner (1992); Roberts and Tybout (1996); Rodríguez and Rodrik (2001).

The macroeconomic environment also played a key role in determining the relative importance of creative and destructive processes in the production sector. The elimination of hyperinflation was certainly a positive factor, as was the improvement of fiscal balances. However, other aspects of macroeconomic management tended to accentuate the destructive effects and weaken some of the creative ones. The strong procyclical behavior of aggregate demand, of external capital flows and of key macroeconomic prices – such as real exchange rates and interest rates – generated tensions that jeopardized the survival of many firms, especially small and medium-sized ones. Producers of tradable goods and services were particularly threatened, as they lost the protection they previously enjoyed (ECLAC, 1998). The sudden elimination of subsidies, as a result of fiscal and credit reform, and the drastic trade reforms that were implemented also caused some activities to be closed down. If, conversely, changes had been carried out more gradually, they would have had a better chance of reconverting. Instead, there was overdestruction. The weakness of the long-term segments of the capital market and the exchange rate appreciations that occurred in many countries between 1991 and 1994 and during the 1996–97 biennium, also weakened the positive trends and contributed to overdestruction.

Throughout the last century, the rapid growth experienced by the developing world occurred in a context of *strategies of structural change*, which, along with *macroeconomic and financial environments* that were conducive to development, led to dynamic capital accumulation processes (Rodrik, 1999).[7] This is clearly illustrated by the rapid rise of the Asian economies. The vigorous growth that took place in Latin America during the period of State-led industrialization was also the product of a strategy of structural change that was based, in some cases, on the deepening of import substitution and, in most cases, on "mixed" models combining import substitution with export promotion (Cárdenas, Ocampo and Thorp, 2000, ch. 1). Unlike the Asian countries, in the Latin American and Caribbean region, there was not always an adequate degree of macroeconomic stability, particularly after the avalanche of external resources that came in during the 1970s.

During the current development stage, therefore, structural change strategies must be implemented that will serve as a framework for

---

[7] This author refers to what we call here strategies of structural change as "investment strategies".

dynamic growth in the production sector. Once strategies and policies are adopted, they should, of course, be consistent with the new external and domestic scenario. In this regard, five basic considerations are in order. First, the main emphasis should be on integrating the region's economies into the world economy. This means developing regional and subregional production chains and clusters within the framework of integration processes, and generating activities complementary to export activities, with a view to enhancing the value-added of exportable goods and services, and their capacity to create momentum for other production activities. Second, there must be a proper balance between individual initiative, which is decisive for getting a dynamic process of innovation started, and the establishment of coordination systems and public incentives. Incentives should, of course, be in line with international rules, especially those of the World Trade Organization. Nevertheless, although priority should be given to taking advantage of the maneuvering room provided under existing agreements, more opportunities should be available to the authorities of developing countries, which were too narrowly restricted after the Uruguay Round. In particular, they should be allowed to apply selective policies and performance criteria to encourage innovation and create the complementarities that are essential to development. Third, all incentives should be granted on the basis of performance. Fourth, public policy should not necessarily be equated with government policy. On the contrary, a broad mix of public and private institutions should be considered, with each country developing the combination that best suits its own particular needs. Finally, these policies should be applied in a macroeconomic context that is conducive to the restructuring of existing capacity and that encourages productive investment.

References

Amsden, A. (2001), *The Rise of the Rest: Non-Western Economies' Ascent in World Markets*, Oxford University Press, Oxford.

Cárdenas, E., J. A. Ocampo and R. Thorp (2000) (eds.), *Industrialisation and the State in Latin America: the Post War Years, An Economic History of Twentieth Century Latin America*, Volume Three, Palgrave Press and St. Martins, New York.

Cimoli, M. and N. Correa (2005), "Trade openness and technological gaps in Latin America: A 'low growth trap'", in J. A. Ocampo (ed.) *Beyond Reforms: Structural Dynamics and Macroeconomic Vulnerability*, Stanford University Press/ECLAC, Palo Alto, Ca.

Correa, R. (2002), "Reformas estructurales y crecimiento en América Latina: un análisis de sensibilidad", *CEPAL Review*, No. 76, Santiago, April.

Dosi, G., C. Freeman, R. Nelson, G. Silverberg, and L. Soete (1988) (eds.), *Technical Change and Economic Theory*, Maastricht Economic Research Institute on Innovation and Technology (MERIT)/The International Federation of Institutes for Advanced Studies (IFIAS), Pinter Publishers, London and New York.

ECLAC (Economic Commission for Latin America and the Caribbean) (2003a), *A Decade of Light and Shadow: Latin America and the Caribbean in the 1990s*, ECLAC Books No. 76, Santiago.

—— (2003b), *Latin America and the Caribbean in the World Economy, 2001–2002 Edition*, Santiago.

—— (2002a) *Globalization and Development*, Santiago.

—— (2002b), *Growth with Stability: Financing for Development in the New International Context*, ECLAC Books, No. 67, Santiago.

—— (2002c), *Latin America and the Caribbean in the World Economy. 2000–2001 Edition*, Santiago.

—— (1998), *América Latina y el Caribe: políticas para mejorar la inserción en la economía mundial*, Second edition, Fondo de Cultura Económica, Santiago and Mexico City. Also see the English version *Latin America and the Caribbean: Policies to Improve Linkages with the Global Economy*, United Nations, Santiago, 1995.

Edwards, S. (1995), *Crisis and Reform in Latin America: From Despair to Hope*, The World Bank, Oxford University Press, Washington, DC.

Escaith, H. and S. Morley (2001), "El efecto de las reformas estructurales en el crecimiento económico de la América Latina y el Caribe. Una estimación empírica", *El Trimestre Económico*, Vol. LXVIII (4), No. 272, Mexico, October–December.

Fatás, A. (2002), "The effects of business cycles on growth", in N. Loayza and R. Soto (eds.), *Economic Growth: Sources, Trends and Cycles*, Central Bank of Chile, Santiago.

Ffrench-Davis, R. (2003), "Financial crises and national policy issues: An overview", in R. Ffrench-Davis and S. Griffith-Jones (eds.), *From Capital Surges to Drought: Seeking Stability for Emerging Markets*, WIDER/CEPAL, Palgrave/Macmillan, London.

—— (2005), *Reforming Latin America's Economies: After Market Fundamentalism*, Palgrave Macmillan, London and New York.

Helleiner, G. K. (1992), (ed.), *Trade Policy Industrialization and Development: New Perspectives*, Oxford University Press, New York.

Hirschman, A. O. (1958), *The Strategy of Economic Development*, Yale University Press, New Haven, CT.

Hnatkovska, V. and N. Loayza (2003), "Volatility and growth", The World Bank, Washington, DC, August.

Hofman, A. (2001), "Long run economic development in Latin America in a comparative perspective: Proximate and ultimate causes", *Serie Macroeconomía del Desarrollo, No. 8*, Economic Commission for Latin America and the Caribbean (ECLAC), Santiago, December.

IDB (Inter-American Development Bank) (1997), *Latin America After a Decade of Reforms, Economic and Social Progress in Latin America 1997*, Washington, DC.

Katz, J. (2001), *Structural Reforms, Productivity and Technological Change in Latin America*, ECLAC Books, No. 64, Economic Commission for Latin America and the Caribbean (ECLAC), Santiago.

—— (1987) "Domestic technology generation in LDCs: a review of research findings", in J. Katz (ed.), *Technology Generation in Latin American Manufacturing Industries*, Macmillan, London.

—— and B. Kosacoff (2000), "Technological learning, institutional building, and the microeconomics of import substitution", in Cárdenas, Ocampo and Thorp (2000).

Kuczynski, P. P. and J. Williamson (2003), (eds.), *After the Washington Consensus: Restarting Growth and Reform in Latin America*, Institute for International Economics, Washington, DC.

Lall, S. (1990), *Building Industrial Competitiveness in Developing Countries*, OECD Development Center, Paris.

Loayza, N., P. Fajnzylber and C. Calderón (2002), "Economic growth in Latin America and the Caribbean: Stylized facts, explanations, and forecasts", World Bank, Washington, DC.

Lora, E. and U. Panizza (2002), "Structural reforms in Latin America under scrutiny". Background paper prepared for the seminar *Reforming Reforms*, Inter-American Development Bank Annual Meetings, Fortaleza, Brazil.

—— and F. Barrera (1998), "El crecimiento económico en América Latina después de una década de reformas estructurales", *Pensamiento Iberoamericano*, Madrid, Special issue.

Mortimore, M. and W. Peres (2001), "Corporate competitiveness in Latin America and the Caribbean", *CEPAL Review*, No. 74, Santiago, August.

Nelson, R. R. (1996), *The Sources of Economic Growth*, Harvard University Press, Cambridge, Mass.

—— and S. G. Winter (1982), *An Evolutionary Theory of Economic Change*, The Belknap Press of Harvard University Press, Cambridge, Mass. and London.

Ocampo, J. A. (2005), "The quest for dynamic efficiency: Structural dynamics and economic growth in developing countries", in J. A. Ocampo (ed.) *Beyond Reforms: Structural Dynamics and Macroeconomic Vulnerability*, Stanford University Press/ECLAC, Palo Alto, Ca.

—— (2003a), "Capital account and counter-cyclical prudential regulations in developing countries", in R. Ffrench-Davis and S. Griffith-Jones (eds.), *From Capital Surges to Drought: Seeking Stability for Emerging Markets*, WIDER/ECLAC/Palgrave, London.

—— (2003b), "Developing countries' anti-cyclical policies in a globalized world", in A. Dutt and J. Ros (eds.) *Development Economics and Structuralist Macroeconomics: Essays in Honor of Lance Taylor*, Edward Elgar, Aldershot, UK.

—— and M. A. Parra (2003), "The terms of trade for commodities in the twentieth century", *CEPAL Review*, No. 79, Santiago.

Pérez, C. (2001) "Technological change and opportunities for development as a moving target", *CEPAL Review*, No 75, Santiago.

Prebisch, R. (1951), *Theoretical and practical problems of economic growth*, Economic Commission for Latin America (ECLAC), United Nations publication, Mexico City.

Ramey, G. and V. Ramey (1995), "Cross country evidence on the link between volatility and growth", *American Economic Review*, Vol. 85, No. 5, December.

Roberts, M. J. and J. R. Tybout (1996) (eds.), *Industrial Evolution in Developing Countries. Micro Patterns of Turnover, Productivity, and Market Structure*, Oxford University Press, Oxford.

Rodríguez, F. and D. Rodrik (2001), "Trade policy and economic growth: a skeptic's guide to the cross-national evidence", Vol. 15, in S. Bernanke and K. Rogoff (eds.), *NBER Macroeconomics Annual 2000*, MIT Press, Cambridge, Mass.

Rodrik, D. (1999), *Making Openness Work: The New Global Economy and the Developing Countries*, Overseas Development Council, Washington, DC.

Ros, J. (2000), *Development Theory and the Economics of Growth*, The University of Michigan Press, Ann Arbor.

Rosenstein-Rodan, P. N. (1943), "Problems of industrialization of Eastern and South-Eastern Europe", *The Economic Journal*, Vol. 53.

Schumpeter, J. (1962), *Capitalism, Socialism and Democracy*, Third edition, Harper Torch Books, New York.

Stallings, B. and J. Weller (2001), "Employment in Latin America: Cornerstone of social policy", *CEPAL Review*, No. 75, Santiago, December.

—— and W. Peres (2000), *Growth, Employment and Equity: the Impact of the Economic Reforms in Latin America and the Caribbean*, The Brookings Institution /ECLAC), Washington, DC.

Stiglitz, J. A. (2003), "Whither reform? Toward a new agenda for Latin America", *CEPAL Review*, No. 80, Santiago, August.

Taylor, L. (1991), *Income Distribution, Inflation and Growth*, The MIT Press, Cambridge.

UNCTAD (1999), *Trade and Development Report, 1999* (UNCTAD/TDR/1999), Geneva.

World Bank (2002), *From Natural Resources to the Knowledge Economy: Trade and Job Quality*, D. De Ferranti, G. E. Perry, D. Lederman, and W. F. Maloney (eds.), World Bank Latin American and Caribbean Studies Viewpoints, Washington, DC.

—— (1997), *The Long March: A Reform Agenda for Latin America and the Caribbean in the Next Decade*, S. J. Burki and G. E. Perry (eds.), World Bank Latin American and Caribbean Studies Viewpoints, Washington, DC.

III

Macroeconomic Stability and Investment Allocation of Domestic Pension Funds in Emerging Economies: The Case of Chile

*Roberto Zahler**

Introduction

Growth has been frustratingly slow in Latin America, notwithstanding a decade and a half of rather intense reforms (Ocampo, 2005). In this period, growth of the region has diverged from that of the major economy of the world and has moved slower than the world average (Ffrench-Davis, 2005). The macroeconomic environment has been one crucial variable underlying both a low capital formation and great instability of economic activity.

Significant reforms have been made in financial markets and the financing of pensions. Most of the analysis of pension funds take as given the macroeconomic environment in which they are inserted, and focuses on the microeconomic conditions under which their return is maximized and/or their risk minimized. This chapter studies macroeconomic implications of the behavior of domestic pension funds as a major institutional investor, in emerging economies (EEs). The paper distinguishes between the long-run savings/investment implications, and the short-run macroeconomic impact on the foreign exchange and/or domestic financial markets.

Section 1 summarizes the main issues associated with the macroeconomic implications of capital flows in EEs. This background is important since institutional investors, given their size and/or regulation,

* The author is grateful to Ricardo Ffrench-Davis, Esteban Jadresić, Felipe Jiménez, Andrés Reinstein, Salvador Valdés and participants in two Seminars organized by ECLAC in 2002 and 2003, for their comments and suggestions, and to Hermann González for his research and statistical support.

when allowed under certain conditions to invest abroad, could play a relevant role in the interrelationship between local and international financial and exchange rate markets. And that interrelationship may cause significant short-run macroeconomic effects.

Section 2 analyses the long-run macroeconomic impact of institutional investors in EE. Because of the substantial amount of funds that they manage, they play an important role in the savings/investment process and their behavior may have significant consequences for the economic growth of EEs. Section 3 describes and explains the main developments of the Chilean pension fund system (AFP).

Sections 4 and 5, which deal with the potential short-run macroeconomic effects of institutional investors, exemplifying with the Chilean experience, constitute the "core" of the paper. Section 4 analyses the eventual impact on the local-term structure of interest rates. Section 5 deals with the effect on the foreign exchange market. Section 6 concludes and proposes macroeconomic policy measures for the regulation of institutional investors in EEs.

1. Capital mobility and macroeconomic stability in EEs

The globalization of capital markets has been pushing EEs to dismantle balance of payments capital controls and integrate more fully their financial systems to those of the rest of the world.

Long-run benefits usually associated with open capital accounts relate mainly to the stabilization of income and consumption paths, diversification of risk and complementation of external and local savings.[1] In the short term and during the transition, however, a completely open capital account can have negative consequences, especially for small EEs.

In the first place, during the transition process from a closed capital account to an open one there could be a significant capital inflow generated both by higher local interest rates and by the "stock" adjustment of international direct investment and portfolios seeking diversification. These capital inflows tend to generate an overshooting (appreciation) of the domestic currency, increase the value of local assets and create excessive and unsustainable current account deficits in their balance of payments. Depending on the length of time during which the inflows and (key relative and asset) price adjustments take place, there could be a substantial disruption in the allocation of

---

[1] This latter benefit requires a stable supply of international finance.

resources in the domestic economy and thus generate the seed of what in many occasions has ended up in a foreign exchange and/or financial crisis (Zahler, 2003a and 2003b).

The impact of the capital inflows depends importantly on the capacity of the economy to absorb domestically and/or reinvest abroad, efficiently, the resources coming from the rest of the world. For small economies, with quite illiquid capital markets and relatively weak banking systems (in many cases due to inappropriate banking supervision and regulation), the absorption and/or rechanneling of excessive inflows is a difficult process, which in many occasions has ended up in significant macroeconomic imbalances. That is one of the reasons why restrictions on short-term financial inflows are justified. The experience and practice of some "well behaved" EEs suggest that when "excessive" short-term voluntary foreign financial flows take place, countries should apply measures to prevent those inflows from undermining their macro-economic objectives as well as the health of their financial system.[2]

A second effect of an open capital account, depending on the EEs exchange rate policy, is a loosening of its autonomy on the design and implementation of monetary policy.

A third effect usually associated to open capital accounts is the excessive volatility of exchange rates and interest rates caused by the very "sensitive" international markets, which tend to react in a procyclical, quick and massive manner to short-term news.

Finally, open capital accounts in EEs tend to amplify the effects of two international market imperfections: "currency runs" and "moral hazard". Currency runs tend to be caused by the contagion of the balance of payments problems in one country to another country. Moral hazard is caused by the explicit or implicit official guarantees in banking debt, external debt or the exchange rate.

In short, *one of the main problems usually faced by EEs that are in transition of becoming fully integrated to international markets, is the massive flow of capital into and out of the country* that they have to confront in relatively short periods of time. Experience shows that those capital movements tend to cause serious disruptions on the local financial system, the foreign exchange market and the economy as a whole. The effects caused by the size and volatility of capital flows depend importantly on the depth and size of the EEs markets being affected: the smaller and less liquid the markets, the greater tend to be the disruptive effects of short-term capital movements.

---

[2] A detailed analysis of those measures can be found in Zahler (2000).

Given the degree of globalization, it is quite difficult, and in many cases undesirable, to isolate EEs from international markets. In recent years many countries have adopted or are adopting more flexible exchange rate systems to allow them more maneuverability for their national monetary policy and to increase the exchange rate risk. That measure though, is usually not enough to prevent the economy from the effects of shocks caused by short-term capital flows and in occasions generates a procyclical behavior of the real exchange rate. Therefore, together with the above mentioned restrictions on short-term financial inflows, EEs should develop, deepen and make more liquid their capital and currency markets so as to absorb those shocks in a less disruptive way.

2. Long-term macroeconomic implications of institutional investors

As is well known, in recent years EEs have engaged in deeper financial liberalization and reform, including both the domestic financial sector as well as financial opening up to the international economy. An important part of this development has been the pension fund reform: through the transfer of all or part of the state-operated pay-as-you-go system to the private sector in a fully funded "individual capitalization system", several EEs have initiated and/or deepened the development of markets for long-term financial instruments.

Pension funds, and also more gradually insurance companies, may have long-run macroeconomic effects in EEs through two main different mechanisms: by channeling important amounts of long-term savings to investment[3] and by creating and developing markets for long-term bonds and stocks.

a) Institutional investors and capital markets

International experience indicates that institutional investors, such as pension funds, insurance companies and mutual funds, are the main

---

[3] However, the *direct* contribution from the pension fund system to capital accumulation is usually overstated since part of the financial intermediation of their funds ends up in consumption rather than investment. Although there is no clear evidence that social security reforms have increased domestic savings rates, they are an important factor in explaining the shift in the composition of saving in EEs towards the long term (Mihaljek *et al.*, 2002). For an analysis of the Chilean case, see Uthoff (2001).

demanders of bonds. In the United States, country with the most developed corporate bond market, families hold only 12% of total corporate bonds and 7% of corporate bonds of non-financial companies. In Japan families also hold 12% of corporate bonds, and only 1.5% of corporate bonds of non-financial firms (Reinstein, 2002). This is due to the fact that families and companies prefer to invest through the intermediation of institutional investors, which specialize in collecting information and carrying out financial analysis.

Some institutional investors, such as pension funds, due to the nature of their liabilities, are natural candidates to demand long-term corporate bonds. As pensions will be paid in the long-term, it is to the workers advantage to have their funds invested in long-term instruments and earn the corresponding risk premium. In terms of currencies, from a pure consumer perspective (not from a producer perspective), pension funds should seek a currency exposure comparable to the traded goods proportion of the basket consumed by a typical pensioner. In principle, in small EEs pension funds should hold a higher share of foreign assets than in large, more self-sufficient countries (Reisen, 1997, pp. 11–12; Reisen and Williamson, 1996, p. 236). However, in EEs long-term insurance for exchange rate differentials are weakly developed and, in those "well behaved", the long-run equilibrium trend of the real exchange rate is that of appreciation. Therefore, if pension funds make "excessive" investments in foreign currency, the pensioners may end up carrying the foreign exchange risk.

In the case of (mainly life) insurance companies, the insured have a long-term horizon and company commitments are mainly in local currency, so they should prefer to make long-term investments in local currency. Mutual funds usually invest on shorter terms.

Thus, institutional investors generate a demand for long-term corporate bonds and provide liquidity to that market, which further increases the demand for corporate bonds.[4] The lack of liquidity, typical of many EEs, is not only a problem because companies must

---

[4] The liquidity is measured by the bid-ask spread of financial assets: if it is high, the liquidity of the markets will be low since investors take a significant loss every time they change position. That is to say, if an investor buys and soon wishes to sell the instrument, his loss will be proportional to the bid-ask spread of that financial asset. Harrison (2002) proposes a model where the lack of liquidity of an asset consists in a problem of information about the fair market price, which gives rise to a "lemons problem", in the sense of Akerloff (1970). In this case, the lemons problem is mitigated by "informed" traders, because they compete with the others for transactions. Thus, the greater the number of informed institutional agents, the greater tends to be the liquidity of the market.

pay a higher cost for funds, but it also results in discouraging underwriters to subscribe issuances.[5] Lastly, institutional investors contribute to improve corporate governance of companies by requiring stricter supervision and regulation of publicly offered stocks and bonds, by imposing discipline over the company's management and by aligning their interests with those of the majority of shareholders, all of which facilitates the development of equity and bond capital markets.

In short, institutional investors play a major role in providing long-term financing to both the private sector and the government. The lack of significant institutional investors has been, with the exception of Chile and to a lesser extent Brazil (which does not have a reformed social security system), a critical limitation for developing the bond market in Latin America. In fact, at the end of 2001, Mexico's pension funds had assets amounting to the equivalent of 3.5% of GDP, while for Peru this figure was 7.3%, for Argentina 7.7%, for Brazil 12.4%, and for Chile 54%.

b) Indexation of long-term bonds

One of the main difficulties in creating a long-term corporate bond market has been the high and uncertain inflation rate experienced by many EEs. A solution to this problem has been the development of an indexed bond market, by which the investor obtains an interest rate that is composed of a real return, plus the variation in an established price index. The latter could be the consumer price index (CPI), the value of a foreign currency or the price of a commodity. The most attractive in terms of its general use is the CPI, since it provides a better overall hedge of the risks to investors and fund suppliers. With bonds indexed to foreign currency, investors are exposed to the risk of local currency appreciation. In their turn, tradable companies could hedge risk by a bond expressed in the relevant foreign currency.

---

[5] In an issuance underwriters must take the bonds and keep them in stock, to later sell them to investors. If there is low liquidity in the market, they will have a lower incentive to subscribe them and, consequently, there will be few bond issuances. With the Russian crisis and the bankruptcy of the Long Term Capital Management in 1998, the US corporate bond market lost most of its liquidity, trading reduced significantly and there were no market prices; therefore, trades could not be realized. This liquidity shock had a significant impact on the US corporate bond market, as well as in the capability of companies to raise funds: corporate bond issuance dropped from 150 issuances per month in May, to 40 in September and October of 1998; and only in early 2001 did bond issues reach the May 1998 level (Harrison, 2002).

Even if there already exists a nominal bond market, indexed bonds allow achieving better progress in the *completion* of financial markets. Market completion consists in generating patterns of payment flows in different states of nature so that investors or companies may hedge or bet on the occurrence of certain states in a way that could not be replicated with the financial instruments existing in the market.

Issuing indexed bonds may significantly reduce financing costs of firms. Equation (1) shows that the nominal interest rate at which companies issue their bonds is equal to the real interest rate plus inflation expectations plus inflation risk premium. The latter is an "insurance" that companies must pay investors for them to assume the inflation risk. For the United States, Campbell and Shiller (1996) estimated that the inflation risk premium was between 50 and 100 base points for a bullet bond at a 5-year term. In EEs, however, this premium is usually much higher. In fact, it is frequently so high that it generates a sort of credit rationing in the sense given to the term by Stiglitz and Weiss (1981), which results in long-term corporate bond markets failing to arise. By issuing indexed bonds, companies will only pay the real interest rate plus the actual inflation, while saving the inflation risk premium.

(1) $$i_t = r_t + \pi_t^e + \delta_t$$

where i_t: Nominal interest rate for period t,
r_t: Real interest rate for period t,
π_t^e : Inflation expectations for period t, and,
δ_t : Inflation risk premium.

Indexed bonds also facilitate companies and the Government to issue long-term debt, since high inflation makes very difficult to extend the duration of bonds[6] (Walker, 1998) and can even cause the disappearance of long-term nominal bond markets.

At present, there are several countries with government inflation-indexed bonds. Even countries with low inflation rates have considered developing an indexed bond market, as it reduces the cost of the public debt. One recent case is the United States, which introduced them in January of 1997.

---

[6] Mihaljek, *et al.* (2002) presents clear evidence that lower inflation is associated with longer average maturities of government bonds.

3. The Chilean pension fund system

In Latin America, Chile is the only country with a relatively large indexed bond market (Reinstein, 2002). By the end of 2000, 89% of all domestic debt issued in Chile was inflation indexed.[7] This compares to less than 20% in other Latin American countries, less than 10% in Central Europe and almost nil indexed debt in Asia (Mihaljek, *et al.*, 2002, table 6).

The main characteristic of the medium- and long-term Chilean fixed income market is that it is denominated in *Unidades de Fomento* (UF),[8] an account in Chilean pesos, linked to past inflation, which has allowed the Chilean economy to have long-term securities denominated in domestic currency. Another important feature of Chile's fixed income market is that banks can use papers with maturities of less than 90 days to meet technical legal reserve requirements, which strongly improves the liquidity for these papers.

a) From 1982 to 1989

In 1982 the Chilean economy confronted a severe balance of payments and financial crisis, which translated into a 14% decrease in GDP, a nominal depreciation of the peso of 100% and the intervention of 22 financial institutions representing 60% of the banking system. To restore growth and the functioning of the financial system, a number of monetary, fiscal and foreign exchange policies, together with debt to equity swaps and financial rescuing mechanisms were implemented. In 1985 the economy started a recovery path that lasted until 1989, when actual output reached the level of the potential output (Ffrench-Davis, 2002).

In May 1981 Chile abolished its pay-as-you-go pension fund scheme and replaced it with mandatory private pension fund managers, Administradoras de Fondos de Pensiones (AFP). At the beginning, AFP were allowed to invest mainly in indexed instruments: Government debt and Central Bank securities, mortgage backed securities, fixed term bank deposits and corporate bonds. No foreign investment was allowed and only since 1985 could equities be held by the AFP (table III.1).

---

[7] Until 2001 there were no nominal papers (denominated in Chilean pesos) with maturity of more than one year.

[8] The UF is adjusted daily, and the factor of adjustment is the previous month's change in the CPI, distributed uniformly between the 10th day of the present month and the 9th day of the next month.

Table III.1   **Main ceilings on AFP holdings, 1981–92 (%)**

	Dec-81	Sep-85	May-92
Central Bank Bonds	100	50	45
Time Deposits	50	40	50
Mortgage backed securities (LH)	80	80	80
Bonds	60	40	50
Equities	0	30	30
Foreign Investments	0	0	1,5

Source: Central Bank of Chile.

Although the AFP didn't have an obligation to invest in Central Bank securities, they did not have many other relevant alternatives, so that the restrictive permissible portfolio permitted the government to achieve two macroeconomic goals: (i) the funding of the transition from a public pay-as-you-go to a fully funded private system; and (ii), the funding of the bankruptcy of the bulk of the Chilean private banking system in a relatively mild inflationary way.

The transition from the pay-as-you-go system to a fully privately funded one had a big impact on the fiscal accounts. It is estimated that the income loss that the new system generated to the fiscal balance was equivalent to 5.7% of GDP per year between 1981 and 1999 (Uthoff, 2001). The funding came mainly through two mechanisms: a reduction in fiscal spending and the issuance of indexed bonds by the Central Bank that was mainly bought by institutional investors (table III.2).[9]

The financing from the AFP was crucial to stabilize the banking system during the crisis of the 1980s. To restore the solvency of the system the Central Bank had to infuse resources for an accumulated amount equivalent to 35 % of GDP (Sanhueza, 2001). To absorb excess liquidity and keep monetary growth in pace with the general macro-economic program and inflation rate objectives, the Central Bank issued bonds that were acquired mainly by AFP and insurance companies. In fact, Central Bank debt in AFP portfolios grew rapidly (table III.2).

---

[9] The development of insurance companies, which reserves increased from 2% of GDP in 1981 to more than 5% in 1989, was also related to the new social security system, which mandated that the risk of disability and death should be covered. Insurance companies initially invested mainly in long-term Central Bank debt.

Table III.2   Chilean Central Bank debt held by AFP, 1981–2003

Year	Central Bank debt (million USD)	Held by AFP (million USD)	Percentage
1981	310	31	10
1985	2,412	315	13
1990	6,258	2,855	46
1995	18,241	9,494	52
1996	20,928	10,744	51
1997	24,834	11,265	45
1998	21,743	11,689	54
1999	21,449	10,535	49
2000	23,065	11,424	50
2001	20,560	10,400	51
2002	19,537	8,867	45
2003	21,251	9,367	44

Source: Central Bank of Chile and Superintendencia de AFP (SAFP).

The other overall important macroeconomic role of the pension system was the provision of long-term financing to the economy. The portfolio managed by the AFP grew from less than 1% of GDP in 1981 to 24% in 1990 (table III.3a). The successful stabilization of the economy and the financial system, in combination with incentives associated to huge income and wealth redistribution and appropriate key macro prices ignited Chile's economic recovery of the second half of the 1980s.

The banking system started issuing long-term indexed mortgage backed securities ("letras hipotecarias", LH) and sold them initially mainly to the AFP and later, gradually, to the insurance companies. The LH, a bank indexed long-term bond, provided a very important source of long-term financing that was critical in the dynamism of the building sector. These securities went from almost non-existent before1982[10] to US$ 1.2 billion in 1990 and US$ 3.8 billion in 1995. At the end of 2002 their stock amounted to US$ 5.3 billion, equivalent to 8% of GDP; 76% of them were held in the AFP portfolio.

Although the economy was in a very dire situation, with few international reserves and almost no access to voluntary international capital markets, the Central Bank was able to maintain real interest rates at a level that contributed to economic growth. In fact, the average real

---

[10] Since 1960 and until the mid 1970s Chile had a similar system to the LH, called Valores Hipotecarios Reajustables (VHR), linked to the Savings and Loans System (Sistema de Ahorro y Prestamos, SINAP).

Table III.3a   Portfolio composition of AFP, 1981–2003 (% of GDP)

	Dec-81	Dec-85	Dec-90	Dec-95	Dec-96	Dec-97	Dec-98	Dec-99	Dec-00	Dec-01	Dec-02	Dec-03
Central Bank Bonds	0.1	2.2	10.3	15.0	14.5	14.2	15.1	15.3	16.3	16.3	13.7	11.7
LH	0.1	3.8	3.9	6.3	6.7	6.6	6.7	7.4	7.3	7.0	6.3	5.4
Time Deposits	0.6	2.2	4.0	2.1	1.6	4.2	5.5	7.9	9.5	9.5	12.0	9.2
Equities	0.0	0.0	2.7	11.7	9.4	8.8	5.8	5.8	5.7	5.4	5.1	8.3
Corporate Bonds	0.0	0.1	2.7	2.0	1.7	1.3	1.1	1.4	1.6	3.3	4.0	4.7
Others	0.2	2.5	0.7	2.7	3.4	3.5	3.8	4.9	5.1	5.5	6.0	7.3
Foreign Instruments	0.0	0.0	0.0	0.1	0.2	0.4	2.3	6.5	5.5	7.2	9.2	14.6
TOTAL	0.9	10.7	24.4	40.0	37.4	39.0	40.3	49.2	51.0	54.3	56.3	61.1
US$ billion	0.3	1,5	6,7	25,3	27,6	30,9	31,1	33,9	35,8	34,7	36,3	48,9

Source: SAFP.

Table III.3b Portfolio composition of AFP, 1981–2003 (% of total assets)

	Dec-81	Dec-85	Dec-90	Dec-95	Dec-96	Dec-97	Dec-98	Dec-99	Dec-00	Dec-01	Dec-02	Dec-03
Central Bank Bonds	10.1	20.3	42.5	37.5	38.8	36.4	37.5	31.0	31.9	30.0	24.4	19.1
LH	9.4	35.2	16.1	15.8	17.9	17.0	16.6	15.1	14.4	12.9	11.1	8.9
Time Deposits	61.9	20.4	16.3	5.3	4.2	10.7	13.6	16.1	18.7	17.5	21.3	15.0
Equities	0.0	0.0	11.3	29.4	25.1	22.6	14.5	11.9	11.1	9.9	9.9	13.6
Corporate Bonds	0.6	1.1	11.1	5.1	4.5	3.3	2.7	2.8	3.1	5.2	7.1	7.7
Others	18.0	23.0	2.8	6.7	9.0	8.9	9.4	9.9	10.1	11.3	9.8	11.9
Foreign Instruments	0.0	0.0	0.0	0.2	0.5	1.1	5.6	13.3	10.8	13.4	16.1	23.9
TOTAL	100.0	100.0	100.0	100.0	100.0	100.0	100.0	100.0	100.0	100.0	100.0	100.0

Source: SAFP.

deposit interest rate between 1986 and 1989 was 5.4%. The monetary instrument employed was the 90-day "real" interest rate, which was fixed through an open window for short-term UF securities issued by the Central Bank.

b) After 1990

In 1989, just before a significant change of the political regime and government in March 1990, a new Central Bank law became effective. The new legislation gave birth to an independent Central Bank, with the objective of preserving price stability and the protection of external and internal payments. To achieve its goal, the Central Bank was given a series of legal instruments. In relation to pension funds, it was given the responsibility of establishing the limits for their investments in different types of assets, within the margins given by the law.

From 1990 until 1997 real GDP grew at an average rate of 7.6% per year. With the Asian crisis and the Chilean macroeconomic response to it, growth slowed quite significantly, to an average of 2.4% from 1998 until 2002.

In 1990 AFP had US$ 2.9 billion (representing 46%) of Central Bank debt in their portfolio; most of that debt was short term. The heavy amount of debt maturing in the short term put important pressures on the Central Bank and could have created instability in the financial markets. To lengthen the maturity of its debt, the Central Bank intensified its issuing of long-term indexed bonds in 1990. For this reason and in order to sterilize significant capital inflows, between 1990 and 1993 the Central Bank debt increased substantially. The AFP were very important buyers of this new debt, and thus contributed to the Central Bank attaining a better structure for its liabilities.

In 1992 the AFP were for the first time allowed to invest in foreign (international) assets (up to 1.5% of their total portfolios).[11] Later, in the same year this ceiling was increased to 3%; in 1995 to 6% and 9%, and in 1997 to 12%. By late 1999 the ceiling was 16%. In 2002 the

---

[11] The regulation and limits applied to the pension funds holdings of overseas assets has caused considerable controversy. See Lee (2000), Reisen (1997) and Vittas (1998). Besides the objective of reducing idiosyncratic risks through diversification, in a relatively mature system as the Chilean one, where AFP accumulated a significant share of assets in the domestic equity market, the increase in the limit on foreign asset holding is also explained by the lack of diversified alternative eligible uses for AFP funds. In this way it may contribute to reduce excessive volatility in domestic asset valuations caused by AFP buying and selling decisions.

Table III.4   AFP investment overseas, 1993–2003

	Actual		Limit	
	US$ million	% of Fund	US$ million	% of Fund
May-93	5	0.0	377	3
Dec-93	91	0.6	482	3
Dec-94	200	0.9	671	3
Dec-95	51	0.2	2,277	9
Dec-96	149	0.5	2,491	9
Dec-97	353	1.1	3,711	12
Dec-98	1,754	5.6	3,738	12
Dec-99	4,504	13.3	5,436	16
Dec-00	3,869	10.8	5,732	16
Dec-01	4,632	13.4	5,552	16
Dec-02	5,966	16.1	7,272	20
Dec-03	11,692	23.9	12,235	25

Source: Central Bank of Chile and SAFP.

Table III.5   Flow of funds into AFP, 1990–96 (% of GDP)

1990	3.0
1991	2.8
1992	3.3
1993	3.6
1994	3.9
1995	4.4
1996	4.3

Source: Uthoff (2001).

foreign asset ceiling was lifted to 20%, at the same time that a sub-limit on the amount of foreign equities was removed (table III.4).

Between 1990 and 1996 Chilean AFP received an annual inflow of funds from labor, which, on average, represented 3.6% of GDP, peaking in 4.4% (table III.5). That was the direct contribution via AFP to national financial savings. Most of these savings flows were invested in bank liabilities (LH and deposits), companies stocks and bonds, and Central Bank bonds.[12] At the end of 2003 AFP assets totaled US$ 48.9 billion, equivalent to 61% of GDP. Foreign assets represented 24% of

---

[12] As mentioned, AFP have played an increasingly important role in providing long-term financing to the Chilean private sector. In addition to LH, which has contributed to the building sector dynamism, between 1995 and 2002 AFP held 36% of bonds issued by private firms. Table III.3 contains information of AFP holdings of different assets as a percentage of total AFP assets and of GDP.

total AFP assets, which compares with only 0.7 % at mid 1997, just before the Asian crisis erupted (table III.3b)

4. Institutional investors and long-term interest rates

a) Closed economy

In a closed economy local investors determine the term structure of interest rates. One of the most important determinants of long-term interest rates is the expected future short-term spot rate. Arbitrage in the credit market makes the relation between short- and long-term interest rates to be:

$$(2) \qquad (1 + r_0^n)^n = (1 + r_0^1) \times (1 + f_1^2) \times ... \times (1 + f_{n-1}^n)$$

where r represents the spot rate and f is the implicit forward for the one period spot rate. According to the "expectations theory" of the term structure of interest rates, f's equal the expected future spot rates. If there is some kind of risk premium, f can be different from the expected spot rate. If investors are short-term oriented, and there is a risk premium for long-term assets, then the forward rates will be higher than the expected spot rates.

Pension funds and insurance companies tend to favor long-term assets. Their development in a modern economy can be a major contribution to reducing long-run risk and the cost of capital, thus stimulating real investment and improving resource allocation. If pension funds "dominate" the long-term asset markets, the risk premium could be zero or even negative, eventually generating a "concavity" at the end of the yield curve. This is called the "preferred habitat" theory of the term structure. In addition to the effect on the shape of the yield curve, the "preferred habitat" of institutional investors can have important implications for the volatility of interest rates in EE, given that a few big institutions tend to dominate its quite illiquid long-term financial asset market.

In Chile the impact of institutional investors on the long-term interest rate market has been an issue of debate. On the one hand, the Central Bank is the largest issuer of domestic bonds, by which it regulates base money, while simultaneously determines a benchmark yield curve of significant length for the economy. Since the early 1990s Central Bank long-term bonds (with a range of maturities that has gone from 8 to 20 years) are issued through predetermined periodic tenders and placed directly through a public auction in which only banks and domestic institutional investors can participate. On the other hand, domestic institutional investors are the main demanders of domestic debt.[13] And although in a declining fashion, transactions in the fixed income market have been dominated by Central Bank bonds.[14] In addition, the pension fund industry has become increasingly concentrated, which has created a virtual monopsony among institutional investors, due to the relatively small size of mutual funds.[15] Finally, it should be mentioned that Chilean pension funds regulation[16] stimulates them to have similar portfolios and therefore, given their significant size, sudden changes in those portfolios could alter the domestic yield curve.[17]

As was seen in table III.2, AFP are the major holders of Central Bank securities. Figure III.1 shows the holding of Central Bank bonds as a percentage of the total AFP portfolio, versus the yield of those securities. It can be observed that when pension funds alter their holdings there are some effects on the yield of the securities.

b) Open economy

According to the theory of interest rate parity, in an open economy, where local investors can buy international securities and international investors can buy local securities, domestic interest rates are connected to those of the rest of the world. The more integrated the markets, the

---

[13] By the end of 2000, domestic institutional investors (AFP and insurance companies) held 62% of total domestic debt issued in Chile. (Mihaljek, *et al.*, 2002, table 8, page 29). Significant holdings of local domestic long-term debt by foreign institutional investors would reduce the monopsony power of local AFP; however, since that market is still quite illiquid, it deters international institutional investors to participate in it, generating a sort of vicious circle of illiquidity and concentration in the Chilean long-term fixed income market.

[14] At the beginning of the 1990s Central Bank bonds represented 80%–85% of transactions and by 2000 their share still amounted to 50% (Cifuentes, *et al.*, 2002, page 90).

[15] The number of AFP increased from 12 in 1982 to 14 in 1990 and 21 in 1994 and fell to 8 in 2000, when the three biggest AFP concentrated more than 70% of the system's total funds.

[16] AFP are committed to get a return on the portfolio they manage of at least a minimum between 50% of the pension fund industry-wide average or that average minus 200 basis points.

[17] This line of reasoning has been used regarding AFP investment overseas. See Fontaine (1996).

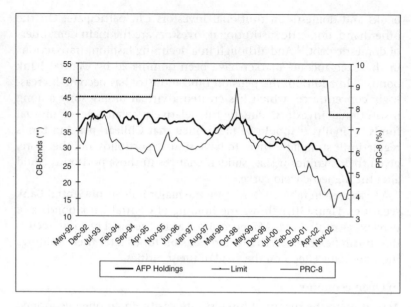

Figure III.1   AFP investments in Central Bank bonds and yield on PRC-8 (*), 1992–2003
Source: Central Bank of Chile and SAFP.
(*) BCU-10 since September, 2002. (**) As a percentage of total AFP assets.

higher should be the correlation of local and international "financial" interest rates.[18]

According to that theory, the integration of local and international financial markets in EEs occurs rapidly through the short-term money market. Banks tend to tap easier than other agents the international market for short-term funds, and open investment accounts abroad. Similarly, international banks penetrate rapidly the short-term money markets to exploit any differences in the covered or uncovered interest rate parities:

(3) Uncovered interest parity $(1 + r_0^n)^n = (1 + r_0^{*n})^n \times (1 + dS_0^n) \times (1 + \delta_0^r)$

(4) Covered interest parity $(1 + r_0^n)^n = (1 + r_0^{*n})^n \times (1 + f_0^n)$

---

[18] However, as analyzed in Zahler and Valdivia (1987), there is usually a big difference between the short-term financial interest rate and the rate associated to the productivity of capital in EEs, with the significant implications of the characteristic of the transition period before and after the EE opens its capital account.

where r_0^n is the local spot interest rate for the period between dates "0" and "n", r_0^{*n} is the international spot interest rate for the period between dates "0" and "n", dS_0^n is the expected change in the exchange rate for the period between dates "0" and "n", δ_0^n is the risk premium for the period between dates "0" and "n", f_0^n is the forward premium for the period "n" and S is the spot exchange rate.

If the uncovered interest parity operates, the forward premium should equal the expected depreciation plus the risk premium. This means that the forward exchange rate is equal to the expected exchange rate adjusted by the risk premium; only if the risk premium is zero the forward rate will equal the expected exchange rate.

According to that theory, long-term interest rates incorporate the short-term interest parities through the expected short-term rates, as shown by equation (5):

(5) $\quad (1 + r_0^n)^n = (1 + r_0^{*1}) \times (1 + dS_0^1) \times (1 + \delta_0^1) \dots \times (1 + r_{n-1}^{*n}) \times (1 + dS_0^1) \times (1 + \delta_{n-1}^1)$

which is equivalent to:

(6) $\quad (1 + r_0^n)^n = (1 + r_0^{*n}) \times (1 + dS_0^n) \times (1 + \delta_0^n)$

Equation (6) states that in an open economy the long-term interest rate equals the international long-term interest rate plus the long-term expected depreciation of the currency plus the long-term risk premium. The long-run expected depreciation should equal the expected long-run inflation differential plus the productivity growth differential plus the short-term overshooting effects caused by short-term interest rates movements.

Assuming that the inflation and productivity growth differentials are relatively stable in the long run, two quite heroic assumptions for EE, the most volatile effect on the long-run expected exchange rate depreciation is the short-run movement of the exchange rate. This happens because of the short-run overshooting effects of expected or actual monetary policy (Dornbusch, 1976). These movements, however, are reflected only partly on the long-run interest rate because they fade out as time passes. In fact, as the price rigidities that cause the overshooting are concentrated in the short term, the long-term overshooting effects tend to be smaller.

The main conclusion of the approach outlined above is that in a small open economy the movements in the long-run interest rate are caused by the movements in the international long-term rates. Its macroeconomic rationale,[19] however, abstracts from some well known imperfections of international capital markets and from the very significant fact that equilibrium in the real sector in EEs usually requires either a huge and extremely rapid increase in investment and/or in asset prices, especially of non tradable financial (i.e., stock) and/or "real" (i.e., land) assets (Zahler and Valdivia, 1987, pp. 257–277).

Regarding financial markets, the one for long-term securities in EEs tends to be illiquid, and thus international investors command a high liquidity premium to access them. This tends to create a wedge between interest rates in these markets and those of the rest of the world, at least for a period of time. If some sort of preferred habitat theory applies, a short-term disconnection between long-term local and foreign interest rates should be observed, if no agents are arbitraging them.[20] Local institutional investors could, if allowed, quickly access international markets if they find them attractive and accessible. Thus, they could become the main link between local and international long-term securities markets.

c) The Chilean experience

After the balance of payments crisis of 1982 the Chilean capital account was "*de facto*" closed: there was very little access to international finance and local investors were not allowed to invest abroad. At the end of the 1980s and early 1990s the economy creditworthiness recovered and foreign investors started to demand Chilean assets. Local companies were able to raise bank debt in international markets again, FDI increased and the Central Bank started to accumulate international reserves at a high speed. There were significant peso appreciation pressures (Ffrench-Davis and Villar, 2005).

---

[19] According to this approach, in EEs integrated to the international economy the expected GDP growth rate is highly dependent on the world economic activity. This follows both from the demand for EEs exports and capital flows available to finance growth.

[20] There is the potential arbitrage between the long-term bond market and the stock market. In fact, international institutional investors (when allowed) tend to be big players in EEs stock markets, and not so much in EEs local bond markets. Then, if for example, international investors push local stock prices higher and expected stock returns lower, arbitrage between the stock and the bond market would push local bond prices higher and their long-term interest rate lower. The extent of the connection depends on the degree of substitution of the two types of assets.

With the new economic environment, which was costing high quasi-fiscal losses, the Central Bank encouraged capital outflows by opening the capital account for foreign investments by most local agents, except for banks and institutional investors, which, for prudential reasons, were also allowed to invest abroad but in a more gradual and selective way. It also established regulations to limit and reduce the speed of excessive short-term capital inflows. The main chronological events in the opening of the capital account were the following:[21]

In 1991 the waiting period for capital remittances for inward investment under the debt-equity swap mechanism (chapter XIX) was shortened from ten to three years; and exporters were authorized to keep their foreign currency abroad for a period of 150 days before selling them in the domestic formal market. Banks were allowed to hold up to US$ 400 million before selling the excess to the Central Bank, versus the previous US$ 200 million limit. In 1993 the minimum repatriation period for FDI was reduced from three years to one year. In 1994 the limit to the holdings of foreign exchange by banks was eliminated and exporters were allowed to sell in the "informal" domestic market up to US$ 15 million. In 1995 insurance companies were allowed to invest overseas up to 13%, and mutual funds up to 30% of their respective portfolios, and exporters were allowed to sell in the informal market all of their exports. In 1996 mutual funds were allowed to invest 100% of their funds abroad. In 1997 every person and firm[22] was allowed to invest abroad freely.

Thus, since 1997 capital outflows have been completely free for persons and for companies, with the partial exception of banks and institutional investors, which were subject to regulatory limitations by their own law, by the Chilean SEC and/or by the Central Bank.

Table III.4 shows the evolution of AFP holdings of foreign assets and the limits set by the Central Bank.[23] Although overseas investments were authorized in early 1992, pension funds did not start using this alternative until 1993. However, *by August 1997 they had invested less*

---

[21] Chile's liberalization and opening-up of the capital account implemented between mid 1991 and mid 1996 was carried forward with a pace coherent with the objective of overall macroeconomic equilibrium. See Zahler (1998).

[22] Except, for prudential reasons, banks, pension funds and insurance companies.

[23] Chilean regulation regarding foreign investments by AFP distinguished between fixed income instruments (mainly bonds) and variable income instruments (mainly equities). However, this distinction is not very relevant for the macroeconomic consequences of AFP investment abroad.

than 1% of their total assets abroad, a pattern that changed in a rather abrupt and significant manner during 1998.

Our hypothesis states that as AFP invested significant amounts of their assets abroad, local long-term interest rates increased their correlation with long-term international rates.

We tested the causality between the Chilean 8 year Central Bank UF bond (PRC – 8) yield and the 5 year USD Treasury interest rates for two periods of time: between June 1996 and September 1998 and between October 1998 and January 2002. We used 1998 as a threshold because the actual investment by AFP abroad "jumped" from US$ 272 million in 1997 (equivalent to 1.1% of their assets) to US$ 1400 million in 1998, equivalent to 5.6% of their assets,[24] an amount which should have given the AFP enough freedom to exploit their visions on the relative value of foreign and local assets.

The equations tested were:

(7) $$PRC_t = \alpha + \sum_{l=1}^{10} \alpha_l \times PRC_{t-l} + \sum_{l=1}^{10} \beta_l \times UST_{t-l}$$

(8) $$UST_t = \alpha + \sum_{l=1}^{10} \alpha_l \times PRC_{t-l} + \sum_{l=1}^{10} \beta_l \times UST_{t-l}$$

where PRC is the yield on the 8 year Central Bank indexed bond and UST is the dollar yield on the 5 year US Treasury bond.

The results were the following:

Pairwise Granger Causality between June 1996 and September 1998

Null Hypothesis:	OBS	F-Statistic	Probability
PRC does not Grange Cause UST	159	1.80836	0.06445
UST does not Granger Cause PRC		0.89516	0.53957

Pairwise Granger Causality between October 1998 and January 2002

Null Hypothesis:	OBS	F-Statistic	Probability
PRC does not Grange Cause UST	122	1.06530	0.39597
UST does not Granger Cause PRC		4.85554	1.1E-05

The test shows that there is a clear change of the influence between the US Treasury long-term interest rates and the Chilean Central Bank

---

[24] In both years they could have invested abroad up to 12% of their total assets.

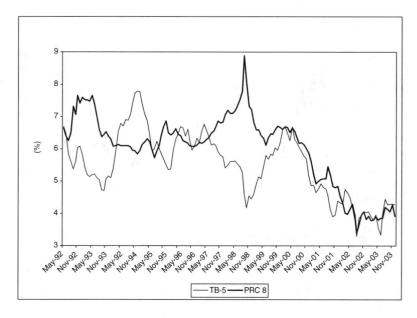

Figure III.2   Yield on Chilean PRC-8 and 5 year UST, 1992–2003 (*)
Source: Central Bank of Chile and www.federalreserve.gov
(*) BCU-10 and TB-10 since September, 2002.

8 year PRC before and after 1998.[25] This result can also be seen in figure III.2.

During 1998 the local long-term interest rate increased substantially, while the 5 year US Treasury yield decreased. This occurred because of an extremely tight monetary policy followed by the Chilean Central Bank in order to face a significant current account deficit, together with an increase in Chile's risk premium (figure III.3) that followed the generalized increases in the EEs risk premiums triggered by the Asian, and later the Russian crisis. Other than that, the correlation between the USD 5 year Treasury bond and the Chilean 8 year PRC increased substantially after 1998.

---

[25] It should be noted that we did not attempt a more rigorous empirical analysis between these two variables, which would have required controlling for changes in liberalization measures regarding openness of the capital account, exchange rate regimes, expectations of devaluation, AFP regulatory limits and Central Bank's interventions in the foreign exchange market.

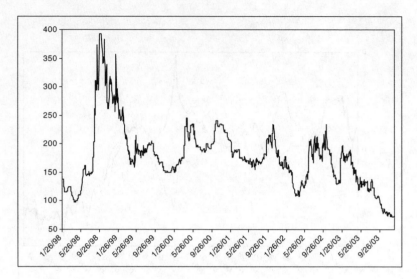

Figure III.3   Chilean government bond risk premium, 1998–2003 (basis points)
Source: Bloomberg data.

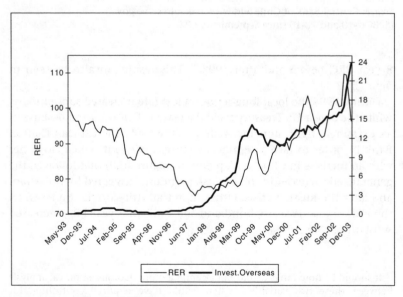

Figure III.4   AFP investments overseas and RER, 1993–2003 (% of funds and indice 1986=100)
Source: Central Bank of Chile and SAFP.

The change regarding the linkage between international long-term rates and local ones did not occur until around three years after the AFP were allowed to invest abroad a rather substantial share of their portfolio, and occurred only after they *effectively* invested quite heavily abroad. This can be explained, at least partially, because the capital account of Chile was less open until 1997. In fact, most of the measures that had been applied until 1996 to graduate the speed of financial integration to the rest of the world were removed in 1997 and 1998, thus augmenting the connection between local and international interest rates. In addition, part of the reluctance to move funds overseas by AFP reflected stronger domestic return prospects. Perhaps more importantly, the trend towards the appreciation of the domestic currency (UF) until late 1997 reinforced expectations of appreciation during that period and biased AFP investments in favor of peso or UF denominated assets, as shown in figure III.4. Only in 1998 started a new cycle of depreciation of the Chilean currency.

5. Institutional investors and the exchange rate

When a closed economy opens its capital account, there should be a stock adjustment of the assets of both local and foreign investors. Local investors will have a desired demand for international securities, and international investors will have a net demand for local securities. It should be expected that, overall, the inward flow to EEs should be significantly higher than the outward flow from EEs. However, the latter movement should be dominated by institutional investors, given the expected benefits associated to risk diversification and enhanced returns.[26]

Given their size, the effect of institutional investors on the foreign exchange market could be substantial (J. P. Morgan, 2002). This should be more intense in a case like the Chilean one, considering the already mentioned concentration of the industry as well as the AFP regulation regarding their committed rate of return. And short-term expected returns are those that tend to dominate the decisions of investors, institutional ones included. Thus, under quite common conditions, *foreign investment decisions by pension funds will tend to be dominated by the short-run expected appreciation or depreciation of the currency relative to the interest rate differentials.* Only through time do

---

[26] These benefits, for the Chilean case, are discussed in Valente (1988, 1991).

long-run investment objectives permeate the policies of institutional agents.

a) The Chilean experience

Together with giving the Central Bank the power to determine autonomously foreign exchange and capital controls, the Central Bank law of 1989 provided a new regulatory framework for foreign exchange transactions: it established that all transactions are free, except those regulated by the Central Bank. The latter was given the authority to regulate balance of payments transactions, but not to prohibit a non-regulated transaction from being done between two agents.

Thus, there coexisted two foreign exchange markets: the formal one, composed by the banking system and the Central Bank, where all the regulated transactions have to be done, and a legalized informal market, where the unregulated transactions are done. This coexistence aimed at two objectives: to preserve the stability of foreign payments and allow the overall foreign exchange market to be free and legal.

The Central Bank issued a comprehensive set of regulations in its "Compendium of Regulations for Foreign Exchange Transactions", applicable to all transactions in the formal market; in particular, those related to foreign investments by institutional investors, the most important of which are the AFP.

Initially there were three main concerns regarding international investments by AFP: (i) a political concern, related to Chilean compulsory savings being invested abroad; (ii) authorities wanted that opening-up to be gradual, in order to smoothen the learning process, which included the proper evaluation of transaction and information costs of overseas investments; and (iii) there was a concern regarding the potential destabilisation of the foreign exchange market if the AFP were to invest or disinvest a significant portion of their assets abroad in a short period of time.

Thus, the strategy was to allow the AFP investments abroad gradually. And although the microeconomic benefits of international diversification were clear, the size, concentration and the regulation of the Chilean AFP industry could cause macroeconomic imbalances if allowed to quickly and sizably invest abroad.[27] Therefore, some macroeconomic considerations were taken into account in the regulation of

---

[27] Associated in general to financial agents' behavior and time-horizon and, more specifically, to the "herd" effect which characterizes the Chilean AFP industry, due to its regulation.

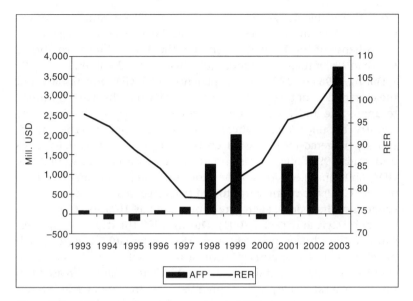

Figure III.5 AFP net investments overseas and RER
Source: Central Bank of Chile.
Minus = AFP net annual inflows; Plus = AFP net annual outflows.

international investments of Chilean pension funds during the first half of the 1990s.[28]

The first capital outflows by AFP occurred in the second quarter of 1993, for an amount of US$ 90 million (figure III.5), which represented only 0.6% of their portfolio and can be interpreted as an initial exploring attempt of overseas investments by AFP.

During most of the 1990s, until the end of 1997, the observed nominal exchange rate was very similar to the floor of the exchange rate band (see Ffrench-Davis and Villar, 2005). This situation, together with the huge increase in international reserves generated strong expectations of persistent real appreciation. These expectations, together with a differential of returns favorable to local (bonds and

[28] Fontaine (1996) presents the case for macroeconomic considerations leading to some sort of regulation of AFP investments abroad. These relate, on the one hand, to the fiscal cost associated to pension fund reforms and the need to develop a sound and liquid domestic capital market; and on the other, to the eventual destabilizing effects, especially on the real exchange rate, of sudden changes in their portfolios when the country faces severe balance of payments problems.

stocks) investments, generated almost no AFP investment overseas until late 1997. In July of 1997, when the Asian crisis was triggered by the collapse of the Thailand economy, the AFP had invested abroad less than 1% of their total funds, quite below the 12% limit.

During 1996 and 1997 Chile experienced high GDP growth rates, but the current account deficit rose significantly while the peso continued to appreciate and foreign short-term debt increased. Therefore, the country became quite vulnerable to foreign shocks. When those shocks, triggered by the Asian crisis, took place from January 1998 until mid 1999 (Chile's terms of trade declined the equivalent of 3% of GDP, and capital outflows by pension funds were equivalent to 4.8% of 1998 GDP) the country was forced to engage in a significant macro-economic adjustment: aggregate demand fell by 10% and GDP by 1% (Ffrench-Davis and Tapia, 2001). During 1998 the depreciating pressures on the Chilean peso were almost unsustainable. The (nominal) price of the dollar increased until near the ceiling of the band. To avoid a more significant depreciation, the Central Bank increased real interest real rates sharply. In September 1998 the 90-day real interest rate reached almost 18% while the 8 year PRC increased by 100 points.

The combination of foreign shocks and inappropriate domestic policies were major determinants of peso depreciation expectations, which triggered quick and substantial international investments by AFP. Figure III.6 shows that even until mid 1998 AFP had invested overseas less than 20% of their ceiling, explained in part by the fact that the yield of Chilean long-term bonds, adjusted for effective devaluation, exceeded international returns. Similarly, Chilean equities, adjusted for effective devaluation, outperformed US stocks until the mid 1990s (figure III.7).

In 1998, as the depreciation pressures on the peso mounted, gross outflows of AFP were US$ 1.6 billion, equivalent to 29% of portfolio outflows in the capital account (figure III.8). AFP gross international investments increased even more in 1999, to over US$ 4 billion in that year, equivalent to 36% of portfolio outflows. During 2000, on the outset of calmer international markets, AFP started to repatriate some of their investments, so that they generated a net inflow of about US$ 100 million. Between 2001 and 2003, AFP invested abroad US$ 33.1 billion in gross terms and US$ 6.5 billion net.

Figure III.8 shows that AFP have become an increasingly important agent in the Chilean foreign exchange spot market, as measured by portfolio capital flows. In fact, while in 1996–97 total AFP flows (inflows and outflows) accounted for 7.5% of total portfolio flows

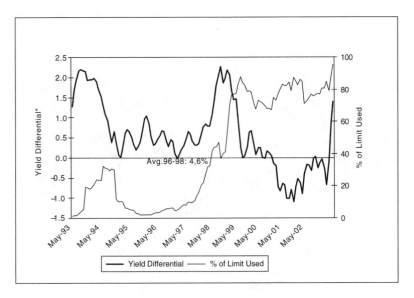

Figure III.6 AFP investment overseas and long term bond yield differential, 1993–2003
Source: Central Bank of Chile, SAFP and www.federalreserve.gov
*Twelve months moving average of dollar yield of PRC – 8 minus TB – 5 (in percentage terms).
BUC-10 and TB-10 since September, 2002.

(inflows and outflows), in 1998–99 that percentage increased to 26%, and in 2000–03 to 57%. However, information available for 2000–03 indicates that around 50% of AFPs investments abroad were hedged in the forward market, which means that AFPs net pressure on the exchange rate market is smaller as compared to their spot position.

This highlights that, contrary to what is usually stated (Turner, 2002, p. 6), allowing institutional investors to hold a high proportion of their assets abroad (denominated in foreign currency), does not imply that EEs will have a buffer against exchange rate volatility. In fact, the Chilean experience of 1998–2003 suggest that if no restriction is placed on the speed at which the stock adjustment can be made, AFP tend to act as a short-term oriented financial agent, seeking for the short-term returns of an appreciating currency and/or protection from a depreciating currency. In the process, *AFP behavior may end up increasing foreign exchange volatility and exacerbating deviations of the real exchange market value from its long-term equilibrium, thus complicating and turning more*

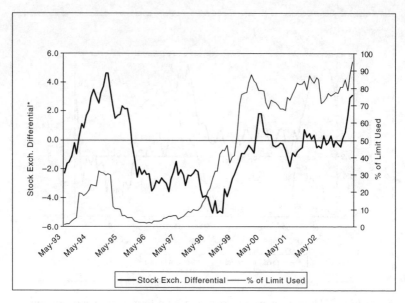

Figure III.7 AFP investment overseas and stock exchange differential, 1993–2003
Source: Central Bank of Chile and SAFP.
*Twelve months moving average of differences in returns on IGPA and Dow Jones indexes (in %).

costly overall macroeconomic management, with very probable negative effects on pensioners, who expect long-run returns.

Additionally, Chilean AFP accounting is mark-to-market; therefore, gains and losses are registered on all their domestic and foreign trading. In spite of the development of the Chilean capital market, domestic bonds and equities eligible to belong to AFP assets are still quite illiquid *vis à vis* the market for similar bonds and equities in developed economies. Therefore, when in need of liquidity or when incentives to trade are present, AFP could prefer, *ceteris paribus*, to trade with their overseas holdings rather than with their quite illiquid domestic holdings. This easiness to trade foreign currency denominated holdings apparently also contributed to the significant destabilizing effect on the exchange rate and need for over adjustment by the Central Bank's monetary policy in 1998.

In short, in every year from 1997 until 2003 Chilean AFP behaved in a procyclical manner regarding the foreign exchange market. As mentioned, given their size, industry concentration as well as its regulation,

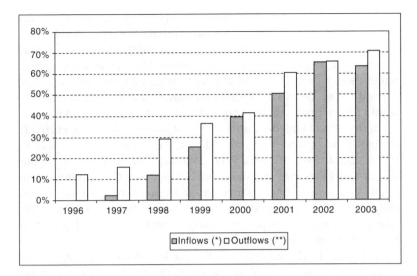

Figure III.8 AFP gross overseas flows, 1996–2003
Source: Central Bank of Chile.
*As percentage of gross portfolio inflows. ** As percentage of gross portfolio outflows.

under quite common conditions AFP decisions related to foreign currency denominated assets will be dominated by the short-run expected movements of the currency relative to the interest rate differentials, thus exacerbating market pressures, except for their hedging in the forward market, on the exchange rate, and very probably requiring a higher degree of macroeconomic adjustment than strictly necessary. In general, it is not clear that the benefits associated to risk diversification associated to institutional investors holding significant investments abroad will be higher than the costs associated to the required macroeconomic over adjustment needed to face the effect of their procyclical behavior on the domestic financial and foreign exchange markets.

6. Conclusions and policy implications

Based on recent Chilean experience, this paper analyzed some of the macroeconomic implications of privately managed pension funds in EEs.

In the middle and long-run pension funds play a role regarding total domestic saving and developing local capital markets. The effect of reformed pension funds on overall domestic savings is not clear. On the one hand, the transfer from a pay-as-you-go system to a fully funded privately managed individual capitalization system generates, during a quite long transitory period, a substantial fiscal deficit. Additionally, the compulsory savings imposed by the reformed system, which is expected to achieve higher returns that the old one, could generate some kind of inter temporal substitution by individuals, who would tend to spend more at present against their pension savings.

On the other hand, development of long-term capital markets in EEs is highly and positively influenced by the existence of these new big institutional investors which: (i) generate a demand for company stocks and long-term corporate bonds; (ii) provide liquidity to the equity and bond markets, which increases the demand for these typically long-term financial assets; (iii) contribute to improve the corporate governance of companies, which facilitates the development of both equity and bond capital markets.

Chile has developed a relevant local long-term bond market in domestic currency (UF). That market developed *pari passu* with the growth of reformed pension funds (AFP), which are the main holders of corporate and Central Bank bonds, so their influence to this development is evident.

But Chilean long-term bonds are indexed to (past) inflation, and the question remains as to whether this indexation is an essential part of the bond market development, especially in inflation-prone countries such as many of Latin America. Inflation indexed bonds solve a series of problems in economies with high and uncertain inflation rates. First, they contribute to complete financial markets. With long-term indexed bonds the long-term real interest rate can be locked, something that cannot be done by rolling over short-term instruments. Second, the issuance of indexed bonds may significantly reduce companies financing costs. Third, indexed bonds also encourage long-term issuances, since with high inflation the incentive to extend the maturity of bonds is low, regardless of the inflation risk premium.

In the case of Chile, indexation has been a major factor in the development of the long-term bond market, but without the significant and increasing buying power of AFP this market would not have developed as much as it did. This can easily be seen by considering that after ten years of bond market development, the AFP held more than 50% of Central Bank and private sector bonds, and near 75% of the mortgage bonds issued by financial institutions (LH).

In terms of the short-run macroeconomic implications of AFP, when the economy is relatively closed, we argued that the effect of pension funds on the term structure of interest rates could be significant, given that they are the main players in the market. In Chile this is reinforced because the pension fund industry has become increasingly concentrated, which has created a virtual monopsony among institutional investors, due to the relatively small size of mutual funds. Additionally, since Chilean AFP regulation stimulates them to have similar portfolios, this also contributes to expect that their trading could significantly affect the domestic yield curve. However, this hypothesis requires further research.

The analysis is then extended to an economy with a more open capital account, where institutional investors are allowed to invest in foreign securities. In this scenario, theory states that the long-term domestic interest rate tends to equal the international long-term rate plus the long-term expected appreciation or depreciation of the currency plus the long-term risk premium. However, as EEs markets for long-term securities tend to be quite illiquid, international investors command a high liquidity premium to access them. This contributes to isolate these EEs long-term markets from those of the rest of the world, at least for a period of time. If some sort of preferred habitat theory of the term structure of interest rates prevails, there could persist some disconnection between long-term local and foreign interest rates, if no agents arbitrate them. Local institutional investors, if allowed to invest heavily abroad, could quickly access international markets when they find them attractive, becoming the main link between local and international long-term securities markets.

Being aware of the potential distorting adjustment mechanisms in the typically quite long transition period until the desired stocks of domestic and foreign assets is attained, the empirical evidence of the Chilean economy suggests that when financial opening-up is increased and when AFP can invest significantly abroad, the movements in the long-run "financial" interest rate are quite correlated to the movements in the international bonds rates. We tested the abovementioned theoretical approach for the Chilean economy during the 1990s. The test showed that there is a clear change of the influence between the US Treasury 5 year bond and Chile's Central Bank 8 year PRC before and after 1998, year when the AFP started to allocate a significant percentage of their assets abroad.

One explanation of this change relates to the fact that between mid 1997 and 1998 most of the measures that had been applied during the first half of the 1990s to partially de-link the Chilean interest rate from the international one were abolished. However, AFP did not play a role as arbitrager until 1998 not only because of the effects of those measures but very crucially because until the end of 1997 expected and actual exchange rate movements indicated that the peso was undervalued. Furthermore, in that period returns on Chile's long-term bonds were higher than in the United States and, although to a smaller degree, returns in the stock exchange were also higher than in the United States.

Since late 1997, financial assets became more profitable in the United States than in Chile. Additionally, there was a big shift in exchange rate expectations towards a devaluation of the peso, due to the direct and indirect effects of the Asian and Russian crises on the, at that moment, highly vulnerable Chilean economy. This increased the expected return of dollar denominated financial assets. The speed and amount of AFP investment overseas allowed for a much greater connection between the local and international rates. That contributed to make more acute the peso devaluation pressures and, consequently, the Central Bank reaction, and required a highly costly macroeconomic adjustment process.

Therefore, the analysis, based on the Chilean experience, suggests that the importance of institutional investors is such that *EEs rules governing their portfolio decisions should incorporate not only microeconomic considerations, but also those regarding macroeconomic stability and growth.*

One macroeconomic issue refers to the (usually quite long) transitory effects on the fiscal deficit of the transfer from a pay-as-you-go pension fund system to a fully funded privately managed individual capitalization system (Fontaine, 1996; Reisen, 1997; Uthoff, 2001). Another macroeconomic consideration refers to delaying the liberalization of outward investment by pension funds as a way to help creating or deepening the size and/or liquidity of domestic long-term capital market. In other words, institutional investors play a major role by filling the gap in the supply of long-term finance that exists in most EEs, as well as by facilitating the privatization of state owned enterprises (Fontaine, 1996; Reisen and Williamson, 1996) and improving the financial sector regulatory framework.

Chilean AFP, in the process of attempting to maximize benefits, affect and are affected by market perceptions, particularly with regard to expectations of changes in monetary policy and exchange rates. Furthermore, once developed, given their significant size, AFP end up leading market expectations. The 1998–99 Chilean macroeconomic recessive adjustment suggests that in the absence of appropriate regulations, AFP desired change in foreign exchange denominated assets took place through sudden, abrupt and large changes in flows of overseas holdings. This contributed, to the extent that those movements were not hedged, to exacerbate actual and expected devaluations, thus deepening the recessive macroeconomic adjustment. *This macroeconomic outcome, by increasing unemployment, lowering real wages and/or reducing AFP domestic profitability affects directly the welfare of future pensioners.* To reduce this undesirable impact, a third macroeconomic policy refers to the convenience of establishing, in addition to the stock limitation on overseas holding, a *regulation that limits the velocity with which pension funds can change their portfolios of international securities.* For example, the Central Bank could establish, depending on the overall macroeconomic policy stance, a limit to the outflow (Fontaine, 1996) or inflow of institutional investors per period of time (a month, for example). This could be implemented as a function of each investors holding of foreign currency or as a fixed amount to be auctioned between institutional investors. This policy should help to reduce the volatility of the exchange rate and the depth of the macroeconomic adjustment, when required. However, care should be taken not to overburden institutional investors with this sort of regulation, since there are situations when, for example, a quicker response by these investors is needed in order to better protect the returns of pensioners.

Finally, a consideration on pension fund regulation aimed at reducing their eventual negative effect on macroeconomic stability relates to their ability to trade. In principle, long-term investors such as pension funds or insurance companies do not have the same need for liquidity as most other participants in financial markets. To ameliorate excessive trading in foreign holdings, regulation could require pension funds to record their holdings in either an *investment account* or a trading *account.* The investment account would be related to a "buy and hold" criteria (and not to make liquid those investments in the short run), and there could be some incentive to allocate an important part of AFP foreign currency holdings in that account. This would induce institutional investors to be less active in trading (not holding) overseas instruments, thus contributing to reduce volatility and procyclical behavior by domestic pension funds in the foreign exchange market.

References

Akerloff, G. (1970), "The market for lemons: quality uncertainty and the market mechanism", *Quarterly Journal of Economics*, August.
Campbell, J. and R. Shiller (1996), "A Scorecard for indexed government debt", *NBER Working Paper* 5587, Cambridge, Mass.

Cifuentes, R., J. Desormeaux and C. González (2002), "Capital markets in Chile: from financial repression to financial deepening", in *The Development of Bond Markets in Emerging Economies*, BIS Papers, No. 11, June.

Dornbusch, R. (1976), "Exchange rate dynamics", *Journal of Political Economy*, December.

Fontaine, J. A. (1996), "Are there (good) macroeconomic reasons for limiting external investments by pension funds? The Chilean experience", in S. Valdés-Prieto (ed.), *The Economics of Pensions: Principles, Policies and International Experience*, Chapter 9, Cambridge University Press, New York.

Ffrench-Davis, R. (2005), "Macroeconomics-for-growth under financial globalization: Four strategic issues for emerging economies", in this volume.

—— (2002), *Economic Reforms in Chile: from Dictatorship to Democracy*, University of Michigan Press, Ann Arbor.

—— and H. Tapia (2001), "Three varieties of capital surge management in Chile", in R. Ffrench-Davis (ed.), *Financial Crises in "Successful" Emerging Economies*, ECLAC/Brookings Institution Press, Washington, DC.

—— and L. Villar (2005), "Real macroeconomic stability and the capital account in Chile and Colombia", in this volume.

Harrison, P. (2002), "The impact of market liquidity in times of stress on the corporate bond market: pricing, trading, and availability of funds during heightened illiquidity", *BIS CGFS Conference Paper*, No. 2, October.

J. P. Morgan (2002), "Pension fund reform: anticipating FX implications", *Global Foreign Exchange Research*, New York, December 17.

Lee, J. Y. (2000), "The role of foreign investors in debt market development: conceptual frameworks and policy issues", *World Bank Working Paper*, No. 2428.

Mihaljek, D., M. Scatigna and A. Villar (2002), "Recent trends in bond markets", in *The Development of Bond Markets in Emerging Economies*, BIS Papers, No. 11.

Ocampo, J. A. (2005), "Overcoming Latin America's growth frustrations: The macro and mesoeconomic links", in this volume.

Reinstein, A. (2002), "Issues in building corporate money and bond markets in developing-market economies", presented at the IDB Bond Market Development Workshop, November.

Reisen, H. (1997), "Liberalizing foreign investments by pension funds: positive and normative aspects", *Technical Paper*, No. 120, OECD Development Center.

—— and J. Williamson (1996), "Pension funds, capital controls, and macroeconomic stability", in S. Valdés-Prieto (ed.), *The Economics of Pensions: Principles, Policies and International Experience*, Cambridge University Press, New York.

Sanhueza, G. (2001), "Chilean banking crisis of the 1980s: solutions and estimation of the costs", in *Documentos de trabajo del Banco Central de Chile*, No. 104.

Stiglitz, J. and A. Weiss, (1981), "Credit rationing with imperfect information", *American Economic Review*, 71.

Turner, P. (2002), "Bond markets in emerging economies: an overview of policy issues", in *The Development of Bond Markets in Emerging Economies*, BIS Papers, No. 11.

Uthoff, A. (2001), "La reforma del sistema de pensiones y su impacto en el mercado de capitales", in R. Ffrench-Davis and B. Stallings (eds.), *Reformas, crecimiento y políticas sociales en Chile desde 1973*, ECLAC/LOM, Santiago.

Valente, J. R. (1991),"Inversión de los fondos de pensiones en el extranjero", *Documento de Trabajo*, No. 159, Centro de Estudios Públicos, Santiago, August.

—— (1988), "Diversificación internacional: una alternativa para las necesidades de inversión de los fondos de pensiones", *Documento de Trabajo*, No. 109, Centro de Estudios Públicos, Santiago, December.

Vittas, D. (1998), "Institutional investors and securities markets: which comes first?", paper presented at the World Bank ABCD LAC Conference, San Salvador, El Salvador, June.

Walker, E. (1998), "Mercado accionario, crecimiento económico y rentabilidad esperada: Evidencia chilena", *Cuadernos de Economía*, 35 (104).

Zahler, R. (2003a), "Conclusions", in E. Demaestri, F. de Mergelina and P. Masci, (eds.), *Financial Crises in Japan and their Implications for Latin America*, IDB publication, Washington DC.

—— (2003b), Comment to "The China Syndrome or the Tequila Crisis", by Francisco Gil Díaz, in J. A. González (ed.), *Latin American Macroeconomic Reforms: The Second Stage*, The University of Chicago Press.

—— (2000), "Policy options for capital importers", in P. B. Kenen and A. K Swoboda (eds.), *Reforming the International Monetary and Financial System*, IMF, Washington DC.

—— (1998), "The Central Bank and Chilean macroeconomic policy in the 1990s", *CEPAL Review*, No. 64, April.

—— and M. Valdivia (1987), "Asimetrías de la liberalización financiera y el problema de las deudas interna y externa", in C. Massad and R. Zahler (eds.), *Deuda Interna y Estabilidad Financiera*, CEPAL/GEL (Grupo Editor Latinoamericano), Buenos Aires.

IV

Real Macroeconomic Stability and the Capital Account in Chile and Colombia

*Ricardo Ffrench-Davis and Leonardo Villar**

Introduction

The management of real macroeconomic balances has shown to be a significant factor in explaining the growth performance and behavior of productive investment in emerging economies (EEs). The environment provided by macroeconomic policies to producers, including the "rightness" of macro-prices and the consistency between aggregate demand and potential GDP, have emerged as significant variables explaining the poor recent performance of LACs. Together with fiscal responsibility and prudential financial regulation, those variables conform a comprehensive set of real macroeconomic balances. In the present stage of globalization of financial volatility, capital flows have played, in emerging economies, a crucial role for the sustainability of those balances and their interplay with growth (Ffrench-Davis, 2005; Ocampo, 2005). Here we examine the macroeconomic policies implemented by Chile and Colombia since 1990, the successes and failures achieved, focusing in growth performance and macroeconomic sustainability.

In 1995, when contagion from the tequila crisis was spreading to several countries in Latin America, Chile and Colombia were exempt from contagion and presented high rates of growth, without significant signs of financial distress. Several elements worked to explain this positive performance. Chile benefited from high copper prices and capital

* We appreciate the valuable comments and suggestions of Guillermo Le Fort, Carlos Quenan, Heriberto Tapia, and other participants at two ECLAC Seminars in Santiago and at a technical meeting of G-24 in Geneva.

flows to Colombia were encouraged by the discovery of an important oil camp. Still, many analysts attribute this positive performance, to a large degree, to the fact that both countries had undertaken prudential measures in order to avoid "excessive" exposure to short term capital flows. In particular, they were at that time using a reserve requirement on short-term foreign indebtedness and several other instruments addressed to reduce domestic vulnerability to capital flows. Also, authorities in Chile and Colombia had effectively worked against the pressures of capital inflows towards excessive real appreciation of their domestic currencies.

The parallelism between Chile and Colombia continued to be present after the Asian and the Russian crises of 1997 and 1998. In this period, however, the results were not so positive. The central banks of both countries had been intervening in the foreign exchange markets through crawling currency bands for many years. In 1998, those bands became strait jackets from which it was extremely difficult to escape from without losing credibility and without exposing the foreign exchange markets to destabilizing dynamics. Despite the fact that short-term debt represented only a small share of total foreign liabilities in both countries, vulnerability to the international financial crisis was significant in those years, real interest rates rose sharply in 1998 and GDP growth was negative in 1999.

The similarities between Chile and Colombia, however, do not go much farther. During most of the decade, Chile presented very high fiscal surpluses and saving and GDP growth rates rose significantly, while in Colombia GDP growth was below historical records, the public sector deficit increased rapidly, and saving rates followed a decreasing trend.

Thus, the macroeconomic outcomes of Chile and Colombia were quite different, but still their response to the international financial crises of 1995 and 1998–99 shared several common elements. This may be due to the fact that both countries used similar instruments to regulate capital inflows and foreign exchange markets. This makes the comparative analysis of the two economies particularly attractive.

Section 1 aims to provide an overview of the macroeconomic frameworks of Chile and Colombia during the 1990s. Section 2 follows the evolution of exchange rate regimes. Section 3 discusses the rationale of capital account regulations and analyses the policy instruments that were adopted in each country to regulate capital flows. Section 4 presents some concluding remarks.

1. Macroeconomic environments of Chile and Colombia during the 1990s [1]

a) Inflation and economic activity

Chile and Colombia had, before the 1990s, a long tradition of relatively high inflation rates, which created strong inertia in the price setting processes. The CPI annual inflation rates were quite similar in both countries during the 1980s. Between 1982 and 1989, they averaged 20.7% in the Chilean case and 22.5% in Colombia (table IV.1). During the 1990s, the central banks – which were quite autonomous – adopted very similar institutional policies, and tried to avoid shock treatments and rather chose a gradual approach to the process of disinflation. The large capital inflows that dominated most of the period created pressures towards the appreciation of domestic currencies and helped the central banks in the process of reducing inflation. However, neither of these countries used exchange rate anchoring in order to reduce inflation. In the early 1990s, the inflation rate started a steady process of reduction, which was more rapid in Chile – this country reached one-digit inflation rates in 1994, while Colombia did it in 1999.

Notwithstanding the similarities in monetary policy, there were deep differences in the behavior of economic activity in Chile and Colombia during the 1990s. The Chilean economy had suffered a deep crisis in 1982–83 – with a 14% drop in GDP and a severe financial crisis – which generated a large gap between effective and potential GDP, discouraging capital formation and the growth of potential GDP. In 1986, actual GDP started to recover, and the gap initiated a gradual reduction trend until it disappeared in 1989. Between 1990 and 1997, both effective and potential GDP grew vigorously, with an average yearly rate of 7.6%. Dynamism of the economy slowed down in 1998, and a 0.8% drop in GDP was observed in 1999. Since 2000, growth resumed at a rate far below the levels that were observed before 1998.[2] In any case, the yearly average in 1990–2003 was 5.5% (table IV.1) – it doubled the 2.9% recorded in 1974–89, the sixteen-year period of the Pinochet regime (Ffrench-Davis, 2002, ch. 1).

---

[1] The table in the Annex shows the relative sizes of both countries: Colombia has a population and a GDP at current prices 2.9 times and 1.3 times those of Chile, respectively, but a GDP per capita that is only $\frac{2}{3}$ that of Chile and $\frac{1}{6}$ that of the USA (at World Bank PPP prices).

[2] It is estimated that potential GDP grew 7% until the arrival of the negative shock brought by the Asian Crisis, and did adjust downward to 4% thereafter (Ffrench-Davis, 2002, ch. 1). Actual GDP growth averaged 3.1% in 1999–2004.

Table IV.1   Chile and Colombia: CPI inflation and GDP growth rates, 1974–2003 (% changes per year)

	CHILE		COLOMBIA	
	CPI Inflation Rate	GDP Growth Rate	CPI Inflation Rate	GDP Growth Rate
1974–81	98.9%	3.3%	24.6%	4.6%
1982–89	20.7%	2.6%	22.5%	3.4%
1990	27.3%	3.7%	32.4%	4.3%
1991	18.7%	8.0%	26.8%	2.0%
1992	12.7%	12.3%	25.1%	4.0%
1993	12.2%	7.0%	22.6%	5.4%
1994	8.9%	5.7%	22.6%	5.1%
1995	8.2%	10.6%	19.5%	5.2%
1996	6.6%	7.4%	21.6%	2.1%
1997	6.0%	6.6%	17.7%	3.4%
1998	4.7%	3.2%	16.7%	0.6%
1999	2.3%	–0.8%	9.2%	–4.2%
2000	4.5%	4.5%	8.8%	2.9%
2001	2.6%	3.4%	7.7%	1.4%
2002_p	2.8%	2.2%	7.0%	1.6%
2003_p	1.1%	3.3%	6.5%	3.7%
Average 1990–2003	8.5%	5.5%	17.2%	2.7%

Source: Chile: Central Bank of Chile. Colombia: DANE.

$_p$ Preliminary

Colombia also experienced a boom by the mid-1990s but it was much milder and shorter than in Chile. Colombian GDP growth averaged 5.3% yearly between 1993 and 1995. For the rest of the 1990s, it was well below the historical standards. The annual GDP growth rate in 1990–2003 averaged only 2.7%. Even during the period of the Latin-American debt crisis, Colombia had attained a higher average growth rate. Moreover, the recession in 1999, with a drop of 4.2%, was much deeper than in Chile and the recovery in more recent years has been slower. As a result, *per capita* GDP in 2003 was at the level of 1994 and 5% below 1997, mirroring a significant output gap.

b) Fiscal balances

The outstanding behavior of economic activity in Chile during most of the 1990s took place in an environment of fiscal surpluses. Until 1997, there was a fiscal surplus of 2% of GDP in average and the central government expenditure as a share of GDP was relatively constant – at around 20% (table IV.2). Since 1998, government expenditure rose

Table IV.2   Chile and Colombia: government expenditure and deficit, 1990–2003 (Shares of GDP in current pesos)[1]

	Central Government Expenditure		Central Government Surplus (+) or Deficit (−)[2]		Non-Financial Public Sect or Surplus (+) or Deficit (−)[2]	
	Chile	Colombia	Chile	Colombia	Chile	Colombia
1990	20.2%	9.8%	0.8%	−0.9%	1.2%	−0.6%
1991	20.6%	10.9%	1.5%	−0.4%	1.5%	0.0%
1992	20.3%	12.6%	2.1%	−1.8%	2.5%	−0.2%
1993	20.5%	12.3%	1.8%	−0.7%	2.1%	0.3%
1994	19.9%	12.8%	1.6%	−1.4%	1.9%	0.1%
1995	18.6%	13.6%	2.4%	−2.2%	2.4%	−0.3%
1996	19.6%	15.7%	2.1%	−3.6%	1.6%	−1.7%
1997	19.9%	16.3%	1.8%	−3.8%	0.8%	−3.3%
1998	21.3%	17.0%	0.4%	−4.9%	−0.6%	−3.7%
1999	22.6%	19.2%	−1.4%	−5.9%	−1.5%	−4.1%
2000	22.4%	19.2%	0.1%	−5.9%	−0.6%	−4.2%
2001	22.9%	21.3%	−0.3%	−5.9%	−0.6%	−4.4%
2002p	22.9%	21.4%	−0.6%	−5.6%	−1.6%	−3.6%
2003p	22.4%	21.1%	−0.8%	−5.0%	−2.2%	−3.0%

Source: Chile: Dirección de Presupuesto (DIPRES) and Central Bank of Chile. Colombia: DNP-CONFIS (Cash basis) and DANE.
[1] GDP figures at current pesos have been adjusted to make old data compatible with the methodology adopted in 1996 and 1994, respectively.
[2] Does not include privatizations.
p Preliminary.

gradually by three percentage points of GDP, reflecting increases in social expenditure as well as a counter-cyclical fiscal policy. Even so, the deficits of both the central government and the consolidated non-financial public sector were very moderate, notwithstanding the tax revenue foregone due to a gap between effective and potential GDP and a depressed price of copper.[3]

In contrast with Chile, the poor performance of economic activity in Colombia along the 1990s coincided with an unprecedented increase in government expenditure and fiscal deficits. Central government expenditure, that before 1990 had been close merely to 10% of GDP for more than three decades, increased to 21% in 2001–03 (similar to the Chilean level). Several analysts have attributed this unprecedented increase in public spending to the Constitutional reform of 1991, which accelerated the process of fiscal decentralization and incorporated into the Constitution new citizens rights that should be covered with public resources. In addition, the transition from the pay-as-you-go system towards a pension regime based on individual capitalization accounts implied, as it had done in Chile in the 1980s, a huge increase in government expenditure as measured by cash flows, although it contributed to reduce the actuarial debt. The absence of an equivalent increase in public revenues implied that the central government fiscal deficit rose from less than 1% of GDP in the early 1990s to almost 6% of GDP between 1999 and 2002. In turn, the consolidated non-financial public sector, which had a surplus until 1994, presents a deficit close to 4% of GDP since 1999.

c) Savings and investment

The contrasting performance of economic activity and fiscal accounts in Chile and Colombia implied a very different behavior of savings and investment (table IV.3). With an economy persistently operating at full employment of installed capacity, high rates of GDP growth and outstanding fiscal surpluses, savings and investment rates in the Chilean case were in the 1990s notably above historical standards. Fixed capital formation reached historical peaks in the 1990s, averaging 28.5% in 1991–98 (in 1986 prices). This figure contrasts with 19.9% during the last quinquennium of the Pinochet era (1985–89) and with an even lower average in the prior years. Although the crisis of 1999 implied a

---

[3] Since 2000 the government has been working with a scheme of structural fiscal budget, estimated with a "normal" price of copper and tax proceeds as if actual GDP were equal to "potential" GDP.

Table IV.3   Chile and Colombia: investment and savings, 1985–2003 (Shares of GDP)

A. CHILE	GROSS FIXED CAPITAL FORMATION (Shares of GDP at constant prices)		GROSS NATIONAL SAVINGS (Shares of GDP at current prices)	
	Constant prices of 1986	Constant prices of 1996	Methodology 1986	Methodology 1996
1985–1989	19.9%		16.5%	
1990	24.2%		23.2%	
1991	22.4%		22.3%	
1992	24.7%		21.5%	
1993	27.2%		20.9%	
1994	27.4%		21.1%	
1995	30.6%		23.8%	
1996	31.0%	26.4%	21.2%	23.1%
1997	32.2%	27.4%	21.6%	23.1%
1998	32.2%	27.0%	21.2%	21.8%
1999	26.9%	22.2%	21.8%	21.0%
2000	26.6%	23.2%	21.9%	20.6%
2001		23.2%		20.5%
2002ᴾ		23.0%		20.6%
2003ᴾ		23.4%		21.0%

(continued)

Table IV.3   Chile and Colombia: investment and savings, 1985–2003 (Shares of GDP) *(continued)*

B. COLOMBIA	GROSS FIXED CAPITAL FORMATION (Shares of GDP at constant prices)		GROSS NATIONAL SAVINGS (Shares of GDP at current prices)	
	Constant prices of 1975	Constant prices of 1994	Methodology 1975	Methodology 1994
1985–1989	15.8%		21.5%	
1990	14.0%		21.4%	
1991	12.9%		22.7%	
1992	13.9%	17.9%	19.0%	
1993	18.0%	21.8%	19.5%	
1994	20.7%	23.3%	18.6%	23.0%
1995	20.2%	22.3%	16.9%	23.0%
1996	18.5%	21.6%	12.8%	18.3%
1997		20.4%		16.2%
1998		19.0%		15.3%
1999		13.0%		13.4%
2000		12.4%		14.8%
2001		13.9%		14.5%
2002p		14.4%		14.7%[1]
2003p		15.7%		15.1%[1]

Source: Chile: Central Bank of Chile and IMF-IFS. Colombia: DANE-DNP
p Preliminary.
[1] Preliminary estimates by the National Department of Planning.

significant decline in investment, fixed capital formation between 1999 and 2003 was still well above its average level in the 1980s.

Fixed investment in Colombia presented large swings, with a significant increase until the mid-1990s and a rapid decline thereafter. However, even during the boom period, between 1993 and 1995, the Colombian ratios of fixed capital formation were much lower than in Chile. After the crisis, since 1999, fixed investment experienced a dramatic drop and stayed below 15% of GDP. These low levels of investment will make it much more difficult for Colombia to recover high and sustainable rates of economic growth in the near future.

The Colombian savings rates plummeted dramatically during the 1990s. They went down by about four percentage points of GDP between the late 1980s and mid-1990s and by nearly eight additional points during the second half of the decade. In the Chilean case, in contrast, in the 1990s the savings ratios were systematically higher than in the 1980s.

d) **Financial sector**

An outstanding contrast between Chile and Colombia during the 1990s has to do with the behavior of the financial sector. In Colombia, the reduction in domestic saving rates and the rise in investment during the first half of the decade were accompanied by an impressive financial boom, which was to a large degree fed with capital inflows (Barajas and Steiner, 2002). Outstanding credit of the financial sector rose from around 24% of GDP at the beginning of the decade to 40% in 1997. During the subsequent crisis this figure went down dramatically, back to 25%, while the quality of the portfolio of the financial system deteriorated substantially (table IV.4).

In the Chilean case, the degree of financial depth was much higher than in Colombia since the beginning of the 1990s and continued to be so after the crisis. In addition, in contrast with most other Latin American countries, the index of credit/GDP behaved counter-cyclically.[4] This helped to explain the fact that the deterioration of quality of the loan portfolio during the crisis was extremely mild. While non-performing loans as a share of outstanding credit reached

---

[4] In a comparative study for the eight largest Latin American economies, Barajas and Steiner (2002) show that the Chilean case was exceptional in this respect.

Table IV.4   Chile and Colombia: financial sector, 1990–2003

| | Outstanding Credit/GDP | | *Non-performing Loans* *Outstanding Credit* | |
	Chile	Colombia[1]	Chile	Colombia[1]
1990	52.4%	24.8%	2.1%	4.0%
1991	48.7%	22.7%	1.8%	4.2%
1992	51.5%	24.4%	1.2%	3.1%
1993	55.7%	28.4%	0.8%	2.1%
1994	52.8%	31.9%	1.0%	2.4%
1995	55.4%	35.5%	0.9%	3.7%
1996	59.5%	37.3%	1.0%	5.1%
1997	64.3%	39.6%	1.0%	5.2%
1998	66.8%	37.8%	1.4%	8.7%
1999	69.2%	33.9%	1.7%	11.5%
2000	69.2%	27.1%	1.7%	9.4%
2001	69.7%	25.5%	1.6%	8.6%
2002	68.2%	24.8%	1.8%	8.0%
2003	67.2%	25.0%	1.6%	5.7%

Source: Chile: Central Bank of Chile, Banks and Financial Institutions Superintendence.
Colombia: Banco de la República.
[1] Outstanding credit data does not include leasing transactions.

11% in Colombia in 1999, they did not surpass 1.8% in Chile.[5] One main reason behind this strength of the Chilean financial system is the strict prudential supervision, built after the generalized collapse of the banking sector in 1983–86 as a result of the debt crisis.

In summary, the cycle in foreign capital inflows was leveraged in Colombia by the behavior of domestic credit, which was not the case in Chile. Together with the stricter supervision of the financial sector in the Chilean case, two other factors may have contributed to these contrasting results. First, in Colombia the boom of capital inflows coincided with a reform in the financial sector, which implied that the central bank undertook an important reduction in the reserve requirements on domestic deposits between 1991 and 1998. Thus, as stressed by Carrasquilla and Zárate (2002), domestic financial regulation in Colombia was highly procyclical. Second, the higher degree of financial depth may have worked in the Chilean case as a buffer against the capital inflows shock. This hypothesis would endorse the

[5] There is heterogeneity in the definition of non-performing loans. In Chile it refers to the installments of loans overdue for more than 90 days. In Colombia, the definition changed several times along the 1990s.

idea that foreign capital account regulations are even more important when the domestic financial system is less developed.

e) Foreign savings and the current account

In the Chilean case, probably as a consequence of very active regulations on capital inflows, the current account deficit was kept under control during the first half of the decade. In 1993, due to a sharp drop in the copper prices, the deficit went up to 5.4% of GDP. However, the current account deficits were below 3% of GDP, averaging 2.3% between 1990 and 1995 (see table IV.5 below). After the tequila crisis, the current account deficits rose to less sustainable levels, close to 5% of GDP between 1996 and 1998. As shown later, this coincides with the period in which the regulation of capital inflows became less active.

In Colombia, in contrast, the deterioration of the current account was particularly acute during the first half of the decade. Between 1991 and 1994 – coinciding with a process of trade opening, currency appreciation and capital flows liberalization – a current account surplus of 4.9% of GDP was transformed into a deficit of 4.5%, level around which it remained until 1998.

The drop in international liquidity after the Asian and the Russian crises implied drastic adjustments in the current account deficits. In 1999, such adjustments represented 5.0% and 5.7% of GDP in Chile and Colombia, respectively. As shown in the next section, the paths followed by the current account balances of Chile and Colombia during the 1990s were matched by the behavior of their real exchange rates.

2. Exchange rate regimes

During most of the 1990s, the exchange rate regimes of Chile and Colombia were dominated by the currency bands, which in both countries were dismantled and replaced by floating regimes only in 1999. Those regimes shared many common elements.

a) Chilean exchange rate regime

After the crisis of 1982–83, and much earlier than Colombia, Chile introduced a minor width currency band. Since the beginning, the upper and the lower bounds of the band were devalued daily, according to an estimate of net inflation. Discrete nominal devaluations, however, were added at various junctures, serving to achieve the notable real depreciation of 130% between 1982 and 1988. In 1989 the band was widened to ±5%, allowing for an orderly and not traumatic depreciation of the peso, which was required to compensate for the rise in imports associated to a sharp increase in economic activity in 1988–89.

The evolution of the foreign exchange regime since 1990 reflected the purpose of the central bank to regulate the surge in capital inflows. Since June 1991, as we will see in the next section, an unremunerated reserve requirement was established on foreign loans, and a tax on domestic loans applied to up to one year of each operation was extended to foreign loans. In January 1992, the currency band was widened to ±10%. In contrast with what had happened three years earlier, the widening of the band in this case was addressed to allow for some additional appreciation of the peso. In June 1992, the dollar was replaced by a basket of currencies as the standard for the exchange rate. Replacing the dollar with the basket meant greater stability for the real exchange rate as perceived by producers of tradables, and introduced greater uncertainty in the peso-dollar exchange rate, thereby reducing incentives for interest rate arbitrage and short-term capital movements (Ffrench-Davis and Tapia, 2001, p. 87). Remember that, by this time, capital inflows were very large and it was already clear that the Chilean economy was booming. As we will see in the next section, the objective of deterring interest rate arbitrage was being simultaneously addressed through the reserve requirement on capital inflows, thus providing space for an active counter-cyclical monetary policy. In the following years capital inflows continued, and the real exchange rate experienced a moderate appreciation (averaging 1% yearly between 1989 and 1995).[6] Naturally, that appreciation contributed to reduce inflation. However, it was an equilibrating, sound, real appreciation. Consistently, as said, the current account deficit between 1990 and 1995 averaged only 2.3% of GDP.[7]

---

[6] Central Bank figures provide a higher estimate of appreciation – an annual average of 2.5% – because it uses wholesale price indexes for measuring external inflation and CPI for domestic inflation. We use figures of ECLAC that also measure external inflation on the basis of CPI. This procedure is consistent with that of Colombia.

[7] Appreciation of the real rate was "equilibrating" in the sense that it was consistent with the net increases of productivity in Chile, as the sustainable external deficit suggests. Keeping a low current account deficit was among the explicit objectives of the exchange rate policy of the Central Bank in that period (see Zahler, 1998).

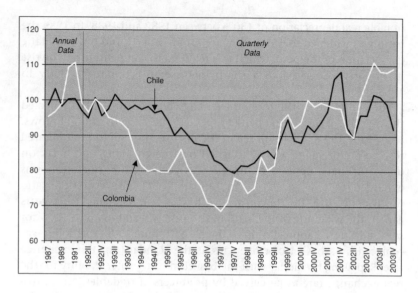

Figure IV.1   Chile and Colombia: real exchange rate index, 1987–2003
Base average 1987–90 = 100
Source: ECLAC figures.
Average real exchange rate with main trading partners, computed with CPI.
A higher real exchange rate indicates a more depreciated domestic currency.

Following the tequila crisis, the behavior of the Chilean economy
was so strong that expectations of appreciation and capital inflows
were greatly reinforced after 1995. The central bank kept accumulating
significant amounts of international reserves with the exchange rate at
the then appreciating bottom of the band, until the end of 1997.
Several parameters of the band were adjusted during that period in
order to allow for some additional appreciation of the peso and to
reduce monetary pressures from the accumulation of foreign reserves.
Since November 1995, the rate of nominal depreciation of the band
was designed to allow for a 2% real appreciation per year, based on the
assumption that Chilean productivity growth would be faster than that
of its trading partners. In addition, the external inflation used to calcu-
late the referential exchange rate was overestimated, which generated
considerable additional revaluation. Furthermore, in early 1997, the
band was broadened from ±10% to ±12.5% as a mechanism to allow
for further appreciation of the peso and served to reduce inflation (see
Ffrench-Davis and Tapia, 2001, pp. 95–96). As a consequence, the peso

appreciated 20% in real terms between March 1995 and October 1997, notably faster than before the tequila crisis (figure IV.1).

When the exchange rate expectations shifted to depreciation, in late 1997, following the Asian crisis, the Central Bank started to sell abundant reserves to avoid a depreciation of the exchange rate even within the lower half of the exchange rate band in order to prevent a rise in inflation. The anti-inflationary bias of the Central Bank interventions in the foreign exchange market became even more evident in mid-1998, when the band was drastically shortened, right at the moment of greatest uncertainty, in order to send a signal that the authorities would not give in to market pressures towards devaluation. This measure implied that the macroeconomic adjustment process that was needed as a consequence of the drastic decline in the terms of trade and of the shortage of capital flows had to be led by interest rate hikes and monetary contraction.[8] Then, the strategy chosen by the authorities of the Bank was more consistent with a fixed exchange rate regime than with a currency band system. Naturally, credibility in the new band rapidly deteriorated. The band was widened again at the end of 1998 and then suspended in September 1999 in order to allow for the exchange rate to adjust freely, now in the context of strongly depressed domestic absorption.

Given the significant appreciation recorded in 1996–97, it was clear that the center of the band had become an "outlier" price, leaving no space within the band to make feasible the necessary exchange rate adjustment (Ffrench-Davis and Larraín, 2003). Actually, most of the depreciation in the real exchange rate in Chile in recent years took place after the dismantlement of the currency band in 1999. Between August 1999 and July 2003 the real exchange rate depreciated by 30%.

b) Colombian exchange rate regime

As in Chile, the Colombian currency experienced a notable real devaluation during the 1980s, which was required by the shortage of foreign savings. The devaluation of the peso was managed within the tradi-

---

[8] The authorities of the Central Bank stated that an adjustment in the exchange rate would have caused both pressure on prices and costs associated to currency mismatches in large non-tradable firms. Ffrench-Davis and Tapia (2001) point out that these effects were overrated and implied an over-adjustment in the productive sector. Corbo and Tessada (2002) estimate a VAR model for Chile and conclude that i) the defense of the exchange rate in January 1998 was well justified by potential inflationary costs and, ii) however, a devaluation in mid-1998 would have not represented an inflationary risk.

tional crawling-peg regime that had been introduced since 1967 and lasted until 1991, and that, in contrast with Chile, avoided any discrete jump in the exchange rate. Even in 1985, when nominal devaluation was almost 50%, it was instrumented through small and continuous daily movements.

In 1989, Colombia decided to depreciate its real exchange rate even further, in order to compensate for the decline in coffee prices after the collapse of the International Coffee Agreement and to prevent negative effects of the sharp opening up of the trade balance on the domestic production of tradables (Ocampo and Villar, 1992). However, this strategy rapidly proved to be inconsistent with the contractionary monetary policy that the central bank was trying to undertake in order to curb inflationary pressures. As in Chile, large capital inflows and pressures towards appreciation of the peso dominated during most of the 1990s, until mid-1997. Most of the adjustments in the Colombian exchange rate regime were introduced in order to manage those pressures.

In June 1991, the traditional crawling-peg regime was modified. The Banco de la República would exchange dollars for "Certificados de Cambio" (dollar-denominated bonds) that could only be redeemed at the "official exchange rate" after a given maturity. The exchange rate would be determined by the secondary market for those bonds. The new regime, which was in place until January 1994, implied a nominal appreciation of the peso, which marked an important shift in the policy strategy that had been in place during almost a quarter of a century. During this period, there was a drastic relaxation in monetary policy addressed to reduce domestic interest rates and to discourage foreign capital inflows attracted by interest rate arbitrage. However, between 1991 and 1994, the real depreciation of the peso that had taken place in 1989 and 1990 was entirely reversed (see figure IV.1 above). In January 1994, the Banco de la República decided to discontinue the mechanism of the "Certificados de Cambio" and introduced an explicit exchange rate band system (Urrutia, 1995). The amplitude of the band was set at ±7% and the center was increased every day at a predetermined crawling rate. In December 1994, however, the exchange rate band was shifted downwards as a consequence of the actual increase in long-term capital flows and of the expectations of additional inflows associated to the development of recently discovered oil camps.

The currency band established in December 1994 was kept without important changes until September 1998. During more than three and a half years, therefore, it helped to reduce the medium-term instability of the exchange rate in an effective manner. For instance, the upper limit of the band helped to avoid an extreme depreciation during the first half of 1996, when there were speculative pressures related to the process against President Samper for allegedly illegal resources in his presidential campaign. Also, few months later, the lower bound of the band helped to avoid extreme appreciation of the peso when it became clear that President Samper would stay in office and large inflows were coming into the country, associated with the privatization of important public companies.

After the Asian crisis had exploded, in the final months of 1997 and during the first half of 1998, the role of the currency band was much more controversial. The exchange rate had depreciated and was hitting the upper limit of the band, so the central bank was forced to sell large amounts of foreign exchange while implementing a highly contractive monetary policy. Nonetheless, due to the slope and of the amplitude of the band, the depreciation of the Colombian peso was quite substantial. The peso price of the dollar by mid-1998 had depreciated by about 8% in real terms, without any change in the currency band mechanism. The upward shift in the currency band was decided in September 1998, when a new government was in office and the macroeconomic program for 1999 had gained some credibility. After a short-lived overshooting, the new currency band worked smoothly during the last quarter of 1998 and the first quarter of 1999. The Central Bank stopped losing reserves and the domestic interest rate experienced a relatively rapid downward trend.

In the second quarter of 1999, the financial crisis, the deeper than expected recession and the further deterioration of the fiscal accounts, damaged the credibility in the macroeconomic program and new pressures towards devaluation appeared. In June, the band was again shifted upwards and its amplitude was widened from ±7% to ±10%. Simultaneously, the government and the central bank announced that they had agreed to design an IMF backed program in order to recover confidence from the international financial community. By late September, immediately after the agreement with the IMF was reached, the currency band was dismantled. Having been shifted twice in less than a year, its credibility had eroded. Also, at the international level, the initial success of other Latin-American countries with their new floating regimes (notably Brazil in February and Chile in early September) had created strong pressures against the band system, both in the market and in the multilateral financial institutions. This facilitated the appearance of speculative attacks. Most analysts however considered at that time, that the real exchange rate was already close to its long-run equilibrium level. Interestingly enough, this was verified *ex post de facto*. Since the currency band was abolished, the exchange rate fluctuated inside the dismantled band during more than two years, despite a very rapid decline of the domestic interest rate.

Therefore, the real depreciation of the peso that took place as a consequence of the crisis was instrumented within the currency band system.[9] Subsequently, between September 1999 and May 2002, the real exchange rate fluctuated around the levels reached by the third quarter of 1999. After May 2002, the contagion from the Brazilian crisis and a higher degree of uncertainty on the sustainability of the Colombian foreign debt, led to an additional real depreciation of the peso, which was reinforced by the end of that year with the effects of the Venezuelan crisis.

Since the last quarter of 1999, Colombia has a floating exchange rate regime. Although this type of regime does not allow the central bank to target any specific nominal or real exchange rate, it contemplates two transparent and publicly known mechanisms for central bank intervention:

(i) The central bank can buy or sell international reserves through *put* or *call options* that are auctioned in limited amounts of foreign exchange at the end of each month. This mechanism has been used mainly to buy international reserves and to recover the international liquidity indicators that Colombia had before the 1998/99 crisis. Since February 2003, however, given the rapid pace of depreciation, the Banco de la República has also used the call options in order to mitigate pressures on the exchange rate that may risk the attainment of the inflation target.

(ii) The second mechanism is addressed to reduce extreme short-run volatility of the exchange rate and consists of additional auctions of *put* or *call* foreign exchange options which are triggered whenever the market rate deviates in an "unusual" manner from its own 20-day moving average.[10] In practice, short-run volatility of the exchange rate has been low and these trigger conditions only took

---

[9] By the third quarter of 1999, before the currency band was dismantled, the real exchange rate had recovered the levels of the late 1980s.

[10] An "unusual" deviation was initially defined as 5% and since December 2001 was redefined as 4%.

place in the second half of 2002, when contagion from the Brazilian crisis implied a rapid depreciation of the peso.

c) Common and contrasting elements of the exchange rate regimes in Chile and Colombia

From the above description, it is possible to highlight some common and some contrasting features of the exchange rate regimes that Chile and Colombia had in the 1990s:

(i) During most of the 1990s, central bank interventions in both countries implied large amounts of international reserve accumulation. In this sense, the currency bands worked as limits against appreciation of the exchange rate and not as anti-inflationary devices.

(ii) As accumulation of international reserves, led by the capital surges to emerging economies, created monetary pressures and (short-run) quasi-fiscal costs of sterilizing monetary intervention, it became more difficult for the central banks to resist the market pressure for appreciation. Giving up to those pressures would contribute to keep inflation under control, so the currency bands were widened and shifted downwards in several opportunities, allowing for a sizeable appreciation of the real exchange rate during most of the decade in Colombia and in the second half in Chile.

(iii) The degree of flexibility of the foreign exchange market in the inner part of the bands proved to be much lower in Chile, where the Central Bank, with intramarginal intervention, was more active in trying to stabilize the exchange rate market than the Colombian one. This is mirrored in the fact that both the accumulation of international reserves during the boom and the losses during the crisis were much larger in Chile (see table IV.5 below).

(iv) In both countries, the limits of the currency bands seemed to be more effective to control pressures towards currency appreciation than towards currency depreciation. As the bands have an explicit or implicit pre-announcement of their limits, the exchange rate regime loses credibility when those bands are shifted or widened. If that happens in response to a speculative attack against the upper limit of the band, the credibility in the anti-inflationary commitment of the Central Bank is also damaged. It is interesting that currency bands in Chile and Colombia disappeared almost simultaneously, in September 1999, when there were strong pressures towards depreciation. However, the simultaneity in the dismantling of currency bands may also say a lot about IMF preferences and fashions in the international financial community.

(v) The floating regime introduced in Chile and Colombia after dismantling the currency bands does not imply absence of Central Bank intervention.[11] What they have in common is the assumption that the Central Bank cannot target specific levels of neither the nominal nor the real exchange rates. Still, Central Banks have some room to alter the short-term foreign exchange market through their interventions, which in turn may be discretionary or follow publicly known rules. While Chile has exerted discretion in intervening the market, Colombia is following strict rules since 1999. In any case, the experiences of both countries show that the optimal exchange rate policy is far from leaving the exchange rate determination to the short-termist markets.[12]

3. Capital account regulations[13]

a) The rationale for capital account regulations

The rationale for capital account regulations arises from the hypothesis that full liberalization of the capital account in a developing economy, is likely to "trap" domestic policies into short-term bias and non-sustainable macroeconomic equilibrium (Ffrench-Davis and Ocampo, 2001).

The exchange rate regimes of Chile and Colombia provide a clear example of the difficulties created by foreign capital flows to macroeconomic policies. Capital flows greatly reduce the autonomy of domestic economic authorities to jointly manage the real exchange rate, the real interest rate, and aggregate demand, even in the short and medium run. Large capital inflows tend to reduce both the exchange rate and the interest rate, and to increase aggregate demand, while capital outflows tend to increase both macro-prices and to reduce economic

[11] Colombia accumulated US$ 2.2 billion since it entered the floating regime. Chile accumulated reserves in 2000 and 2002 but lost US$ 600 million in 2001 and US$ 400 million in 2003 (table 5).

[12] Ffrench-Davis (2003, p. 12). See also Edwards (2002), who argues that "it is perfectly possible that the optimal policy ... is one where the central bank intervenes from time to time" (p. 17). Those interventions, also, may be consistent with an inflation targeting regime without implying a "fear of floating".

[13] Revised and updated version of a paper presented in a Geneva meeting of the G-24, September 2003.

activity. As far as capital flows to developing economies have been proved to be highly procyclical, the real exchange rate, the real interest rate and aggregate demand become highly procyclical too. As a general rule, the capital account regulations that have been used both in Chile and in Colombia are oriented to:

(i) Enhance the ability of monetary and exchange rate policies to act in a counter-cyclical way. When capital inflows are very large, they push the domestic demand into a boom and lead to a deficit in the current account. Under those circumstances, the capital account regulations are addressed to discourage capital inflows in order to mitigate pressures towards lower real interest rates – which would artificially reinforce the aggregate demand boom – and towards a real appreciation – which would increase the current account deficit.

(ii) Reduce the vulnerability of the domestic economy to sudden changes in the international financial environment. This explains the emphasis of those regulations in reducing the share of short-term and liquid liabilities in total capital flows, and in imposing limits on the net uncovered foreign exchange positions of the domestic economic agents.

(iii) Improve the capacity of a country to use foreign savings as complementary to domestic savings and not as substitute. Again, this explains the emphasis of those regulations in reducing the share of short-term capital, which tends to finance consumption, *vis-à-vis* long-term capital, which usually finances productive investment.

b) Reserve requirement on capital inflows: A price-based capital account regulation

The most famous mechanism of capital account regulation used in both Chile and Colombia during the 1990s is the reserve requirement on capital inflows. As we will see, the height of the requirement and several details of its operation changed along time and were different in each country. The regulations used in both countries, however, shared three very important characteristics: (i) they were not quantitative controls but price-based regulations, (ii) they affected capital inflows and not capital outflows, and (iii) they were designed to have more impact on short-term than on long-term capital flows.

As with any price-based mechanism, the reserve requirement on capital inflows was not intended to block the way for those inflows, but to discourage them at the margin, *placing sand in their wheels.*[14] In order to make capital inflows more costly under a large external supply, two key elements were present as complements to the reserve requirement: (i) restrictive policies on any type of dollarization of deposits in the domestic financial system, and (ii) strict prudential regulations on the net foreign exchange position allowed to financial intermediaries. These two elements together guaranteed that the domestic financial intermediaries could provide foreign exchange denominated loans only when they were funded with foreign credit and subject to the reserve requirement. At the same time they inhibited the domestic financial system from becoming a major actor in the speculation in favor or against the peso.

The introduction of a non-remunerated reserve requirement in Chile in June 1991 was explicitly addressed to soften appreciatory pressures and provide more breath and autonomy to monetary policy (Zahler, 1998, p. 69). The deposit of the reserve requirement was initially equivalent to 20% of foreign loans and had to be kept for a minimum of 90 days and a maximum of one year, according to the term of the operation. In order to increase its effect, in May 1992, it was raised to 30% and the term of the deposit was raised to one year, independent of the maturity of the loan, which increased the bias against short-term capital inflows. In July 1995 it was extended to the purchase of Chilean stocks (secondary ADRs) by foreigners.

Although the objective of regulating capital flows continued to be present in Chile after 1996, the attitude of policy-makers was much less proactive. Despite the fact that there was a significant surge of capital inflows in 1996 and 1997, and that the effectiveness of any regulation tends to decline with time, the authorities did neither accommodate the height of the reserve requirement to the increased supply of funding nor generalized its scope.[15] The surge clearly weakened the fundamentals of the Chilean economy: the current account deficit

---

[14] As any kind of regulation or tax, the reserve requirement implies some efficiency costs at the microeconomic level. Forbes (2004) stresses some of those costs and argues that, more than "sand in the wheels", capital controls are "mud in the wheels of market discipline". However, prudential regulations, of which the reserve requirement is one, are directed to reconcile the interests or freedom of all agents, discouraging negative externalities and time inconsistencies.

[15] Le Fort and Lehmann (2003) argue that in order to mitigate elusion, it would have been required to eliminate exemptions to direct suppliers credit and to some investment inflows, but these measures faced strong opposition from the private sector and the previous coherent consensus within the public sector had been weakened.

increased, the exchange rate appreciated much faster and the stock of liquid foreign liabilities grew. When the Asian crisis contagion arrived, therefore, these fundamentals of the Chilean economy were much weaker than they had been during the tequila crisis of 1995. This fact contributed to increase the magnitude of the crisis of 1998 and 1999 when, as we will see, private capital outflows were quite large, including funds of the domestic private pension system (see Zahler, 2005). The reserve requirement was reduced from 30% to 10% in June 1998 and then to 0% in September.

Inspired by the Chilean experience, the Colombian reserve requirement on capital inflows was decreed in September 1993, coinciding with the final steps of the process of dismantling administrative capital controls that had started in 1991. The size of the reserve requirement was high enough to make it prohibitive in practice. Exemption made for trade financing, the requirement applied to any "short-term" foreign loan. "Short-term" was initially defined as less than 18-month maturity: this term was raised in March and August of 1994 to three and five years, respectively.[16] In 1996, when the exchange rate was at the most depreciated limit of the currency band and the central bank was loosing reserves, the minimum maturity of the foreign loans to be exempted from the reserve requirement went down to three years.

After the huge increase in international reserves that took place in the last part of 1996, the Colombian government issued a State-of-Emergency Decree, which, among other measures, established an explicit Tobin tax on all capital inflows (trade financing included) in addition to the reserve requirement regulated by the Central Bank. The Decree was declared unconstitutional in March 1997 but the central bank rapidly increased the reserve requirement again.

In May 1997, the Colombian Central Bank introduced several changes in the reserve requirement system, making it simpler and more similar to the Chilean one. A flat deposit in local currency (instead of a dollar denominated deposit) was required for all loans, independently of the maturity. The minimum maturity was thus abandoned but, as in the Chilean case, the new mechanism implied that the tax equivalent of the deposit was lower the longer the maturity of the loan. Initially, the size of the reserve requirement was 30% of the foreign loan and had to be kept during 18 months. These numbers were reduced in January and again in September 1998 as a response to

---

[16] A history of the reserve requirement on capital inflows in Colombia is summarized in Ocampo and Tovar (2003).

the weakened capital inflows. Between September 1998 and May 2000, the reserve requirement was only 10% of the foreign loan and had to be kept during 6 months. In June 2000, the reserve requirement was reduced to zero. Colombian authorities stated, however, as had done the authorities in Chile, that this was not the end of the mechanism, but only a resetting of the parameters, and the mechanism could be used again if needed to confront renewed capital surges.

Besides the similarities among the Chilean and the Colombian reserve requirement instruments to deter capital inflows, it seems clear that Chile used them more proactively during the first half of the 1990s than after 1995. In contrast, Colombia used them more proactively in the second half of the decade.

c) Non-FDI private capital flows and the effectiveness of private capital account regulations

The behavior of non-FDI private capital flows shows significant common elements in Chile and Colombia (see table IV.5, column e). Those flows were highly positive for several years until 1997 and became highly negative in both countries during the crisis of 1998/99.

In Chile, these flows averaged US$ 2.4 billion yearly between 1990 and 1996 and did not have extreme swings during that period. Even in 1995, when the tequila crisis was taking place, they amounted to US$ 2.0 billion. In contrast, between 1998 and 1999 they implied a net outflow of US$ 8.4 billion. Capital outflows had a pause in 2000 but were high again since 2001.

In Colombia, private non-FDI capital inflows became important only after 1992. During the initial years of the decade, net capital flows were negative, reflecting perhaps the existence of direct controls which were more effective to discourage inflows than to restrain outflows. As already mentioned, those controls were dismantled between 1991 and 1993. Private non-FDI capital flows averaged US$ 2.7 billion per year between 1993 and 1996. As in Chile, they were high even in 1995, when they amounted to US$ 2.5 billion, despite the tequila crisis. The reduction in this type of inflows took place in 1997, probably because of an increase in the costs of the reserve requirement implemented at the beginning of that year, before the Asian crisis started. In 1998 they became very small but still positive, and starting in 1999 they turned highly negative (see table IV.5).

Based on these figures, it appears easy to doubt the effectiveness of the reserve requirement that was used to regulate capital inflows. Both in Chile and in Colombia, net capital inflows were highest precisely during the periods in which that regulation was being used. However, the coexistence of large capital inflows and the reserve requirement may reflect a policy reaction function in which the introduction of capital regulations is caused by the large supply of capital inflows.[17] That was, evidently, the actual sequence in both cases.

In any case, it is clear that the regulations on capital inflows used in Chile and Colombia were not able to avoid the large net capital *outflows* that took place in the final years of the 1990s and the beginning of the new century. Our hypothesis may be summarized as follows: the reserve requirement was useful and effective as a temporary policy tool during the boom of capital inflows. Its effectiveness may be seen from two different perspectives. First, as a *short-run macroeconomic policy*, it enhanced the ability of the domestic authorities to act in a counter-cyclical way and to deal with the trade-offs between exchange rate and monetary policies. Second, as a *liability-flows policy*, it was effective in reducing the short-term component of capital inflows. Thus, the reserve requirement enhanced the absorptive capacity of a given total inflow, by raising the share of funds more associated to productive investment and, consequently, reduced the vulnerability to sudden stops; by contributing to resist appreciating pressures on the exchange rate, it contributed to increase the share of tradables in GDP.

On the other hand, however, the reserve requirement and, more generally, the set of policies adopted by Chile and Colombia, were not fully effective to deal with a major and lasting crisis as the one observed after 1997. This is not a reason to discard the temporary use of this type of policies under new capital surges, but to stress the need of other complementary regulations. The experiences of Chile and Colombia since 1998 highlight the need for more strict controls on the behavior of the stocks of foreign exchange denominated assets and liabilities. For example, as we will argue later, there should be financial regulations addressed to discourage large currency mismatches in the balance sheets of firms in the non-tradable sectors. Also, there should be regulations on the ability of institutional investors to manage portfolios in foreign currency. Opening the way for outflows of domestic capital in periods of abundance proved to be ineffective in reducing the excess supply, while in periods of scarcity of external supply led to

---

[17] Cardoso and Goldfajn (1998) successfully test this hypothesis for the Brazilian case.

Table IV.5   Chile and Colombia: capital flows and current account financing, 1990–2003 (US$ Millions)

	a. Current Account		b. International Reserves Accumulation	c. Net Direct Foreign Investment	d. Net Foreign Credit to Public Sector[1]	e. Other Flows of Private Capital = b-a-c-d
	US$ Millions	Shares of GDP				
A. CHILE						
1990	-485	-1.5%	2,121	654	-222.0	2,174
1991	-99	-0.3%	1,049	697	-955.1	1,406
1992	-958	-2.2%	2,344	538	42.2	2,723
1993	-2,553	-5.4%	173	600	-357.0	2,483
1994	-1,585	-2.9%	2,919	1,672	-313.8	3,146
1995	-1,345	-1.9%	741	2,205	-2,085.5	1,967
1996	-3,083	-4.1%	1,122	3,681	-1,540.3	2,064
1997	-3,660	-4.4%	3,320	3,809	-125.7	3,297
1998	-3,918	-4.9%	-2,194	3,144	430.0	-1,850
1999	99	0.1%	-738	6,203	429.0	-7,469
2000	-897	-1.2%	337	873	-85.3	446
2001	-1,100	-1.6%	-596	2,590	481.1	-2,567
2002	-885	-1.3%	199	1,594	886.2	-1,397
2003	-594	-0.8%	-366	1,587	1,859	-3,218

(continued)

Table IV.5 Chile and Colombia: capital flows and current account financing, 1990–2003 (US$ Millions) *(continued)*

	a. Current Account		b. International Reserves Accumulation	c. Net Direct Foreign Investment	d. Net Foreign Credit to Public Sector[1]	e. Other Flows of Private Capital = b−a−c−d
	US$ Millions	Shares of GDP				
B. COLOMBIA						
1990	544	1.2%	610	484	−45	−373
1991	2,347	4.9%	1,763	437	−347	−675
1992	876	1.5%	1,274	745	−56	−292
1993	−2,221	−3.4%	464	865	−158	1,978
1994	−3,669	−4.5%	199	1,298	−1,224	3,795
1995	−4,524	−4.9%	2	712	1,388	2,425
1996	−4,642	−4.8%	1,721	2,784	856	2,723
1997	−5,751	−5.4%	277	4,753	1,146	129
1998	−4,858	−4.9%	−1,390	2,032	1,469	−34
1999	671	0.8%	−315	1,392	647	−3,025
2000	628	0.9%	870	2,069	614	−2,441
2001	−1,250	−1.5%	1,217	2,509	1,484	−1,525
2002p	−1,580	−1.8%	138	1,258	388	73
2003p	−1,389	−1.8%	−184	837	469	−101

Source: Central Bank of Chile, IMF, Banco de la República.

p Preliminary.

[1] Chile: Includes Central Bank's operations and excludes operations by the state-owned commercial bank (Banco del Estado). Colombia: Corresponds to the net loans to public sector plus the net investment in bonds issued by the public sector.

an extremely procyclical outcome.[18] In the Colombian case, it is clear that the large growing fiscal imbalances that took place since the mid-1990s implied a rapid increase in foreign exchange liabilities and made it much more difficult to manage the crisis.

d) The reserve requirement as a macroeconomic policy tool

In evaluating the effectiveness of the reserve requirement on capital inflows as a macroeconomic policy tool, most analysts have focused on the effects of this regulation on the volume of total capital inflows. Empirical results on this topic are mixed.

Some econometric studies for both Chile and Colombia failed to find effects of the reserve requirement on the total volume of capital inflows, even though they found an effect on the composition of flows.[19] Those studies argue that there is a high substitution between capital inflows of different maturities, which implies a compensatory increase in long-term inflows when the reserve requirement induces a reduction in the short-term ones. From there, they conclude that this type of price-based regulation does not have an impact on net capital flows.

Other recent studies, however, obtain very different results. Le Fort and Lehman (2003) and Ffrench-Davis and Tapia (2004) show that, in the Chilean case, the reserve requirement did have an effect on the total volume of private capital inflows, once the effects of interest rate differentials and the evolution of the supply of funds are well taken into account. Gallego *et al.* (2002), find a significant effect of the reserve requirement on capital inflows when actions taken by the Central Bank to close loopholes are considered, highlighting the need for an active approach as a necessary condition for succeeding in the use of capital controls.

---

[18] It is interesting to underline that Korea, assumed to be at present a case of open capital account (evidently, it was the opposite in its period of "miraculous" growth), still applies restrictions on outflows of domestic savings.

[19] Critical evaluations are developed in Valdés-Prieto and Soto (1998) and Cárdenas and Barrera (1997) for the Chilean and the Colombian cases, respectively. De Gregorio, Edwards and Valdés (2000) also conclude that the Unremunerated Reserve Requirement (URR) did not affect net capital inflows in Chile, but they find that it allowed for a larger interest rate differential with the rest of the world, providing room of maneuver to monetary policy.

Similarly, Ocampo and Tovar (2003) find that the reserve requirements in Colombia "were effective in reducing the volume of capital inflows, both due to the increased costs of short-term borrowing and to the discrete effects of regulations, associated to the imperfect substitution of borrowing at different maturities" (p. 29).

Villar and Rincón (2003) argue that the econometric results on the effectiveness of this type of regulation on the volume of capital inflows do not solve the simultaneity problem that arises from the fact that those regulations affect the domestic interest rates, which in turn affect capital inflows. The papers mentioned in the previous paragraphs obtain partial equilibrium results: given the differential between domestic and foreign interest rates, a tax on capital inflows reduces their volume. The tax, however, should increase the domestic interest rate and it is likely that its total effect on the volume of capital inflows will be ambiguous when this channel is taken into account.

Following Villar and Rincón, the effectiveness of the reserve requirement as a macroeconomic policy tool should be evaluated also from the perspective of its impact on the domestic interest rates and the real exchange rate. Their econometric work show indeed that, in Colombia, the reserve requirement was a useful macroeconomic policy tool in a period characterized by large capital inflows, excess aggregate demand, pressures towards domestic currency appreciation and large current account deficits. This tool facilitated a counter-cyclical policy, allowing the domestic authorities to increase the domestic interest rates *vis-à-vis* the foreign rate, and hence reducing aggregate demand while avoiding additional pressures towards domestic currency appreciation.

Chile, in 1992 offers one quite illustrative case of the contribution of the reserve requirement to macroeconomic stability. Then, the USA, with a rather low interest rate, was further reducing it in order to face domestic recession, while Chile experienced some overheating and large supply of external funds. The response of Chile was to increase the reserve requirement, thus making space for monetary policy to raise its domestic interest rate with net stabilizing effects on aggregate demand. The effectiveness of capital controls to make room for monetary policy is supported by all econometric studies (see De Gregorio *et al.*, 2000; Edwards, 1999; Ffrench-Davis and Tapia, 2004; Gallego *et al.*, 2002). Thus, the Central Bank could induce a policy of *mini adjustments* to avoid *maxi adjustments*.

We can conclude, therefore, that the reserve requirement was a useful macroeconomic policy tool. However, as any other macroeconomic policy addressed to affect interest rates and the exchange rate, it is essentially a short-term policy instrument,[20] and to be used only in periods of an "excessive" supply. It is a counter-cyclical policy tool.

e) On microeconomic effects of capital controls

While the positive effects of the reserve requirement have been acknowledged by academic circles and authorities of institutions such as the BIS, IMF and the World Bank, some research on microeconomic effects has appeared. Although this chapter focuses on macroeconomics, we have included this brief section on microeconomic effects because of the notoriousness that this research, particularly related to the Chilean case, has gained recently.

Forbes (2003) finds that the reserve requirement affected more intensively "small" firms by imposing financial constraints. Gallego and Hernández (2003) conclude that the reserve requirement affected the financial structures of the Chilean firms reducing their leverage, increasing their reliance on self-generated funds (retained earnings), and increasing the maturity profile of their debt. Both microeconomic works use as a sample a group of listed companies in stock markets.[21]

Without discussing now the specifics of those two studies, it is evident that any tax imposes some cost to taxpayers and, in doing so, changes relative prices. The crucial point is what is the net effect of capital controls on overall welfare, after contrasting both their eventual microeconomic costs and their macroeconomic benefits. As mentioned, overall, evidence show that in Chile capital controls worked well, despite the existence of loopholes and a progressive elusion, which was not monitored by authorities as they had done systematically in 1991–95. In fact, at least in terms of its intermediate objectives, the reserve requirement was able to open space for monetary policy, contributed to reduce the stock of foreign liabilities and improved their maturity profile.

From the point of view of investment and growth, the impressive growth performance of the 1990s seems to support the idea that the positive effect of the whole approach, including the capital controls and their management, was much stronger than any associated micro-

---

[20] As already discussed, the "short-term", in this respect, can refer to several years, associated to the extent of the capital surge.

[21] Most listed companies in Chilean stock markets are among the biggest in the economy, therefore conclusions from these works cannot apply directly to SMEs.

economic costs. Actually, the investment ratio of Chile in the 1990s was the highest recorded in its history. In this sense, "financial constraints" as defined and reported by Forbes (2003) were not impediment for expanding the productive capacity.[22] Moreover, the microeconomic switch from debt to retained earnings in the financial structure, as well as the shift toward longer-term liabilities of "small" firms, found by Gallego and Hernández (2003) can be considered as a positive by-product of Chilean capital controls. Indeed, the main source of private savings in EEs, tends to be non-distributed profits and depreciation reserves of firms.

On the other hand, the Chilean economy became one of the less vulnerable in the region, escaping from the contagion of the Mexican crisis. In the case of the Asian crisis, the negative effect was rather moderated and, according to Ffrench-Davis and Tapia (2004), was mostly linked to policy errors like careless liberalization of outflows by residents during the boom phase. The reserve requirement, in turn, contributed to reduce the stock of liabilities and to improve its profile (both from a micro and macro perspective). According to most international research these two factors determine strongly both the probability of crises and its associated costs. In other words, the Asian crisis would have had a stronger negative effect on the Chilean economy if the capital controls had not been there.

Finally, evidence appears to be strong in the direction that access to financing and spreads of SMEs are more intensively affected than large firms during crises. Avoiding crises via discouraging capital inflows during the boom stage tends to imply for SMEs paying higher interest rates during the boom, but contributes to avoid sharp increases during the eluded bust and the corresponding actual financial constraints that they face during recessions.

f) The reserve requirement as a liability policy: Flows policies vs. stock policies

Empirical studies in both Chile and Colombia coincide in showing that the reserve requirement on capital inflows contributed to keep a rela-

---

[22] Forbes (2003) defines "financially constrained" firms as those that depend on their own sources of financing to invest. This definition is quite disputable, as reflected in the literature on the issue (see, for example, Kaplan and Zingales, 1997).

tively longer maturity of private foreign liabilities in the 1990s.[23] From this point of view, this was an effective tool as a *liability policy*. With a long-term maturity of foreign debt stock, a sudden stop in the supply of capital flows towards emerging markets has a much lesser impact on those markets as far as the refinancing needs are lower. In those conjunctures, what matters are gross financing needs rather than net needs. When the tequila crisis spread over most Latin-American countries in 1995, the maturity structure of foreign debt in Chile and Colombia was perceived as a significant strength of these economies and helped to make them almost immune to the crisis.

However, a high average maturity of private foreign debt is not a sufficient safeguard against a strong and long-lived shortfall in the supply of inflows. The experiences of Chile and Colombia in 1998–99 suggest that, when the economy receives that type of shock, what was originally contracted to be long-term debt may become shorter-term debt by the decision of debtors. They, indeed, buy dollar-denominated assets to hedge their positions. Also, under the pressure of weak economic activity and expectations of devaluation, they may be allowed to prepay their foreign currency liabilities before maturity, as actually happened in Colombia.[24]

Table IV.6 presents the evolution of the stocks of foreign debt in Chile and Colombia. The figures help to highlight the very rapid increase in the private sector foreign debt that took place during the second half of the 1990s, though from moderate initial levels. The rapid process of private debt accumulation marked a deep contrast between the period of the tequila crisis and the 1998–99 crises. At the end of 1994, when the tequila crisis was starting, total private debt was US\$ 12 billion in Chile and US\$ 8 billion in Colombia. Only four years later, at the end of 1998, these numbers had more than doubled (to US\$27 billion in Chile and to US\$18 billion in Colombia). Although the short-term component of these debts continued to be low, the

---

[23] For the Colombian case, see Cárdenas and Barrera (1997); Ocampo and Tovar (2003). For the Chilean case, see Agosin and Ffrench-Davis (2001); De Gregorio, Edwards and Valdés (2000); Le Fort and Lehmann (2003); Gallego *et al.* (2002).

[24] Since 1997, the Banco de la República of Colombia allowed private debtors to prepay long-term liabilities (which had not deposited the reserve requirement on short-term capital inflows), provided that half of the original maturity had elapsed.

huge increase in total private debt made the foreign exchange balance sheet much more vulnerable to the crisis.[25]

Behind the behavior of private foreign debt during the 1990s there is a rapidly growing currency mismatch in the private sector balance sheets. Both firms and households increased their foreign exchange denominated liabilities without a corresponding increase in foreign exchange denominated assets. Households and firms producing in the non-tradable sectors increased their indebtedness in foreign currency during the period in which the peso was expected to appreciate, which suggests that the reserve requirement on capital inflows was not binding enough. Only when the crisis of 1998–99 exploded and the Chilean and the Colombian peso started to depreciate, the private sectors started to look eagerly for hedging instruments, which reinforced the pressures towards depreciating the domestic currencies.[26] The regulations in both Chile and Colombia were not strong enough to discourage the financial intermediaries passing currency mismatches through to their clients. As a consequence, when the peso actually depreciated, they had to pay a significant cost. In the Colombian experience, to some degree, the financial crisis of 1999 was explained by the sudden increase in the peso value of foreign liabilities due to the peso depreciation. Prudential regulation should have prevented this from happening by reflecting these risks in the balance sheets of the banks that used to lend to clients with this type of currency mismatch. In the case of Chile, the devaluation that was needed, because of the too appreciated exchange rate reached in 1996–97, was delayed thus giving time to private firms to reduce foreign debt with cheap dollars, at the expense of the Central Bank balance sheet and a costly monetary contraction: the delayed correction of the exchange rate was compensated with a sharp increase in the interest rate.

One main problem with the regulations that were used in Chile and Colombia is that they act on the flow of new foreign exchange liabilities

---

[25] Bleakley and Cowan (2002) use microevidence at firm level for several Latin-American countries to show that the detrimental effect of the depreciation of domestic currencies during the crisis (balance sheet effect) was outweighed by the effect of the income elasticity of firms to the exchange rate. This result suggests that firms in the tradable sectors had higher foreign debt ratios than those in the non-tradable ones. However, in the Colombian case, there is evidence that the increase in private foreign debt was more acute in firms of the non-tradable sectors. See Banco de la República (2002), p. 27.

[26] In 1998–99, the Central Bank of Chile issued dollar denominated bonds for an amount equivalent to 2% of GDP, at an exchange rate evidently overvalued, to enhancing hedging operations.

Table IV.6 Chile and Colombia: international reserves and debt stocks, 1990–2003 (US$ Millions)

End of:	Foreign Private Debt		Foreign Public Debt	Total Foreign Debt[1]	International Reserves
	Short term[2]	Long Term			
A. CHILE					
1990	1,398	4,235	11,792	17,425	6,710
1991	1,135	4,675	10,554	16,364	7,638
1992	3,027	5,592	9,623	18,242	9,742
1993	2,999	7,167	9,020	19,186	10,252
1994	3,339	9,004	9,135	21,478	13,740
1995	2,816	11,419	7,501	21,736	14,783
1996	2,823	17,438	6,011	26,272	15,805
1997	1,438	22,126	5,470	29,034	18,274
1998	1,712	25,087	5,792	32,591	16,292
1999	1,198	27,571	5,989	34,758	14,946
2000	2,694	28,464	6,019	37,177	15,110
2001	2,051	30,363	6,124	38,538	14,400
2002	2,324	31,154	7,478	40,956	15,351
2003	3,710	30,391	9,227	43,328	15,851

(continued)

Table IV.6   Chile and Colombia: international reserves and debt stocks, 1990–2003 (US$ Millions) *(continued)*

End of:	Foreign Private Debt		Foreign Public Debt	Total Foreign Debt[1]	International Reserves
	Short term[2]	Long Term			
B. COLOMBIA					
1990	1,409	1,113	15,471	17,993	4,595
1991	1,184	981	15,171	17,335	6,500
1992	1,612	1,250	14,416	17,278	7,728
1993	2,587	2,046	14,254	18,887	7,932
1994	3,213	4,806	14,718	22,737	8,104
1995	3,920	6,880	15,540	26,340	8,453
1996	3,151	11,572	16,394	31,116	9,939
1997	3,436	14,191	16,785	34,412	9,908
1998	3,002	14,891	18,787	36,680	8,740
1999	2,267	14,267	20,199	36,733	8,103
2000	2,315	13,207	20,610	36,132	9,006
2001	2,802	12,838	23,471	39,111	10,245
2002ᵖ	3,063	11,492	22,785	37,340	10,844
2003ᵖ	3,210	10,455	24,531	38,197	10,921

Source: Central Bank of Chile, Banco de la República.

ᵖ Preliminary.

[1] Colombia: Includes financial leasing transactions.

[2] Refers to transactions originally contracted for one year or less.

and not on the stock of liabilities. Thus, *liability-flows policies* should be complemented with *liability-stock policies*. These stock policies should be primarily based on prudential regulation and supervision, imposing very stringent regulatory provisions to the banks lending to households and firms with large foreign currency mismatches (Villar and Rincón, 2003).[27] In addition, as suggested in Ocampo (2003), they could be reinforced with tax provisions applying to foreign currency liabilities. For instance, deductions for interest payments on international loans could be restricted to firms with foreign exchange revenues.

g) Foreign portfolio investment

While foreign direct investment (FDI) was entirely free in both Chile and Colombia since the beginning of the 1990s,[28] these countries maintained restrictions on foreign portfolio investment as a complementary policy to the reserve requirement on foreign loans.

Chile kept a one-year minimum stay for foreign portfolio investment (except ADRs) up to May 2000. Also, as already mentioned, since 1995 the reserve requirement was applied to the purchase of Chilean stocks by foreigners (secondary ADRs). Still, foreign portfolio investment in equity played a very pro-cyclical role, as can be seen in table IV.7. Colombia applied a less restrictive regulation. ADRs were not subject to the reserve requirement on capital inflows and foreign investment in equity was freely allowed, provided that it was done through special purpose funds administered by financial institutions with residence in Colombia. Moreover, in order to accelerate the process of deepening the domestic capital markets for public debt, Colombia facilitated foreign investment in fixed interest securities in 1996. This purpose was certainly met during 1996 and 1997, before the crisis exploded. The stock of foreign investment in domestic public debt went from zero in 1995 to US$400 million by March 1998. Less than one year later, however, this amount had gone back to almost zero. Therefore, foreign portfolio investment in public securities, which was liberalized in order to facilitate public financing, reinforced the procyclicality of foreign investment in equity.

---

[27] Ffrench-Davis and Ocampo (2001) argue that the main problem with this option is that non-financial agents may borrow directly abroad; actually, restrictions solely on banks tend to encourage that direct borrowing.
[28] In the Chilean case, however, there was a one-year minimum stay before capital repatriation of FDI was allowed, and loans associated to FDI were subject to the reserve requirement.

Table IV.7   Chile and Colombia: net flows of foreign portfolio investment in equity, 1990–2003 (liabilities)[1] (US$ Millions)

End of:	Chile	Colombia
1990	367	0
1991	24	5
1992	338	66
1993	561	145
1994	1,109	478
1995	–248	165
1996	700	292
1997	1,720	278
1998	580	47
1999	524	–27
2000	–427	17
2001	–217	–42
2002p	–320	17
2003p	312	–52

Source: Central Bank of Chile, Banco de la República.
[1] ADRs and Investment Funds.
p Preliminary.

h) The role of domestic institutional investors in the foreign exchange markets

The stronger impact that the crisis of the final years of the 1990s had on the Chilean and the Colombian economies, compared with the impact of the tequila crisis, may be explained in part by factors already mentioned: the more appreciated exchange rates, the stronger and longer reduction in the supply of funds, the higher stock of debt and the higher exposure to volatile portfolio investment. An additional relevant factor may have been the role that major domestic institutional investors started to play in the foreign exchange markets during the second half of the 1990s.

Initially, the restrictions on the activity of domestic institutional investors in the foreign exchange markets were an essential part of the policy framework in which Chile and Colombia introduced the reserve requirement on capital inflows. However, the trend towards financial liberalization that dominated the international economy in the 1990s implied that some of these restrictions were gradually relaxed in the second half of the decade. This relaxation made it more difficult to avoid sudden capital outflows and portfolio reallocations as the ones that took place between 1997 and 1999, when the Asian and the Russian crises exploded. The effectiveness of the reserve requirement on capital inflows to reduce the financial vulnerability was therefore diminished by such relaxation.

The clearest example of this process of relaxation was related with the investment regime applied to the private pension funds. These funds became very important actors in the domestic capital markets in both countries. Paradoxically, their role in the foreign exchange markets was promoted during the second half of the 1990s, when the authorities in both Chile and Colombia considered that the effects of foreign capital inflows could be partly compensated by capital outflows originated by these institutional investors. They were then allowed to invest larger shares of their portfolios in foreign currency, expecting that they would play a counter-cyclical role. In practice, however, the role of these funds was highly procyclical. They did not invest much abroad during the period prior to the Asian crisis, in which there were expectations of domestic currency appreciation. Instead, after the crisis exploded, they took advantage of their more relaxed regulation in order to rapidly reallocate huge amounts of their portfolios abroad, thus reinforcing the demand for foreign currency and the pressures towards depreciation.

Hence, as argued in Ffrench-Davis and Tapia (2001), the attempt to use a more relaxed regulation on the pension funds proved not to be successful in order to encourage capital outflows during the boom. On the contrary, that attempt induced a higher degree of vulnerability of the foreign exchange markets and a reduction in the degrees of freedom of domestic monetary policies during the downturn (see also Ocampo, 2003; Zahler, 2005). Actually, the main source of the recessive adjustment experienced by Chile in 1998–99 was associated to capital outflows by the private social security agents; their net outflow was equivalent to nearly 5% of GDP.

i) Public capital flows and FDI

As mentioned in section 1, the behavior of fiscal accounts in the 1990s was entirely different in Chile and Colombia. Chile kept an average fiscal surplus of nearly 2% of GDP. Colombia, instead, experienced large and growing fiscal deficits during the last part of the decade. This implied that public financing was not an issue in Chile, while it certainly was in Colombia.

Table IV.5 (above) highlights the contrast between Chile and Colombia on this matter. Until 1994, both countries could use their fiscal surpluses counter-cyclically, reducing their public external debt in a period of large private capital inflows. In the Chilean case, this continued to be true in the following years. Most notably, in the biennium 1995–96, net public foreign borrowing was negative in US$ 3.6 billion, partially countervailing private inflows.

In Colombia, in contrast, there were net inflows of foreign credit to the public sector since 1995. Due to the size of the public sector deficit in Colombia, those flows became quite large, averaging US$ 1.1 billion between 1995 and 2001. Between 1995 and 1997, those flows acted procyclically, reinforcing the pressures created by private capital inflows towards the appreciation of the Colombian peso.[29]

The impact of the Colombian fiscal deficit on capital flows did not only show up through foreign credit to the public sector. We already mentioned that foreign portfolio investment in Colombia was closely linked with the development of a public debt market, which in turn was urgently needed to finance the government deficit. In addition, the behavior and the characteristics of FDI in Colombia were largely influenced by the size of that deficit. This implied an important contrast with Chile.

Net flows of FDI were higher in Chile than in Colombia. The yearly averages between 1990 and 2003 were US$ 2.1 billion and US$ 1.6 billion, respectively (table IV.5). The difference between the two countries in terms of FDI in greenfield projects was even larger than suggested by these figures, which implies that the contribution of FDI to increase domestic capital formation and productivity was much higher in Chile. Indeed, until 1998, there was a clear positive relationship between FDI and gross capital formation in that country. Such relationship was lost in 1999, when most FDI became related to mergers and acquisitions (see Ffrench-Davis, 2002, p. 15). Still, it is interesting to notice that FDI played a counter-cyclical role in Chile in 1999 as compared to other private capital flows.

In contrast with Chile, FDI in Colombia corresponded mostly to privatizations and to investment in the oil sector. This implied that its relationship with domestic capital formation in the country was extremely week and that FDI played a procyclical role. The period in

---

[29] Paradoxically, after 1997 net inflows of foreign credit to the public sector behaved again as stabilizers of total foreign financing. They, indeed, help to explain the fact that in 1998 the reduction in international reserves was much smaller, and that in the following years the recovery of those reserves was much faster in Colombia than in Chile. In that sense, the existence of larger fiscal deficits in Colombia, provided that they were financed abroad, helped to reduce the vulnerability of the Colombian economy to the changes in the mood of international financial markets.

which FDI was highest – 1996 through 1998, according to table IV.5 – corresponds with a rapidly declining ratio of capital formation as a whole (see table IV.3). Actually, mergers and acquisitions (M&A) accounted for 58% of total gross FDI in that period (UNCTAD, 2003). A large part of FDI in Colombia was in practice an instrument of public deficit financing. This source of financing almost disappeared after 1998. Also, the natural cycle of investment in the Cusiana oil well implied a rapid decline of that source of FDI after 1998.

4. Concluding remarks

Chile and Colombia seemed to have done things right when the tequila crisis arrived in 1995, as far as they kept growing and had no signs of financial distress. After the Asian and the Russian crises, however, both Chile and Colombia were heavily affected. Does this mean that the capital account regulations that these countries had in place did not work? Was this the result of a badly designed exchange rate regime? Of course, any single answer to these questions would be extremely simplistic. From the analysis above we can extract the following conclusions:

(i)   The type of capital account regulations that were used both in Chile and Colombia did work successfully in reducing the share of the short-term component of total capital inflows.

(ii)   Also, they allowed monetary policy to increase the domestic interest rates relative to foreign interest rates, without strengthening the pressure to overvalue the domestic currencies. This was a positive outcome in the period of the boom of capital inflows, as far as it allowed monetary policy to behave counter-cyclically, and contributed to more sustainable real macroeconomic balances.

(iii)   Some liberalization of the rules applied to both foreign portfolio investment and investment of domestic institutional investors in foreign securities, during the second half of the 1990s, created a more procyclical environment for the management of the crisis of 1998–99.

(iv)   The comparison between the Chilean and Colombian experiences illustrates the importance of fiscal austerity in periods of large capital inflows. The ability of governments to undertake counter-cyclical fiscal policies critically depends on what they do during the boom periods. The government can partially outweigh the effects of private capital inflows by reducing – counter-cyclically – its public debt during booms, as Chile actually did until 1997. Also, if there is a developed market for domestic public debt, substitution of domestic debt for foreign debt may be a good mechanism to reduce pressures towards appreciation in periods of large capital inflows.

(v)   Still, what Chile suffered in the crisis of 1998–99 shows that fiscal restraint is not enough and that private capital flows (particularly of outflows of domestic capital in that biennium) may introduce too much vulnerability, even in presence of capital controls. In fact, the capital account regulations on inflows used in Chile and Colombia were not enough to avoid that critical risk. Even with a low exposure to short-term debt, capital outflows may be very large when the domestic residents are able to invest abroad and long-term debtors can pre-pay their liabilities. This vulnerability may be mitigated with controls on the net foreign exchange position of the financial intermediaries, of the main institutional investors (like private pension funds) and of households and firms. Prudential regulation of the financial sector should require banks to reflect the risks that are implicit in lending to households or firms with important currency mismatches between their assets and their liabilities. Those mismatches could also be discouraged through tax provisions.

(vi)   The exchange rate management may have played a role in aggravating the effects of the reversal in capital flows that took place in 1998–99. The exchange rate bands that were in place in Chile and Colombia were useful arrangements along most of the 1990s. The crawling bands, however, were more efficient to deal with pressures towards currency appreciation than with pressures towards currency depreciation. The credibility problems that were created by the bands led the authorities to restrict the exchange rate flexibility and to undertake very contractionary monetary policies during the crisis. The lack of exchange rate flexibility during the crisis was much more evident in Chile than in Colombia.

(vii) During the 1990s, the experiences of Chile and Colombia with domestic credit were entirely different. In Colombia, the impact of foreign capital flows was leveraged by domestic credit, thus reinforcing their procyclical behavior. In Chile, the index of domestic credit/GDP behaved in a counter-cyclical way. Two lessons arise from these contrasting experiences. First, that a higher degree of financial depth and a stricter financial supervision may work as buffers against the shocks of foreign capital flows, as probably did in Chile. Second, that domestic financial regulation should not reinforce the procyclical behavior of capital inflows, as actually happened in Colombia with the reduction of reserve requirements on domestic deposits before 1998.

Annex IV.1   Comparative Economic Size of Chile and Colombia, 2002

	Population (million)	GDP (current prices) TOTAL (US$ billion)	Per capita (US$)	GDP (PPP) TOTAL (US$ billion)	Per capita (US$)	Gross exports of goods and services (% of current GDP)
Argentina	38	102	2,694	402	10,594	27.7
Brazil	174	452	2,593	1,312	7,516	15.8
Chile	15	64	4,244	149	9,853	34.1
Colombia	44	82	1,879	265	6,068	19.6
Mexico	101	637	6,314	879	8,707	27.2
Latin America (19)	512	1,640	3,200	648	6,962	23.4
Malaysia	24	95	3,915	217	8,922	113.8
Republic of Korea	48	477	10,006	784	16,465	40.0
East Asia (6)	449	1,215	2,707	2,893	6,444	52.0
South Africa	45	107	2,352	449	9,922	33.3
United States	288	10,417	36,123	10,138	35,158	9.4
World	6,201	32,252	5,201	47,426	7,648	24.4

Source: Based on figures from ADB, ECLAC, IMF and the World Bank.
East Asia includes Indonesia, Republic of Korea, Malaysia, Philippines, Taiwan and Thailand.
Latin America includes 19 countries.

References

Agosin, M. and R. Ffrench-Davis (2001), "Managing capital inflows in Chile", in S. Griffith-Jones, M. F. Montes and A. Nasution (eds.), *Short-Term Capital Flows and Economic Crises*, Oxford University Press/WIDER, London and New York.

Banco de la República (2002), "Reporte de estabilidad financiera", Banco de la República, Subgerencia Monetaria y de Reservas, Bogotá, July.

Barajas, A. and R. Steiner (2002), "Credit stagnation in Latin America", *IMF Working Paper*, WP/02/53, March.

Bleakley, H. and K. Cowan (2002), "Corporate dollar debt and depreciations: Much ado about nothing?", Federal Reserve Bank of Boston, *Working Paper Series*, No. 02–5.

Cardoso, E. and I. Goldfajn (1998), "Capital flows to Brazil: The endogeneity of capital controls", *IMF Staff Papers*, 45, September.

Cárdenas, M. and F. Barrera (1997), "On the effectiveness of capital controls: The experience of Colombia during the 1990s", *Journal of Development Economics*, Vol. 54.

Carrasquilla, A. and J. P. Zárate (2002), "Regulación bancaria y tensión financiera: 1998–2001", in ANIF (ed.), *El Sector Financiero de Cara al Siglo XXI*, Tomo I, ANIF, Bogotá.

Corbo, V. and J. Tessada (2002), "Growth and adjustment in Chile: A look at the 1990s", in N. Loayza and R. Soto (eds.), *Economic Growth in Chile: Sources, Trends, and Cycles*, Central Bank of Chile, Santiago.

De Gregorio, J., S. Edwards and R. Valdés (2000), "Controls on capital inflows: Do they work?", *NBER Working Paper*, 7645, Cambridge, Mass.

Edwards, S. (2002), "The great exchange rate debate after Argentina", *NBER Working Paper*, 9257, October.

—— (1999), "How effective are capital controls", *Journal of Economic Perspectives*, Fall.

Ffrench-Davis, R. (2005), "Macroeconomics-for-growth under financial globalization: Four strategic issues for emerging economies", in this volume.

—— (2003), "Financial crises and national policy issues: An overview", in R. Ffrench-Davis and S. Griffith-Jones (eds.), *From Capital Surges to Drought*, Palgrave Macmillan, London.

—— (2002), *Economic Reforms in Chile: From Dictatorship to Democracy*, University of Michigan Press, Ann Arbor.

—— and J. A. Ocampo (2001), "The globalization of financial volatility: Challenges for emerging economies", in R. Ffrench-Davis (ed.), *Financial Crises in "Successful" Emerging Economies*, ECLAC and Brookings Institution Press, Washington, DC.

—— and H. Tapia (2004), "The Chilean-style capital controls: an empirical assessment", mimeo, ECLAC.

—— and H. Tapia (2001), "Three varieties of capital surge management in Chile", in R. Ffrench-Davis (ed.), *Financial Crises in "Successful" Emerging Economies*, ECLAC and Brookings Institution Press, Washington, DC.

—— and G. Larraín (2003), "How optimal are the extremes? Latin American exchange rate policies during the Asian crisis", in R. Ffrench-Davis and S. Griffith-Jones (eds.), *From Capital Surges to Drought*, Palgrave/WIDER/ECLAC, London.

Forbes, K. (2004), "Capital controls: Mud in the wheels of market discipline", *NBER Working Paper*, 10284, January.

—— (2003), "One cost of the Chilean capital controls: increased financial constraints for smaller traded firms", *NBER Working Paper*, 9777, June.

Gallego, F. and L. Hernández (2003), "Microeconomic effects of capital controls: the Chilean experience during the nineties", *Working Paper*, No. 203, Central Bank of Chile, February.

Gallego, F, L. Hernández, and K. Schmidt-Hebbel (2002), "Capital controls in Chile: were they effective?", in L. Hernández and K. Schmidt-Hebbel (eds.), *Banking, Financial Integration, and International Crises*, Central Bank of Chile, Santiago.

Kaplan, S. and L. Zingales (1997), "Do investment-cash flow sensitivities provide useful measures of financial constraints?", *The Quarterly Journal of Economics*, 112, February.

Le Fort, G. and S. Lehmann (2003), "The Special Reserve Requirement and net capital inflows: Chile in the 1990s", *CEPAL Review*, No. 81, December, Santiago.

138 *Seeking Growth under Financial Volatility*

Ocampo, J. A. (2005), "Overcoming Latin America's growth frustrations: The macro and mesoeconomic links", in this volume.

—— (2003), "Capital account and counter-cyclical prudential regulations in developing countries", in R. Ffrench-Davis and S. Griffith-Jones (eds.), *From Capital Surges to Drought*, Palgrave/WIDER/ECLAC, London.

—— and C. Tovar (2003), "Managing the capital account: Colombia's experience with price-based controls on capital inflows", *CEPAL Review*, No. 81, Santiago.

—— and L. Villar (1992), "Trayectoria y vicisitudes de la apertura económica colombiana", in *Pensamiento Iberoamericano*, No. 21, Special edition, Madrid.

UNCTAD (2003), *Foreign Investment Report 2003*, United Nations, Geneva.

Urrutia, M. (1995), "El sistema de bandas cambiarias en Colombia", *Notas Editoriales, Revista del Banco de la República*, Vol. LXVIII, No. 807, Bogotá, January.

Valdés-Prieto, S. and M. Soto (1998), "New selective capital controls in Chile: Are they effective?", *Empírica*, 25(2).

Villar, L. and H. Rincón (2003), "The Colombian economy in the 1990s: Capital flows and exchange rate regimes", in A. Berry (ed.), *Critical Issues in Financial Reform: A View from the South*, New Brunswick, NJ, Transaction Publishers.

Zahler, R. (2005), "Macroeconomic stability and investment allocation of domestic pension funds: The case of Chile", in this volume.

—— (1998), "The Central Bank and the Chilean macroeconomic policy in the 1990s", *CEPAL Review*, No. 64, April.

V
Macroeconomic Adjustments and the Real Economy in Korea and Malaysia Since 1997

*Zainal-Abidin Mahani, Kwanho Shin, Yunjong Wang**

Introduction

The financial crisis that broke out in Thailand in July 1997 and then spread to other parts of East Asia brought about a deep recession, causing a sharp decline in living standards, rising unemployment, industrial breakdown, and social dislocation in the region (Park and Wang, 2002). In 1997–98, five East Asian countries – Indonesia, Korea, Malaysia, the Philippines, and Thailand – experienced deep currency and banking crises. Although a few other East Asian countries were affected to a limited extent, the Asian financial crisis was region-wide.[1]

Korea and Malaysia have managed impressive recoveries at remarkable speed, as compared to other emerging economies (EEs). These economies started to bottom out in the second half of 1998 and then showed a remarkable turnaround in 1999. While the real GDP growth rates of Korea and Malaysia were –6.7% and –7.4% in 1998, they rebounded to 10.9% and 6.1%, respectively, in 1999.

* The authors gratefully acknowledge Ricardo Ffrench-Davis for detailed comments on the earlier and revised draft. We would also like to thank Ariel Buira, Roy Culpeper, José de Gregorio, Barry Herman, Manuel Montes, José Antonio Ocampo, Arturo O'Connell, John Williamson, Heriberto Tapia, and other participants of two seminars organized by ECLAC, for their useful suggestions and comments on the revised version.

[1] The Singapore and the New Taiwan dollar experienced a relatively small depreciation. During the crisis, no significant devaluation took place in China, which remained relatively insulated from world financial markets.

This chapter reviews the post-crisis macroeconomic adjustment and the impact of policy responses on the real economy in Korea and Malaysia. Both countries suffered under the Asian financial crisis, and initially both applied the orthodox crisis solution measures; subsequently, their policy responses were quite different in several aspects. Korea sought liquidity assistance from the IMF, which obliged it to comply with the IMF's structural adjustment program, while Malaysia was able to maintain policy independence in the process of crisis resolution. Korea and Malaysia adopted policies at opposite extremes with respect to capital flows and the exchange rate during the crisis. For example, Korea drastically liberalized capital inflows and adopted a floating exchange rate regime (although maintaining several restrictions on outflows by residents, and with huge accumulation of reserves during recovery). Contrariwise, Malaysia implemented stringent capital controls with a return to a fixed (but devalued) exchange rate. Despite the different policy stances in terms of capital account and exchange rate regime, a swift change toward a vigorously expansionary macroeconomic policy stance helped the two economies recover notably faster than other EEs. There was a positive role of counter-cyclical macroeconomic policies, including sharp fiscal and monetary positive shocks. Their effectiveness shown for the post-crisis economic recovery raises the question of whether the initial sharp tightening of monetary and fiscal policy was kept for too long and, as a consequence, deepened the crisis in both Korea and Malaysia.[2]

This case study highlights the dynamics of the macroeconomic adjustments that came with responses such as monetary, fiscal, and exchange rate policies and their effects on variables such as capital formation and output, of the real economy. This comparative analysis will provide policy implications to the question of what policy responses will be most effective in dealing with future crises.

Section 1 focuses on post-crisis macroeconomic adjustments in Korea and Malaysia. Section 2 reviews their policy responses for crisis resolution. Section 3 assesses the adjustment process and compares both country cases. Section 4 concludes with some remarks on policy implications.

[2] As an initial response to the crisis, Malaysia followed the orthodox IMF policy prescriptions without the IMF involvement – namely, tightened fiscal and monetary policies, introduced measures to redress the balance of payment weakness, and floated the exchange rate.

1. Post-crisis macroeconomic adjustments in Korea and Malaysia

a) Korea

i. What caused the crisis?

The crisis in Korea was certainly unexpected. As late as June 1997, the World Economic Forum had classified Korea as the fifth most secure place to invest in the world (Agosin, 2001). At the onset of the financial crisis, notwithstanding that macroeconomic fundamentals appeared to be sound, the Korean miracle was suddenly unraveled. Actually, Korea became vulnerable because of its large exposure to short-term external liabilities (Radelet and Sachs, 1998; Rodrik and Velasco, 2000).

Korea's external debt increased dramatically over the three-year period 1994–96. The major portion of the increase in external debt involved the financial sector. For instance, foreign currency liabilities of Korean banks nearly tripled in that period, to US$ 104 billion. Two sources contributed to the increase in the financial sector's external debt: one was debt securities that were issued abroad, while the other was external borrowing by the domestic financial institutions. Out of the total increase in external debt during the three years, the financial sector accounts for about 70%. The remaining 30% corresponded to corporate sector liabilities.

In fact, short-term foreign currency liabilities of the domestic financial institutions were much larger than those recorded in capital inflows. As part of the liberalization measures, banks were allowed to open and expand operations of overseas branches. By exploiting the foreign capital channeled through overseas branches, banks actively engaged in foreign currency denominated business. Overseas branches handled about half of the foreign currency operations of the banking sector and, therefore, their transactions were not reflected in domestic monetary indicators (see table V.1). Moreover, the management of foreign currency liquidity risks at the individual bank level was not adequate enough to forestall the liquidity crisis, either.

A relevant part of excessive short-term external liabilities can be explained by asymmetric regulations on short-term borrowing *vis-à-vis* long-term borrowing. The government boosted incentives for short-term debts by making it mandatory to provide detailed information and obtain permission from the regulatory authorities in the case of long-term borrowing, whereas short-term borrowing was regarded as trade related financing and therefore not strictly regulated under the

Table V.1 Korea: Short-term foreign currency liabilities of the financial sector, 1992–97 (US$, billion)

	1992	1993	1994	1995	1996	1997
Short-term external debt	11.3	11.4	19.4	29.7	39.2	27.4
Short-term liabilities of overseas branches	18.5	21.1	28.0	33.4	39.0	20.3
Total	29.8	32.5	47.4	63.1	78.2	47.7
Foreign reserves	17.1	20.2	25.6	32.7	33.2	20.4

Source: Bank of Korea.

Foreign Exchange Management Law. Thus, banks and firms had been operating on a long-term basis with short-term foreign borrowings, leading to a significant discrepancy in the maturity structure (Kim, *et al.*, 2001).

Furthermore, the maturity mismatch was more severe for merchant banks.[3] For example, the liquidity ratio in foreign currency for merchant banks was only 3 to 6% for all the period up to the financial crisis. Thirty merchant banks became heavily engaged in offshore operations by borrowing cheap short-term Japanese funds from Hong Kong to finance mostly long-term investment projects. With 80% short-term debts put into 70% long-term assets, the maturity mismatch blew up when Korea's credibility plummeted. Pressured to obtain foreign currency to repay their debts, merchant banks ultimately ended up buying foreign currency on the spot market with won-denominated call loans from commercial banks. Furthermore, those merchant banks were not properly supervised. Neither unified accounting standards nor standards for classifying non-performing loans existed, and supervision had been perfunctory at best. This lax supervision allowed merchant banks to enjoy freedom without any discipline. When Korea embarked on the IMF structural adjustment program, merchant banks were the first to go through restructuring because their voluminous short-term

---

[3] Most merchant banks in Korea started as investment banks after 1972, to provide legitimate channels to utilize black market funds. Later in 1994 and 1996, the 24 existing investment banks were allowed to become merchant banks, joining the six existing ones. Several merchant banks, owned by chaebols, served as important vehicles for raising the funds required for the chaebols' voluminous investments; these affiliate banks failed to conduct adequate loan assessments of their parent companies.

external debts and imprudent investments were inconsistent with the customary practices of the world financial market.[4]

ii. Overall macroeconomic and sectoral performance

The impact of the financial crisis on the real economy became apparent in the first quarter of 1998 as GDP contracted by 4.6% on a year-on-year basis. Throughout 1998, the deterioration of macroeconomic conditions far exceeded the expectations of both Korean policy makers and IMF economists. For example, the second IMF agreement forecast that real GDP would fall by 1% or less in 1998, but it actually shrank 6.7%.

In 1998, private consumption, investment, and imports dramatically declined (see table V.2). Non-tradable sectors, such as construction, were hit harder than the manufacturing sector, which is more trade-oriented. As output contracted, unemployment quickly increased from 2.1% in October 1997 to 8.7% in February 1999. The real wages of workers in the manufacturing sector fell by 11% in 1998.

After a sharp contraction, the Korean economy started to bottom out in the first quarter of 1999. In 1999, real GDP growth recorded 10.9%. Due to the strengthening of the economy, the unemployment rate sharply declined from the record level of 8.7% in February 1999 to 4.4% in November 1999, while inflation remained low, notwithstanding significant depreciation.

The sharp contraction and the rapid recovery of Korea's growth are broadly consistent with the V-shaped adjustment patterns observed in cross-country analyses. However, the 6.7% decline in 1998 and the 10.9% recovery of GDP in 1999 are far greater than predicted by the cross-country evidence. Malaysia also experienced a huge jump in GDP growth from a 7.4% decline in 1998 to a 6.1% recovery in 1999.

One fundamental question relates to whether the output reduction after the Asian crisis was a temporary deviation downward from the trend level, which was to be reversed as output reverted to trend, or alternatively, whether the level of output tended to shift down permanently. Cerra and Saxena (2003) find that the recovery phase is predominantly characterized by a return to the normal growth rate of an expansion. Thus, the level of output is permanently lower than its initial trend path. A permanent loss is associated with a downward shift of potential output.

---

[4] The Korean government suspended the operations of the 14 unhealthiest merchant banks in December 1997.

Table V.2   Korea: Selected economic indicators, 1996–2002

Indicators/year	1996	1997	1998	1999	2000	2001	2002
Growth of GDP (%)	6.8	5.0	–6.7	10.9	9.3	3.0	6.3
Growth by final demand category (%)							
Consumption	7.2	3.2	–10.1	9.4	6.7	3.7	6.2
Private	7.1	3.5	–11.7	11.0	7.9	4.7	6.8
Government	8.2	1.5	–0.4	1.3	0.1	1.3	2.9
Gross fixed capital formation	7.3	–2.2	–21.2	3.7	11.4	–1.8	4.8
Growth by sector (%)							
Agriculture, forestry and fishing	3.3	4.6	–6.6	5.4	2.0	1.9	–4.1
Industry	7.0	5.8	–6.1	11.0	9.8	3.8	6.7
Mining and quarrying	–0.1	–0.9	–24.0	5.3	2.5	0.5	3.9
Manufacturing	6.8	6.6	–7.4	21.0	15.9	2.1	6.3
Construction	6.9	1.4	–8.6	–9.1	–3.1	5.6	3.2
Services	7.5	6.5	–4.7	10.0	8.7	5.0	8.6
Unemployment rate	2.0	2.6	6.8	6.3	4.1	3.7	3.1
Inflation rate (%)							
Consumer price	4.9	4.4	7.5	0.8	2.3	4.1	2.8
Producer price	3.2	3.9	12.2	–2.1	2.0	1.9	1.6
Fiscal performance (central government) [a/]							
Government expenditure as % of GDP	10.2	10.1	11.0	10.4	10.1	10.4	10.6
Budget surplus (central government) as % of GDP	0.3	–1.5	–4.2	–2.7	1.3	1.3	4.1
Total public debt as % of GDP	8.8	11.1	16.1	18.6	19.5	20.8	–
Money and credit (end of period)							
M3 growth (%)	16.7	13.9	12.5	8.0	7.1	11.6	13.6
Annual average bank lending rate (%)	11.2	11.8	15.2	9.4	8.6	7.7	6.7
Overnight rate	12.4	13.2	15.0	5.0	5.2	4.7	4.2
Non-performing loans as % of total loans [b/]	4.1	6.0	7.4	8.3	6.6	2.9	2.3
KOSPI index	833.4	654.5	406.1	806.8	734.2	572.8	757.0

(continued)

Table V.2   Korea: Selected economic indicators, 1996–2002 (continued)

Indicators/year	1996	1997	1998	1999	2000	2001	2002
External transactions							
Merchandise exports (US$, FOB billion)	130.0	138.6	132.1	145.2	175.9	151.3	162.6
Merchandise imports (US$, FOB billion)	144.9	141.8	90.5	116.8	159.1	137.8	148.4
Current account balance (US$, billion)	–23.0	–8.2	40.4	24.5	12.2	8.2	6.1
Current account balance as % of GDP	–4.4	–1.7	12.7	6.0	2.7	1.9	1.3
Direct investment (US$, billion)	–2.3	–1.6	0.7	5.1	4.3	1.1	–0.7
Portfolio investment (US$, billion)	15.1	14.4	–1.2	9.2	12.2	6.7	–0.1
Other investment (US$, billion)	11.1	–21.9	–7.2	–1.1	–3.6	–4.6	2.7
Foreign reserves (US$, billion)	34.0	20.4	52.0	74.0	96.1	102.8	121.3
Total external debt as % GDP	31.4	33.4	46.8	33.8	28.5	27.5	27.5
Short-term foreign debt as % of total debt	57.1	39.9	20.6	28.6	36.4	33.3	38.0
Short-term foreign debt as % of foreign reserves	274.2	312.5	59.1	53.0	42.7	48.5	41.0

Sources: The Bank of Korea, Monthly Bulletin; Ministry of Finance and Economy, Financial Statistics Bulletin; Financial Supervisory Commission, IMF, International Financial Statistics.
a/ End of period.
b/ Non-performing loans of domestic commercial banks.

Important structural factors driving the speedy adjustment in Korea were flexibility and openness (Park, 2001). With a relatively large trade sector oriented towards exports, Korea was able to benefit from a substantial depreciation of the real exchange rate and fall in real wages. As a consequence, after the manufacturing sector recorded a large decline of 7.4% in 1998, it quickly rebounded to record a growth of 21.0% in 1999.

iii. Exchange rate

Thailand's sudden decision to float the baht in July 1997 subjected all regional currencies to extremely high depreciation pressure. However, the Korean won remained relatively stable until it began to slide in October 1997. Following futile attempts of currency defense, the Korean government widened its won trading band from 2.25% to 10% on November, and finally abolished its band, allowing the won to float on December. With a free floating regime in place, the sudden collapse of investor confidence and concomitant capital outflows caused the nominal exchange rate to overshoot during the crisis.

Large support packages by the IMF did make some contribution to restoring the confidence of foreign investors. The funding helped to reduce the short-term liquidity constraints and provided financial resources to contain the exchange rate depreciation. The Korean government expected that its agreement with the IMF, reached on December 3, 1997, would stop the outflow of foreign capital. However, foreign banks withdrew their short-term credit at an accelerated pace, thereby worsening Korea's foreign reserve position (see table V.2). In response to this unfavorable development, the Korean government asked the major creditor countries, including the US and Japan, to use moral suasion to influence their creditors to refrain from retrieving their short-term credit, and cooperate in reaching an agreement to lengthen the maturity of short-term foreign loans. Only when foreign creditors were convinced that they would be repaid with handsome returns, were the debt-extension agreements signed and finalized on March 1998.[5] Thereafter, the exchange rate came to stabilize at around 1,300–1,400 won per US dollar.

iv. Equity market

After hitting its highest level (1,138 points) on November 8, 1994, the Korean stock price index (KOSPI) started sliding before the crisis broke out. This was one of the earliest signs of trouble. During 1996, stock prices (in domestic currency terms) fell by more than 20% in Korea. Several of the largest chaebols posted losses in 1996 and 6 of the top 30 chaebols went bankrupt in 1997. The crisis aggravated the situation and severely undermined investor confidence in the stock market. As a result, the stock price index fell to 376 points by the end of December 1997.

Having hit the bottom, the KOSPI quickly recovered by early 1998, with the aid of purchases by foreign investors. However, after peaking at 574 points on March 1998, the KOSPI once again began to slide

---

[5] The Korean government was able to issue US$4 billion in bonds, in international capital markets, immediately following the debt-extension agreement.

downward. Following the sudden weakening of the Japanese yen, the KOSPI plunged below 300 points on June. Again, foreign investors left the Korean market, and more bankruptcies were predicted while corporate and financial restructuring proceeded. Stock prices remained stagnant until the end of September, while the won-dollar exchange rate stabilized remarkably. During the post-crisis period, starting in October 1998, foreign portfolio investment boosted stock prices in 1999, but stock prices sharply dropped in mid-2000 and 2001 (over 50%). With respect to exchange rates, appreciation was limited because of evident intervention of the BOK.[6]

v. Current account balance

The current account deficit averaged less than 1% of GDP in 1992–95. In real effective terms, the exchange rate had been around the equilibrium level until 1994, but was somewhat overvalued on the eve of the 1997 currency crisis.[7]

A remarkable feature of Korea's economic performance following the crisis has been the large turnaround in the current account balance. It improved from deficit to surplus after one year, changing from –4.4% of GDP in 1996 (US$23 billion) to 12.7% in 1998 (US$40 billion). The current account balance was the only component that made a positive contribution to GDP in 1998. Imports of goods and services were severely compressed due to the sharp depreciation of the Korean won and the sharp domestic contraction.[8]

[6] The Korean government took drastic measures to liberalize capital markets as well as adopting an officially flexible exchange rate system since the crisis set in. Thus, it would be natural to conjecture that if the Korean government truly has a hands-off policy in the foreign exchange market, there must be some close interaction between stock prices and exchange rates. However, Park, *et al.* (2001) find that empirical results do not support that conjecture during the post-crisis period. This puzzling evidence indirectly hints that the Korean government heavily intervened in the foreign exchange market against volatile foreign portfolio investment flows. This was strongly supported by the huge accumulation of reserves by the BOK.
[7] Our calculation based on a trade-weight, consumer prices index, shows that the real effective exchange rate appreciated by around 5% between January 1993 and July 1997.
[8] To help meet the urgent need for foreign exchange, a national drive to export second-hand goods and recycled gold jewelry was initiated in early 1998. Financial institutions collected gold products, refined and exported them, and then sold the foreign exchange proceeds to the Bank of Korea. The drive enjoyed widespread national support, and is estimated to have contributed about US$4.2 billion to total exports in 1998.

External demand, particularly in Asia, remained weak in 1998 and hampered the response of Korean exports to the real depreciation. Reflecting the disparity in economic conditions between regions, exports to China, Japan, and Southeast Asia in 1998 fell by 17% in value terms, while exports to the US and the EU rose 6.5%. The strong US economy was a significant source of growth for Korean exports in 1998, in particular for both light and heavy industrial products. Much of the decline in exports of industrial products to Japan (mainly in electronics and metal goods) was redirected to the US and to a lesser extent the EU.

vi. Capital flows

The capital account adjustment was also sharp. Immediately following the onset of the crisis, the capital account switched from a surplus to a deficit as a result of the large outflow of portfolio investment and curtailment of short-term bank loans. The capital account showed a deficit of US$64 billion in 1998.

By the first quarter of 1999, the capital account registered a surplus led by strong inflows of portfolio and foreign direct investment, a decline in overseas investment by Korean companies, and a slight pickup in short-term trade financing related to the economic recovery. In particular, FDI picked up sharply in 1998 as companies began to rely increasingly on foreign capital to finance their corporate restructuring efforts. During the pre-crisis period including 1997, net FDI recorded a deficit. But, there was an impressive turnaround in the net balance of FDI as a component of the capital account. This was due to the increased mergers and acquisitions of Korean firms by foreign firms – supported by the government policies aimed at selling liquidity constrained ailing domestic firms to foreigners.[9]

With regard to portfolio investment, private equity flows picked up markedly in the first half of 1999 after international credit rating agencies raised Korea's sovereign rating to investment grade. International spreads also came down to near pre-crisis levels after a period of extreme volatility. With this development, Korean companies could raise capital from the international financial markets by issuing global depository receipts (GDRs).

---

[9] To induce FDI, all institutional restraints on mergers and acquisitions of domestic firms by foreign investors were completely abolished on May, 1998.

vii. Foreign reserves and external debt

After having fallen to a low of US$3.9 billion on December 18, 1997, foreign reserves increased steadily, reaching US$52 billion by the end of 1998. The increasing trend continued in 1999–2000: foreign reserves stood at US$96 billion by year-end 2000. During the early period of crisis resolution, the front-loaded disbursements from the ADB, IMF and World Bank, successful maturity-extension agreement in March 1998, and issuance of global bonds in April 1998 contributed to the sizable reserve accumulation. Nonetheless, the most important increase in foreign reserves closely corresponded to the current account surplus, absorbed by sterilized interventions of the Bank of Korea.

Consequently, Korea's external debt position did significantly improve. The ratio of short-term debt to foreign reserves decreased from 313% in 1997, to 53% in 1999, implying that short-term debt could be covered by official foreign reserves (see table V.2). Total external liabilities during 1999 decreased by US$13 billion from the previous year, while external assets increased by US$22 billion. In terms of debt maturity, the ratio of short-term debt to the total stood at below 0.3 in 1999. With the strengthening of reserve and external asset/liability positions, Korea accelerated its repayments to the IMF to fully settle its loans ahead of schedule.

viii. Financial market

Prior to the crisis, there was some concern over the persistent expansion of domestic credit to the private sector at double-digit rates. Domestic credit increased from 57% of GDP in 1994 to almost 70% in 1997. It is possible that the credit supply has grown as usual while profitability of the real sector was declining for reasons such as delayed adjustments of non-performing companies. In the pre-crisis period, there was easier access to bank credit for firms associated with chaebols, while non-chaebol firms' access to bank credit was more influenced by market considerations (Borensztein and Lee, 2000). The relatively small chaebols (those ranked 11th to 30th) were significantly under-performing even during the 1994–96 boom period. When the terms-of-trade shock arrived in April 1996, the situation of the highly leveraged corporate sector was aggravated and the number of defaults increased significantly far ahead of the crisis. As large chaebols went bankrupt, the financial sector began to bear a substantial burden.

Following the decline in the Hong Kong stock market in October 1997, and the downgrade of Korea's sovereign risk, financial markets in

Korea came under increasingly severe pressure. As in the other Asian crisis countries, with reserves essentially depleted, the choice was made to raise interest rates to restore market confidence and stabilize the exchange market. By December, the Bank of Korea had dramatically raised short-term interest rates, which had fluctuated around 12% prior to the crisis, to over 30% in order to engineer a rapid stabilization of the exchange rate. However, there were a number of malignant side effects accompanying the high interest rate policy along with financial sector restructuring.

The contraction in bank loans was extremely severe as a combined result of both monetary conditions and structural changes in the financial sector. Borensztein and Lee (2000) explain several factors, which affected the pattern of credit allocation after the crisis broke out. First, financial institutions became more reluctant to extend loans to enterprises because of the new financial sector regulations (enhanced financial standards) and high credit risks. In particular, some banks did not meet capital adequacy ratios and could not raise equity capital in times of financial difficulties. Thus, they started to curtail credit to firms by a larger magnitude. Second, the higher level of interest rates further weakened the situation of borrowers' balance sheets. In particular, highly leveraged corporate firms were more vulnerable to the interest rate hikes. The level of non-performing loans rose from 13% of GDP in December 1997 to 22% by June 1998.[10] Third, the fiscal deficit increased from a small surplus in 1997 to a deficit of over 4% of GDP. Consequently, the traditional "crowding-out" effect reduced credit available to the private sector as the government had to tap domestic financial markets to a large extent. Fourth, as foreign credit lines dried out, banks had to repay their short-term foreign debts by curtailing domestic credit.

Once the immediate task of stabilizing the exchange rate market was accomplished in early 1998, the stance of monetary policy was cautiously eased. Since small and medium-sized enterprises (SMEs) were hit harder by the credit squeeze compared to larger firms, the Korean

---

[10] In July 1998, there was a major revision of loan classification standards and provision requirements, which classified loans in arrears of three months or more as substandard or below, and loans in arrears of one to three months as precautionary loans. Asset quality classification standards were further implemented in 1999 by adopting the forward-looking criteria (FLC), which includes expected future performance into account as a criterion. Before July 1998, non-performing loans included loans in arrears of six months or more.

government took a number of steps to ease the financing constraint for SMEs.[11]

b) Malaysia

i. What caused the crisis?

In mid-1997, like the other affected economies, Malaysia did not expect to encounter a severe crisis although the economy was considered "overheated" due to the high growth registered during the 1990s. In June 1997, Michael Camdessus, then Managing Director of the IMF, drew attention to the soundness of the Malaysian economy: "Malaysia is a good example of a country where the authorities are well aware of the challenges of managing the pressures that result from high growth and of maintaining a sound financial system, amid substantial capital flows and a booming stock market."

Inflows of short-term capital (mainly portfolio investment) started to become significant in 1993, amounting to US$9.5 billion (14% of GDP), exceeding FDI inflows (US$5 billion). Those inflows generated the super bull run of the Kuala Lumpur Stock Exchange. The capital inflows also financed the current account deficit: at its peak in 1995, the current account deficit was 10.4% of GDP. By 1997, the current account deficit was still significant at 5.4% of GDP, although this did not directly put a downward pressure on the ringgit exchange rate. Rising services account shortfalls and higher capital goods imports were the reasons for the persistent deficits. The large inflow of portfolio investment had created a window of vulnerability for the Malaysian economy in the event of a sharp, quick and large outflow. The stock of portfolio capital had increased from US$4.6 billion in 1990 to US$36 billion in 1997, which meant that a large and uncontrolled withdrawal would do serious damage to the economy and to the ringgit.

Another vulnerable point for Malaysia was the seemingly stable ringgit exchange rate. The large weight of the US dollar in the currency basket (estimated at about 70%) had indirectly created a *de facto*

---

[11] SMEs are defined as enterprises employing less than 300 workers in the manufacturing sector and 20 workers in services. In order to ease financial difficulties of SMEs, the Bank of Korea raised the ceiling on total loans from KRW 3.6 trillion (in November 1997) to KRW 5.6 trillion (in February 1998). Further, the Bank of Korea overhauled the 90-day maturity clause on commercial bills, which qualify for discount (beginning May 1998). In addition, the government gave an extension of maturity of loans to SMEs.

nominal peg regime for the ringgit. Even with the large capital inflow in the second half of the 1990s, the ringgit was traded within a very narrow band at around RM2.5 for one US dollar. This exchange rate stability had given the impression that there was no risk associated with the flows of funds and subsequently attracted large short-term capital into Malaysia without the fear of possible exchange rate losses.

With sufficient international reserves to meet foreign exchange demand, there was little concern that Malaysia would confront an economic crisis when the baht was floated in July 1997.[12] In 1997, Malaysia's international reserves of US$28 billion were sufficient to cover the short-term debt of US$14 billion in 1997 (table V.3). However, from another perspective, this level of reserves was insufficient to meet the demands of liquid capital, which was composed of a combination of short-term foreign debts and portfolio capital. Hence, the loss of market confidence in the regional economies that resulted with the floating of the baht, in particular about the sufficiency of the international reserves, triggered a massive outflow of capital from the Malaysian stock market. The outflow of private short-term capital reached US$4 billion in 1997 and became even larger in 1998 at US$5.3 billion.

This outflow caused steep ringgit depreciation. Equally severe were the effects of ringgit depreciation on the banking sector. Malaysian banking had been relatively strong compared to the banking sectors in other countries in the region – in the mid-1990s, the average capital adequacy ratios for all banks in Malaysia remained above 10% (Athukorala, 2001) and the level of non-performing loans was 3.7% in 1996. Despite this strong position, the rapid credit growth had created areas of weakness because of the concentration of loans in selected non-tradable sectors, in particular, to the real estate sector and for share purchases. This credit growth had a significant link to stock market boom as shares were used as collateral for these loans. Thus, when the value of the shares decreased as the stock market collapsed, many loans turned non-performing. When faced with the prospects of a more fragile financial position, many banks began withdrawing loan facilities or

---

[12] Due to the prudential measures exercised by the Bank Negara Malaysia (Central Bank), there was no massive build-up of short-term foreign borrowings. Malaysian companies are required to have a natural foreign exchange hedge before being allowed to borrow overseas. By natural hedge it was meant that the companies would have foreign currency income to service loans.

Table V.3   Malaysia: End-of-year stock of volatile capital and foreign exchange reserves, 1990–97

	1990	1991	1992	1993	1994	1995	1996	1997[c]
Mobile capital,[a] US$ billion	6.3	6.5	12.4	23.9	27.7	31.9	38.9	50.1
Composition of mobile capital (%)	100	100	100	100	100	100	100	100
Short-term debt[b] (%)	26	40	41	28	20	20	26	28
Banking sector (%)	26	40	41	28	14	14	18	22
Non-bank private (%)	0	0	0	0	6	6	8	6
Portfolio investment (%)	74	60	59	72	80	80	74	72
International reserves, US$ billion	10	11	19	30	26	26	28	28
Reserve/mobile capital ratio (%)	158	171	149	124	94	80	72	56

Source: Athukorala (2001).
[a] Short-term debt plus portfolio investment.
[b] Debt with a maturity of one year and less.
[c] First half of the year.

demanding more collateral. As a result, businesses faced a credit crunch and higher cost of funds, which culminated in a recession.

ii. Overall macroeconomic and sectoral performance

Although the Asian crisis began by mid-1997, its impact on the Malaysian economy was felt only in late 1997. GDP grew at a commendable rate of 7.3% in 1997 but the economic contraction was very deep at –7.4% in 1998 (table V.4). This severe contraction was due to a combination of several factors: the recessive force of the regional economic slowdown, massive capital outflows, public sector expenditure reduction and a tight monetary policy.

This economic contraction brought about a severe collapse in private investment (–57.8%) and consumption (–10.8%). The public sector also experienced a decline but at a lesser rate – for example, public investment fell 10% and consumption 7.8%. The drop in private investment was caused by a lack of liquidity in the banking system due to the introduction of a tighter monetary policy in late 1997. Prior to the crisis, credit grew on average about 28% annually between 1994 and 1996 and the Bank Negara Malaysia introduced a credit plan to curb the excessive lending especially to the non-productive sector such as real estate and loans to buy shares. In addition to a credit growth target of 25% by year-end 1997 and 15% by year-end 1998, the plan also dis-

Table V.4   Malaysia: Selected economic indicators, 1996–2002

Indicators/Year	1996	1997	1998	1999	2000	2001	2002
Growth of GDP (%)	10.0	7.3	–7.4	6.1	8.3	0.4	4.2
Growth by final demand category (%)							
Consumption (59.3)	4.9	4.9	–10.3	6.7	10.5	5.8	8.8
Private (45.6)	6.9	4.3	–10.8	3.1	12.5	2.8	4.2
Public (13.7)	0.7	7.6	–7.8	16.3	3.0	17.6	13.8
Gross domestic fixed investment (46.8)	9.7	8.4	–44.9	–5.9	25.7	–2.8	0.3
Private (34.2)	13.3	8.4	–57.8	–18.5	32.1	–20.6	–6.1
Public (12.6)	1.1	8.6	–10.0	11.7	19.9	15.5	4.6
Growth by sector (%)							
Agriculture, forestry and fishing (9.8) [a]	4.5	0.7	–2.8	0.5	2.0	1.8	0.3
Industry (41.5)	11.0	10.5	–6.5	5.4	14.2	–4.2	4.0
Mining and quarrying (7.7)	2.9	1.9	–0.4	6.9	1.9	1.6	4.5
Manufacturing (29.1)	18.2	10.1	–13.4	11.7	19.1	–6.2	4.1
Construction (4.4)	16.2	10.6	–24.0	–4.4	1.0	2.3	2.3
Services (48.7)	8.9	9.9	–0.4	4.5	5.7	5.7	4.5
Growth of manufacturing output (%) [b]	12.2	12.4	–10.2	12.9	25.0	–6.6	4.5
Export-oriented (weight: 72)	11.0	13.2	–5.1	13.5	25.8	–10.4	5.1
Domestic-oriented (weight: 28)	15.6	10.4	–23.5	11.1	22.1	5.9	3.5
Imports of capital goods (growth of value)	–6.5	17.1	–17.4	–9.9	38.6	–0.9	10.6
Manufacturing capacity utilization index	81.2	83.2	59.5	80.7	84.2	78.8	83.5
Unemployment rate	2.5	2.6	3.2	3.4	3.1	3.6	3.2
Inflation rate (%)							
Consumer prices	3.5	2.7	5.3	2.8	1.6	1.4	1.8
Producer prices	2.3	2.7	10.7	–3.5	3.1	–5.0	4.4
Local goods	2.8	2.5	11.2	–3.9	3.6	–6.1	5.7
Imported goods	0.1	2.8	9.2	–0.6	1.1	–6.3	–0.7
Total external debt as % GDP	38.7	43.9	42.6	42.1	46.1	50.7	51.7
Short-term foreign debt as % of total debt	25.7	25.2	19.9	14.3	11.1	13.7	17.2
Short-term foreign debt as % of reserves	36.9	53.7	33.2	19.1	17.7	19.9	24.5
External debt service ratio	6.6	5.5	6.7	5.9	5.3	5.9	6.2

Sources: Malaysia, Treasury Economic Report, Ministry of Finance, Kuala Lumpur, various issues and Bank Negara Malaysia, BNM Annual Reports, Kuala Lumpur, various issues.
[a] The sectoral share in GDP in 1996 is given in brackets.
[b] Based on manufacturing production index (1993 = 100).
n.a = Data not available.
MIER = Malaysian Institute of Economic Research

allowed credit for "unproductive" sectors. Higher interest rates added further pressure to the funding costs of companies and had caused an immediate slowdown of business activities.

The Malaysian economy began to recover in the second quarter of 1999. This recovery came sooner than expected, with GDP registering a strong expansion of 6.1% in 1999 and 8.3% in 2000. The revival of domestic consumption, particularly from the public sector, contributed significantly to recovery. Aggregate consumption expanded by 6.7% in 1998 and 10.5% in 1999. Public consumption led this expansion with an increase of 16.3% in 1999.

Although the public sector pumped up its investment expenditure (11.7%) in 1998, total domestic investment still declined (–5.9%) due to the 18.5% contraction of private sector investment. In 2000, there was a significant improvement in domestic investment, which grew by 25.7%, led by the private sector, which expanded its investment by 32.1%. However, private investment retreated once again (–20.6%) under an adverse external environment in 2001. In contrast, public sector investment maintained an active role in leading the recovery with an increase of 11.7% in 1999 and an even higher jump of 19.9% in 2000. In view of the global economic slowdown in 2001, public investment was expanded 15.5% to ensure that the Malaysian economy did not enter into a recession again.

It was not surprising that the construction sector suffered the most during the crisis: the sector had over-invested during the period of high growth (1987 to 1997), which resulted in a massive excess capacity. Sectoral GDP shrank by 24% in 1998. Manufacturing also recorded a large decline of 13.4%. On the other hand, the agriculture sector experienced a relatively mild contraction (–4.5%) while the services sector declined –0.4%.

The manufacturing sector was the engine of recovery in 1999 and 2000. Malaysia benefited from the global recovery of demand for semi-conductors, which resulted in double-digit growth for the manufacturing sector – 11.7% in 1999 and 19.1% in 2000. The construction sector only managed to grow marginally in 2000 (1%) after a dismal performance (–4.4%) in 1999.

iii. Exchange rate

At the onset of the crisis, when regional currencies were under pressure to devalue, Malaysia tried to defend the ringgit but found this strategy unsustainable and costly. In July, the ringgit was floated and it depreciated sharply during the second half of 1997 – the ringgit exchange rate slipped from RM2.50 per US dollar to its lowest level of RM4.88 in January 1998. After showing some signs of stability during February and March 1998, unlike the currencies of the other crisis-hit economies, the ringgit continued to deteriorate with wide volatility in the following months until it was fixed at RM3.80 per US dollar in September 1998. The sharp depreciation and volatility of the ringgit was associated with large capital outflows and strong market reaction to Malaysia's vocal stand on currency speculation.

iv. Equity market

The equity market, not surprisingly, was among the worst hit sectors in the crisis; the Kuala Lumpur Stock Market lost 80% of its market valuation between February 1997 and September 1998, when selective capital controls were finally imposed. The price/earnings ratio of the Kuala Lumpur Stock Exchange Composite Index (KLCI) dropped from 22.6 in June 1997 to 11.8 twelve months later.

The stock market slide was much earlier than the ringgit depreciation, beginning in February 1997. The credit plan issued by Bank Negara Malaysia (BNM), which was concerned about the overheating economy and large credit expansion to the real estate sector, had caused investors to sell their banking and property shares. By late April, the KLCI had dropped 10%. In August 1997, the BNM imposed a RM2 million limit on non-trade ringgit swaps to reduce currency speculation. As a result, investors liquidated their holdings in the stock market and repatriated these proceeds. To stop the free fall of its market, the KLSE made an unprecedented move, classifying the 100 stocks of the KLCI as designated stock, which meant that investors had to have the scripts in their central depository account before they could be traded. The KLCI plummeted an additional 10% before the ruling was lifted in September 1997.

The government also instituted other measures to shore up the stock market; for example, it allowed companies to buy back their shares to overcome steep share price deterioration. Concerns about the unsettled trading losses of stockbroking houses also fuelled negative speculations and pushed the market downwards.

The Malaysian stock market was also characterized by the existence of an active offshore securities market in Singapore, known as Central Limit Order Book International (CLOB). This over-the-counter market was created when the Malaysian government announced its plans to de-list Malaysian companies from the Singapore Stock Exchange in 1990. These CLOB shares were about 3% of the total KLSE capitalization, as of September 1998, and trade was carried out in Singapore dollars through Singapore brokers.

Although the domestic stock market stabilized in the first four months of 1998, the slide recommenced after May and reached its bottom of 262 points (and a total 80% drop) on September 1998, when the selective capital control was introduced. The stock market rebounded strongly in 1999 – the KLCI rose to a high of 991 points on February 2000, but declined thereafter.

v. Current account balance

During the initial phase of the crisis, exports decreased as the troubled East Asian economies (50% of Malaysia's export market) massively cut their demand for imports. In 1998, merchandise exports fell 6.9% (in US dollar terms) but actual export ringgit revenues increased because of the steep currency depreciation. When the ringgit was pegged (at RM3.80 per US dollar), other regional currencies appreciated, increasing Malaysia's relative price competitiveness. This price competitiveness allowed Malaysian exporters to take advantage of the robust US export demand. In nominal ringgit terms, total exports grew by 30%. The larger ringgit export revenue was an important contributor to higher domestic liquidity.

Malaysia's large merchandise balance of US$18 billion in 1998 was achieved not only from large export proceeds but also from the collapse of imports. Capital and intermediate goods dominate the Malaysian import structure, including inputs for exports. In contrast, consumer goods only constituted about 10% of total imports. Thus, when investment activities and export volume dampened, the demand for imports also declined – merchandise imports decreased by 26%.

Due to the strong performance of the merchandise account balance, the balance on goods and services reversed from the deficit trend that had prevailed during the 1990–97 period (on average about 5% of GDP) into a surplus of US$12 billion in 1998. As a result, the perennial current account deficits were transformed into a surplus of 13% of GDP in 1998.

The trade balance registered an unprecedented surplus of US$19 billion in 1999. This surplus came from the 15.7% merchandise export growth in 1999. Although imports also rebounded strongly (12.5% in 1999), the current account surplus reached a record level of 15.9% of GDP in 1999 and remained around a healthy 8 to 9% in 2000–02.

vi. Capital flows

Capital inflows were important in financing the current account deficit as well as in generating new investments. Prior to 1993, capital inflows into Malaysia mainly took the form of FDI but thereafter short-term capital, primarily portfolio flows, also became significant. Large portfolio inflows in 1993 followed the regional pattern of financial inflows into local stock markets.

After the Asian crisis, there was a reduction in FDI inflows into Malaysia, declining from US$9 billion in 1996 to an annual average of US$3 billion in 1998–2001. The slowing down of FDI inflow is due to both internal and external factors. The crisis has resulted in production over-capacity, thus discouraging new investments into the region. In addition, China tends to attract most of FDI flows to the region. Unlike other crisis-hit economies, Malaysia has been cautious in promoting foreign purchases of distressed assets from the crisis through mergers and acquisitions, and this has inhibited the opening of another channel of larger FDI inflows.

Not unexpectedly, the short-term capital account showed a substantial net outflow of US$5 billion and US$6 billion, in 1997 and 1998, respectively, due to the decline in net external liabilities of the commercial banks and the liquidation of portfolio investments by foreign investors. The lower net external liabilities by commercial banks were in response to the stagnation in domestic demand and the unwinding of trade-related hedging activities. The outflow became larger in 1999 (US$9.9 billion), to some extent reflecting the reluctance of many foreign investors because of concerns about the re-imposition of regulations on capital flows and uncertainty about the exchange rate peg.

vii. Foreign reserves and external debt

The strong performance of the external sector contributed to the improvement in the international reserves position. In August 1998, Malaysia had reserves of US$20 billion, which increased to US$31 billion at year-end 1999, equipping the country to finance five months of imports. However, the level of international reserves did not change much in 2000 and 2001, even though Malaysia continued to record trade surpluses. This is partly explained by pre-payments of external debt and portfolio outflows.

Malaysia's total external debt increased from 44% of GDP in 1997 to 51% in 2001. This increase is attributed to higher long-term debt from both the public and private sectors. Public sector external debt is financed mostly through sales of sovereign bonds. In contrast, the share of short-term foreign debt in total debt burden was substantially reduced from 25% in 1997 to 14% in 2001. The international reserves were more than adequate to cover the short-term foreign debt – the ratio of short-term foreign debt to international reserves was on average below 20% during the 1999–2001 period.

viii. Financial market

The crisis placed a strain on the banking system. The high interest rate and collapse of the stock market increased the non-performing loans (NPLs) of financial institutions to a level considered seriously threatening. As Malaysia had a very high ratio of domestic debt to GDP (152%), the interest rate hike quickly turned many loans into NPLs. Prior to the crisis in 1997, the level of NPLs at financial institutions was 4%, but by August 1998, this figure had jumped to 16%. The higher cost of financing and tighter liquidity discouraged private investment. The cost of funds for investment increased substantially when the base lending rate rose from 10.3% in June 1997 to 12.3% in July 1998: in some cases, the effective interest rate reached a high of 20%.

2. Policy responses for crisis resolution

Concerning macroeconomic policies, the swift change in policy stance from tightening to easing supported the quick recovery of the crisis-hit economies. In Korea, although fiscal and monetary policies differed in the points at which the policy stance changed (fiscal stimulus first, monetary easing more cautiously), the policy target under the IMF program shifted from stabilization of the foreign exchange market to economic recovery around April 1998. In Malaysia, although independent macroeconomic policies could be adopted from the beginning of the crisis, counter-cyclical policy measures only became fully effective from August 1998 due to internal politics.

The positive role of counter-cyclical macroeconomic policies in the post-crisis recovery raises the question of whether the initial tightening of monetary and fiscal policy was kept high for too long, in effect deepening the crisis. In the case of Korea, the IMF initially prescribed a tight monetary policy together with fiscal austerity. But, Malaysia also initially adopted the orthodox approach without IMF involvement. There is also the question of whether the tight monetary and fiscal policy with or without the IMF involvement was inevitable in the early resolution of the crisis. Radelet and Sachs (1998) asserted that the austerity measures were unnecessary because the Asian crisis countries were suffering from a liquidity problem. They implied that the traditional IMF policy prescriptions might have done more harm than good as they drove many highly leveraged but viable firms out of business, thereby deepening the downturn of the economy. Feldstein (1998) further criticized the IMF for moving beyond its traditional macroeconomic adjustment role by including a large number of structural elements.[13] The contribution of initial IMF austerity programs and the presence of structural elements in the IMF programs still remain controversial. However, it is generally agreed that the swift change toward a more expansionary macroeconomic policy stance helped these economies to recover quickly.

a) Policy responses in Korea

i. Early resolution

The macroeconomic policy goals at the outset of the IMF program for Korea had been to stabilize the foreign exchange market and build up foreign reserves through contractionary aggregate demand policies. In particular, the high interest rate policy prescribed by the IMF for Korea and other Asian program countries has generated immense public and academic debates. Proponents argued that i) higher interest rates tend to slow capital outflows by raising the nominal return to investors from assets denominated in domestic currency, ii) higher interest rates make speculation more expensive by raising the cost of going short on the currency, iii) tight monetary policy reduces expectations of future inflation and therefore of future currency depreciation, and iv) monetary tightening – by lowering expectations of currency depreciation – reduces default risk for those with unhedged foreign currency debt exposure (IMF, 2000). By contrast, critics contended that although it may have been necessary to increase interest rates initially, they were kept high for too long, plunging the economy into a vicious cycle of declining output, increasing bankruptcies, and further weakening

---

[13] In the East Asian crisis countries that received IMF assistance, short-run policy goals were not necessarily consistent with medium-run structural reform objectives. A wide array of reform packages would entail medium- or long-run development goals, which cannot be easily achieved in a short span of time. If pursued aggressively without due consideration of implementation difficulties and adjustment costs, even if desirable, structural reforms could delay economic recovery or would end up being perfunctory gestures (Park and Wang, 2002).

of the financial sector – all of which served to weaken rather than shore-up investor confidence (Furman and Stiglitz, 1998). A number of studies have tried to assess empirically whether high interest rates have been useful in supporting the exchange rate. In general, the empirical evidence is inconclusive.

During the early period of crisis resolution, several other measures were also simultaneously implemented to stabilize the exchange market. Tight macroeconomic policies were only one component of many. Thus, it is extremely difficult to single out the impact of stringent macroeconomic policies on the exchange market. Additional policy measures included (i) the IMF's financial support; (ii) maturity extension agreement with foreign creditors on restructuring short-term debt; (iii) accelerating capital account liberalization; and (iv) global bond issuance. This multi-pronged approach successfully restored external stability and allowed foreign reserves to be rebuilt.

ii. Macroeconomic policy responses to the crisis

From fiscal austerity to fiscal stimulus   Prior to the crisis, fiscal policy prudence had been the norm in Korea with the consolidated central government remaining in balance or surplus. In fact, during the 1990s, the government consistently reduced its sovereign indebtedness, with the central government debt falling to a low of 9% of GDP by 1996 (IMF, 2000, p. 56).

When the crisis broke out, the initial IMF program presupposed that the policy of fiscal conservatism should be continued. The original 1998 budget, passed on November 1997 before the crisis became full blown, was based on a forecasted real GDP growth rate of 6% and targeted a budget surplus of 0.25% of GDP. By early December 1997, however, growth estimates had been downgraded to 3%. Under this revised macroeconomic outlook, the overall balance was expected to worsen to a deficit of around 0.5% of GDP. The objectives of the IMF's required fiscal balance were to support the monetary contraction, enhancing confidence in the exchange rate and providing the funds necessary to rehabilitate the financial system.

By late 1997, the effects of the crisis were becoming more severe. Then, the program was revised to focus on allowing automatic stabilizers to operate and tolerating a short-term deficit. However, greater fiscal stimulus was programmed later. The supplementary budget was implemented in March 1998, putting greater emphasis on increasing safety net spending, but this policy stance was still deemed too tight given the worsening economic outlook. In face of a vicious spiral of economic recession and corporate insolvency, counter-cyclical fiscal policy actions were strongly called for. Accordingly, the fiscal policy stance was changed toward expansion. Upon consultation with the IMF, the target for consolidated budget deficits was adjusted upward from the initial 0.8% of GDP (February 1998) to 1.75% (May 1998) and 4% (July 1998). In September 1998, the secondary supplementary budget was implemented with expanded budget deficit target of 5% of GDP. However, the actual deficit for the year turned out to be 4.2% of GDP because tax proceeds began to recover.

The expansionary fiscal policy continued in 1999 in order to stimulate the economy, support economic restructuring and increase spending for the social safety net. The budget deficit target was set at 4% of GDP in 1999, and 70% of the resources for public investment projects were front loaded in the first half of the year. The deficit in 1999 was much smaller than the forecast because the economic recovery was much stronger than expected. As the economy grew by a remarkable 10.9%, the fiscal deficit shrank to 2.7% of GDP. Because of the strong economic recovery, Korea reached again a fiscal surplus in 2000.

Korea's history of fiscal soundness is what allowed for these expansionary policy measures. Korea's public debt as a percentage of GDP stood at only 11% in 1997. A figure far lower than the average of the OECD countries of about 70% (OECD, 2001). After the crisis, public debt as a percentage of GDP jumped to 16% in 1998 and 19% in 1999.

From tightening to easing monetary policy   Once the task of stabilizing the foreign exchange market was accomplished in early 1998, the stance of the monetary policy was progressively eased. In the second quarterly agreement (May 1998), the IMF agreed to relax the pressures that were adversely affecting the domestic credit crunch by lowering the high interest rates and resolving financial difficulties. Continued caution was warranted in view of the unsettled global financial markets. However, by June 1998, interest rates had been brought down to below the pre-crisis level. The relaxation of the monetary policy continued in 1999. The short-term interest rate was further lowered to support a recovery in economic activity, with the overnight call rate falling below 5% in April 1999. The sustained low interest rate boosted stock prices, thereby facilitating economic restructuring and the reduction of debt-to-equity ratios through new equity offerings.

Exchange rate policy and capital market liberalization   After Korea allowed the won to float on December 1997, the IMF requested that the Bank of Korea refrain from intervening in the foreign exchange market, except in the event of dramatic exchange rate fluctuations. With the floating exchange rate system in place, the Korean government also substantially accelerated its ongoing capital account liberalization plan. Under the IMF program, the Korean government agreed to undertake bold liberalization measures; in fact, the Korean government can be credited for much of the initiative behind the reforms. All of the capital markets, including the short-term money markets, were liberalized. But most importantly, the real estate market, which had been off limits and considered non-negotiable, was completely opened to foreigners in the second quarterly agreement with the IMF (May, 1998).

Nevertheless, a number of regulations on capital outflows of residents still remain for the purpose of preventing capital flight. For example,

- Institutional investors are permitted to hold deposits abroad for asset diversification purposes without a quantitative ceiling. But general corporations and individuals are permitted to hold deposits abroad only up to $5 million and $50,000 a year, respectively.
- The monthly allowance for residents staying abroad for over 30 days is $10,000. For those staying abroad over one year, a remittance of $50,000 (including basic travel allowances) is allowed.
- Residents traveling abroad may, in general, purchase foreign exchange up to the equivalent of $10,000 a trip as their basic travel allowance.
- The basic monthly allowance for students under 20 years old is $3,000; for students with a dependent family, an additional allowance of $500 for a spouse and each child is allowed. Residents are allowed to remit up to $5,000 a transaction to their parents and children living abroad for living expenses and to their relatives abroad for wedding gifts or funeral donations, with no restrictions on the number of remittances.
- Residents may make payments abroad by credit card for expenditures relating to travel and tourism; for amounts exceeding $5,000 a month, the foreign exchange authorities must verify the authenticity of payments.
- Loans by residents to nonresidents have to be approved by the Ministry of Finance and Economy.
- For gifts, endowments, inheritance, and legacies, payments that exceed $5,000 have to be approved by the Bank of Korea.

- Overseas direct investment in the leasing and sale of real estate, construction, and the operation of golf courses are prohibited. No approvals or notifications are required for acquisition of overseas real estate by foreign exchange banks, government authorities, and residents if given as gifts or through inheritance from nonresidents. However, just a notification to the BOK is required for the acquisition of real estate, necessary for approved business activities, costing up to $10 million. For this real estate exceeding $10 million, permission from the BOK is required.

Under a free floating system with free mobility of capital flows, the Korean won/dollar exchange rates might be expected to be excessively volatile. However, the Korean won has exhibited an impressive degree of stability since the latter half of 1998. As the Korean won steadily appreciated in 1998–99, the Korean government continued to accumulate huge amounts of foreign reserves by intervening in the foreign exchange market: the stock of reserves rose by US$100 billion between 1997 and 2002.

iii. Structural reform measures

Structural reforms and restructuring measures have been actively carried out on two fronts: the financial sector and the corporate sector.

Financial sector   Restructuring of the financial sector has been central to the structural reform program in Korea. As a first step before starting swift and prudential financial reforms, the government established an institutional and legal framework to coordinate and monitor the reform process. The IMF also advised the Korean government to implement a plan for the closure of nonviable financial institutions, which showed no possibility of being revamped, and the rigorous restructuring of others for rehabilitation.

Good progress has been made in consolidating the financial system and strengthening prudential regulations and supervision. During financial restructuring, public funds were provided to ailing financial institutions. By 1999, the Korean government had mobilized fiscal resources of 64 trillion won, out of which 44 trillion won was used to recapitalize financial institutions, and the remaining 20 trillion won supported the disposal of non-performing loans (NPLs). The Korea Asset Management Company (KAMCO) was in charge of purchasing and recovering NPLs, while the Korea Deposit Insurance Company (KDIC) pays off deposits and recapitalizes financial institutions.

Soon, the 1999 plan to spend a total of 64 trillion won was regarded as wholly inadequate. Consequently, the government injected more public funds, amounting to 156 trillion won in total by May 2002 (equivalent to nearly 30% of GDP in 2001). To raise the money, KAMCO and the KDIC issued a total of 104 trillion won in restructuring bonds. The government guarantees the repayment of these bonds and pays the interest accruing on them from the budget. An additional 20 trillion won was raised through other means, and the government recycled some recovered funds and loans from the ADB and IBRD. These funds were spent purchasing NPLs, recapitalization, repayment of deposits and the purchase of assets and subordinated debt.

Although a great deal has been accomplished in restructuring and strengthening the financial sector in Korea, much more remains to be done. The IMF program did not consider the institutional and other constraints that could limit the effectiveness of financial sector reform measures. When the crisis broke out, the bank-oriented financial system was often blamed for the crisis. The IMF program, therefore, included a capital market development plan, in which capital markets complement and substitute for the banking system as a source of corporate financing. Although this plan is a reform objective, it can only be a long-term priority because the bank-dominated system cannot be replaced by a market-oriented system overnight (Park, 2001, p. 37). Rapid dismantling of the existing system (even flawed system) could create an institutional void.

Corporate sector   The high level of corporate debt and weak corporate governance in Korea resulted in the debt-financed expansion by business conglomerates, raising Korea's vulnerability to the financial crisis. In the wake of the crisis, the Korean government made corporate restructuring a priority of its reform agenda. Relevant laws and institutions have been reorganized to enable a market-based corporate restructuring. Since, the changes to the legal and regulatory framework would have little immediate effect on improving companies' capital structure and profitability, the government actively intervened in pushing forward corporate debt restructuring.

The government decided to classify corporations into three tiers that mirrored the structure of the Korean economy. At the top was the small cluster of powerful conglomerates, the so-called Top Five, that controlled a vast share of the country's productive and financial resources; next, a large group of medium-sized chaebols (ranked 6 to 64); and finally, SMEs. The government pushed the Top Five to submit voluntary restructuring plans. The main banks were to review these plans and work with the chaebols to prepare final plans by December 1998. The government also announced its proposal to use mergers and swaps among the Top Five to consolidate overlapping subsidiaries in key manufacturing industries (aircraft, autos, petrochemicals, power generation, rolling stock, semiconductors and ship engines). For the second tier, the government established an out-of-court workout scheme. The scheme was modeled along the Bank of England's London Approach.[14] The government set up several schemes to help SMEs obtain working capital and trade credit.

Market-led operational restructuring in times of a systemic crisis is extremely difficult. In the case of Korea, nearly all of the corporations suffered from liquidity problems. Reducing the debt-to-equity ratio is deemed desirable, but it is unclear why the Korean government under the IMF program aimed for such a drastic reduction in the corporate debt in such a short span of time.

The adoption of the London Rules for corporate restructuring was to some extent understandable in the absence of the market for bankruptcies and well-functioning court-based bankruptcy laws and institutions. In out-of-court workout, the government was supposed to play the role of mediator, facilitating an orderly debt resolution, and banks were supposed to act as creditors, managing the workout of corporate debt; in most cases, however, the government dictated the process (Park, 2001).

When a bank was recapitalized through the injection of public funds, the government invariably controlled its management. The government-appointed bank managers were unwilling to change the status quo. They also had little incentive to collect overdue loans or to engage in workouts of weak but potentially viable corporate borrowers. The restructured banks have avoided corporate workouts as much as possible, so as not to increase their holdings of NPLs or to lower their profits. This moral hazard problem has therefore delayed corporate restructuring and resulted in a deterioration of bank asset quality (Park, 2001).

---

[14] The London approach to corporate workout (out-of-court workout) differs from a court-supervised rehabilitation or receivership. The approach was taken because unlike the Top Five chaebols, most of the medium-size companies lacked access to bank credit or capital markets and needed debt workouts or new loans to have any chance of meaningful restructuring. Preferential treatment was given in order to encourage banks to participate in the corporate restructuring process and to extend new loans. However, it subsequently became clear that the lax provisioning requirement was a disincentive for banks to recognize true losses in debt workout cases and led to superficial corporate restructuring with debt rescheduling and long grace period. See Chopra, *et al.* (2002).

b) Policy responses in Malaysia[15]

i. *Early responses*

For a while, Malaysia followed the orthodox approach to such a crisis, namely tightened fiscal and monetary policies, introduced measures to redress the balance of payment weakness, and floated the exchange rate. This approach was adopted because the economy was taken to be overheated, thus the main objective was to reduce excess demand. The government had proposed a 3% surplus for the 1998 budget on October 1997. The budgetary measures introduced included a 2% reduction in government expenditure, deferment of mega projects, and cutbacks on the government purchase of foreign goods.

On December 1997, an additional package of policy measures was announced. These measures were aimed at strengthening economic stability and instilling confidence in the financial system as the regional instability proved to be more protracted than was earlier anticipated. The package included a further 18% reduction in government expenditure, strict approval requirements for new investments and deferment of implementation of non-strategic and non-essential projects.

Regarding the financial aspects, a comprehensive set of measures was implemented such as reclassifying the non-performing loans (NPLs) in arrears from six to three months, greater financial disclosure by financial institutions and increasing general provisions to 1.5%. The reclassification of the NPLs was aimed at adhering to international financial practices and ensuring an earlier warning of the rising NPLs. The Bank Negara also raised the three-month intervention rate from 10% to 11%, increased the minimum risk-weighted capital adequacy ratio from 8% to 10% for finance companies and reduced the single customer limit from 30% to 25%. The level of provisions against uncollateralised loans was also raised to 20%. In addition, minimum capital for finance companies was increased from RM5 million to RM300 million and subsequently to RM600 million. The capital adequacy framework was also expanded to incorporate market risks. In view of the tight liquidity in the system, the statutory reserve requirement was reduced from 13.5% to 10%.

As a measure to strengthen the balance of payment position, a target was set to reduce the current account deficit from 5% to 3% of GDP in 1998 by limiting imports and increasing import duties. Stricter criteria

---

[15] See Jomo (2001) and Mahani (2002) for two comprehensive analyses.

were also introduced for new overseas investments to reduce the outflow of domestic capital.

ii. Counter-cyclical measures

The implementation of the stabilization policy did not improve the economic situation. In fact, the economy continued to contract, capital outflow worsened and the ringgit exchange rate remained volatile and depreciated. Then, rejecting the IMF type prescription, Malaysia reversed its earlier response policies and adopted counter-cyclical measures to boost the domestic economy. This approach recommended the introduction of fiscal stimulus, relaxation of the monetary policy, and measures to ensure the stability of the banking system as well as selective capital controls. However, due to internal differences among the top political leadership on the question of crisis resolution, these measures only became fully effective in mid-1998.

Fiscal stimulus programs   With the reversal of fiscal policy stance in mid-1998, an additional development expenditure of US$1.8 billion was allocated for agriculture, low and medium-cost housing, education, health, infrastructure, rural development and technology upgrading. The fiscal stimulus programs concentrated on infrastructure projects and an Infrastructure Development Fund (US$1.6 billion) was established to finance essential projects. Social support was also given to the lower income group through direct transfers. These programs were aimed at keeping domestic activities going, particularly for small and medium scale contractors and industries that were dependent on government projects.

The expansive fiscal policy turned the government fiscal position from a 2.4% surplus in 1997 to a deficit. In 1998, the fiscal deficit was 1.8% of GDP and it became larger subsequently to exceed 5% in 2000–01. These deficits were financed primarily from past savings, as the public debt level did not increase significantly during the 1998–2000 period (it hovered around 36% of GDP). However, the Malaysian government had to raise funds to continue with its fiscal expansion – in 2002 the ratio of public debt to GDP jumped to 46%. This was mainly financed from domestic sources (see table 4).[16]

---

[16] Since the early 1990s, the public sector had attained a surplus budget. Thus, there were some savings that could be used to finance the deficit. In addition, Malaysia had a high savings rate (35% of GDP) and a compulsory savings scheme where the government could access cheap financing.

Easing the monetary stance   An important early measure was to increase liquidity and reduce the cost of funding. In this regard, the statutory reserves requirement (SRR) was gradually reduced from 13.5% in February 1998 to 4% in December 1998. With the reduction of the SRR, an additional US$10 billion was injected into the banking system, helping to overcome the tight liquidity problem caused by the introduction of the credit plan and cautious stance taken by banking institutions.

The initial response of increasing the interest rate had seriously affected the business community. In February 1998, the effective lending rate averaged 24%. Therefore, the immediate task was to reduce the cost of funds. The base lending rate (BLR) was reduced from a high of 12.3% in June 1998 to 6.8% in October 1999. Lending rates were consequently reduced from the 24% peak in February 1998 to 7.9% in October 1999 and subsequently, in stages, to 6.4% in 2002. The lower borrowing costs and higher liquidity did not, however, produce high loan growth. Loan growth was only 1% in 1998 and 1999 as compared to 27% in 1997. The low loan growth was due to both demand and supply factors: business conditions were still so lethargic for reviving new investments. Moreover, bankers were more cautious in extending loans to businesses.

Selective capital controls

A key policy response target was to stabilize the ringgit. In September 1998, Malaysia implemented selective capital controls consisting of two inter-related parts: stabilization of the ringgit (which was pegged to RM3.80/US$1) and restrictions on short-term capital outflows, which was needed to ensure that the ringgit peg could be sustained. The measures implemented to support the peg and control capital flows were as follows:

- All settlement of exports and imports was to be made in foreign currency.
- Travelers were not allowed to import and export ringgit exceeding RM1,000 per person.
- Limit on export of foreign currency by resident travelers was set at RM10,000.
- Residents were required to seek prior approval for remitting funds in excess of RM 10,000 for overseas investment purposes.
- Residents were permitted to obtain credit facilities in foreign currency up to the equivalent of RM5 million. Any amount exceeding the permitted limit required prior approval.

- Residents were not allowed to obtain credit facilities in ringgit from non-residents without prior approval.
- Proceeds in ringgit received by non-residents from the sale of any securities were retained in the external account and converted into foreign currency after one year.
- The ringgit was declared not legal tender outside Malaysia.

The capital control measures affected the transfer of funds among non-residents via non-resident external accounts, the import and export of ringgit by travelers (both residents and non-residents) and investments abroad by Malaysian residents. Similarly, non-residents were proscribed from raising credit domestically for the purchase of shares. Non-resident portfolio investors were required to hold their investments for a minimum of twelve months in Malaysia. However, capital controls did not impede current account transactions (trade transactions for goods and services), repatriation of interest, dividends, fees, commissions and rental income from portfolio investments and other forms of ringgit assets.

The selective capital controls were modified on February 1999 with the quantitative control (the requirement stipulating that proceeds from the sale of ringgit assets be kept in the country for one year) being replaced by a price-based regulation called an exit levy. This easing of capital control consisted of two parts, as described below.

(i) For capital brought into Malaysia before February 1999, an exit levy was imposed on the principal at the following rates:
- 30% for a maturity period of 7 months.
- 20% for a maturity period of 9 months.
- 10% for a maturity period of 12 months.
- No levy was charged on capital with a maturity period exceeding 12 months.

(ii) For capital brought in after February 15, 1999, a levy was imposed on the profits made at the following rates:
- 30% for a maturity period of less than 12 months.
- 10% for a maturity period of more than 12 months.

Although these relaxations were introduced, controlling the flow of short-term capital was still the primary objective. A further relaxation was introduced in September 1999 on the exit levy – the two-tier system was reduced to a flat rate of 10% on profits repatriated. The exit levy was abolished on May 2001. By early 2005, the only remaining capital controls are the pegging of the ringgit and the limitations on the outflow of domestic capital.

Another measure that significantly affected portfolio investors was the requirement that all dealings in securities listed on the KLSE were to be affected only through the Kuala Lumpur Stock Exchange or through a stock exchange recognized by the Malaysian authority. Consequently, trading of the 112 Malaysian companies on CLOB, the over-the-counter market of Malaysian securities in Singapore, was discontinued by the Singapore Stock Exchange in September 1998.

Ensuring the stability of the banking sector   Besides reviving economic activities, the Malaysian policy measures also focused on restoring the stability of the banking sector. The core problem was the rising NPLs that had weakened the capital base of some banks. As a result, these institutions were unable to perform their intermediary function. Thus, in order to restore the stability of the banking sector and to restructure corporate debt, the Malaysian government established three institutions, namely an asset management company to remove the NPLs, a recapitalization agency to inject new capital into the troubled banks, and a corporate debt restructuring committee.

An asset management company (Danaharta) was established in June 1998 to manage the NPLs of financial institutions. Its main objective was to remove the NPLs from the balance sheets of financial institutions at a fair market value and to maximize their recovery value. This would free the banks from the burden of debts that had prevented them from providing new loans to their customers.

As the capital base of banks had been affected by the decline in share prices and NPLs, these banks needed to be recapitalized. For this purpose, a Special Purpose Vehicle (Danamodal) was set up in July 1998 to capitalize banks facing difficulties and especially to top-up their capital, which was reduced when Danaharta took over the NPLs. The injection of capital was intended to enhance the resilience of the banks and to increase their capacity to grant new loans so to speed up economic recovery.

To complement the restructuring of the financial system by Danaharta and Danamodal, the Corporate Debt Restructuring Committee (CDRC) was set up in August 1998 to facilitate debt restructuring of viable companies, through voluntary solutions. The aims of the restructuring exercise were to minimize losses to creditors, shareholders and other stockholders, to avoid placing viable companies into liquidation or receivership, and to enable banking institutions to play a greater role in rehabilitating the corporate sector. The CDRC devised a market-approach debt-restructuring plan to enable creditors and debtors to solve their debts without resorting to legal procedures. It also brought together all interested parties to assist in the corporate debt restructuring.

As of December 2001, Danaharta had successfully disposed of a total of US$13 billion in NPLs. In the process of removing the NPLs, financial institutions had to share the losses – the average discount rate for NPLs was 55%. Danamodal injected US$2 billion into 10 financial institutions, pre-empting any potential systemic risks to the financial sector. As a result, the capital adequacy ratio of the recapitalized financial institutions rose to 11.7% to become almost at par with the industry level (12.6%). Most of the recapitalized institutions have subsequently repaid Danamodal's capital injection. By 15 August 2002, the CDRC had resolved 47 cases with a total debt amounting to RM44 billion. The CDRC ceased its operations on August 2002.

Malaysia has moved to another stage in its banking sector restructuring – the 58 financial institutions have now been merged into 10 banking groups. Each of the banking groups may offer a complete range of financial services such as merchant banking, fund management and stockbroking services.

Liberalization of foreign direct investment   Realizing the contribution that foreign capital could make to the recovery of the economy, the Malaysian government liberalized selected sectors in which it was comfortable with foreign presence and in which it could maximize the gains from foreign capital injection. Thus, in the manufacturing sector, Malaysia relaxed its rules on equity ownership by allowing 100% foreign ownership for investments made before the end of December 2003. Previously, only companies that fully exported their products were allowed full foreign ownership.

Equity liberalization was also carried out in other areas. Meanwhile, the 30% pre-crisis limit on foreign ownership in the telecommunications, stockbroking and insurance industries was raised to 61%, 49%, and 51%, respectively, although the limit for the telecommunications industry was scheduled to be reduced to 49% after five years.

In addition, foreigners were permitted to purchase all types of properties above RM250,000 for new projects or for projects that are 50% completed to reduce excess real estate supply. Previously, there were restrictions on foreigners buying landed properties.

Corporate governance   To complement the recovery measures, Malaysia also strengthened its corporate governance regime. Although Malaysia had implemented measures for good corporate governance practice, the crisis highlighted some of the shortfalls of the existing regime. Additional measures were introduced in order to achieve improved transparency and disclosure standards, more accountability of company directors and protection of minority shareholders' rights, among other intermediate objectives.

3. Assessment of the adjustment processes in Korea and Malaysia

Both Korea and Malaysia experienced the crisis starting in 1997. The exchange rate in both countries severely depreciated and GDP plunged in 1998. Then they showed a sharp V-shaped recovery. Despite this shared successful recovery, as explained, several detailed measures they used to deal with the crisis were remarkably different. The main differences are summarized as follows. First, while Korea sought IMF assistance immediately after the crisis and adopted the macro-economic structural adjustment therapies prescribed by it, Malaysia refused to rely on the IMF and paved its own path to recovery. Second, while Korea liberalized its capital market more extensively after the crisis, Malaysia imposed capital controls instead; however, both retained or imposed some restrictions on outflows by residents. Third, Korea's exchange rate became, at least officially, completely floating, but Malaysia's exchange rate was completely fixed, pegged to the US dollar.

However, in response to the crisis, both countries shared counter-cyclical fiscal policies since mid 1998 and in 1999. Both reduced rather rapidly interest rates and kept some restrictions on financial outflows by residents. The most outstanding feature is that both countries used actively fiscal policy, moving from a surplus before the crisis toward a significant deficit. Korea made a faster move into a mild deficit in 1997 and to a large one, 4.2% of GDP, in 1998. Interestingly, with the resulting recovery of economic activity, the deficit was reduced to 2.7% in 1999, and the balance returned to a surplus in 2000. Malaysia moved somewhat later into counter-cyclical fiscal policy in 1998 and subsequently has remained in deficit.

Among the differences, the most striking ones are those related to capital controls and the exchange rate regime. In particular, it is the capital controls that allowed Malaysia to maintain the fixed exchange rate and to start to reflate its economy right away. Hence, most researchers have focused on the role that capital controls played in Malaysia's recovery process.

Despite these differences, rebounds of both Korea and Malaysia were as drastic as their plunges. Park and Lee (2001) find that the sharp recoveries have been faster than earlier similar episodes in other parts of the world.[17] The growth rates in Korea and Malaysia show a remarkably similar patterns from 1997 when the Asian crisis started. Both countries experienced the most severe recession in 1998, exactly one quarter apart: Korea's lowest growth rate was –8.1% in 1998 Q3 and Malaysia's was –11.2% in 1998 Q4. Thereafter, both countries rebounded quite rapidly so that the growth rates for the following three quarters were –5.9%, 5.8% and 11.2% for Korea and –1.0%, 4.8% and 9.1% for Malaysia.

The above findings indicate that, at least, the capital controls did not produce adverse results for Malaysia. However, a number of researchers discount the role of the capital controls in Malaysia's recovery on the ground that Korea managed to recover without imposing capital controls. Krugman (1999), one of the earliest proponents of capital controls (Krugman, 1998), asserts that the financial panic was coming to an end just about the time that Malaysia decided to impose the controls. Nonetheless, he also states that "it would now be foolish to rule out controls as a measure of last resort".

On the other hand, there are also a number of studies showing that Malaysia's capital controls have been more successful than in other cases. Kaminsky and Schmukler (2000) and Edison and Reinhart (1999) find that in Malaysia the capital controls did produce the intended results of greater interest rate and exchange rate stability and more policy autonomy.

Kaplan and Rodrik (2001) go even further, asserting that the capital controls allowed Malaysia a speedier recovery than would have been possible via the orthodox policies of the IMF. This assessment crucially depends on the different timing they impose on Malaysia's recovery process. Most other studies, explicitly or implicitly, assume that the crisis and recovery occurred simultaneously in Korea and Malaysia. However, Kaplan and Rodrik argue that Malaysia's situation at the time of its capital controls was much worse than Korea's. In fact, they claim that Malaysia's imposition of capital controls could be viewed as the

---

[17] All the data in this section have been obtained from the Asian Recovery Information Center (http://aric.adb.org).

equivalent of Korea's appeal to the IMF for assistance. The difference in timing is about three quarters. Because Malaysia's recovery process, which started with its introduction of capital controls, was superior to Korea's, which started three quarters earlier, Kaplan and Rodrik conclude that the capital controls were more effective, eradicating Malaysia's financial pressures so quickly that the country was able to recover faster than Korea.

While Kaplan and Rodrik's research is quite interesting, juxtaposing Malaysia's recovery process three quarters later to Korea's is disputable. In fact, Korea's minimum GDP growth rate leads Malaysia's by just two quarters. Malaysia's recovery of GDP lags behind Korea's by one quarter. Further, while Malaysia bounces back more quickly (from –11.2% to –1.0% *vis-à-vis* –8.1% to –5.9% in Korea), its peak growth rate is lower than Korea's. Hence, it is not evident which recovery process is unequivocally better. What is evident is that both recovered notably faster than the rest of crises-hit East Asia and Latin American economies victims of the Asian contagion.

If we examine the components of GDP in the recovery process, there are additional differences between Korea and Malaysia. Figure V.1 shows changes in the share of private consumption and investment in GDP from 1996 Q1 to 2002 Q1. Panel A is the consumption share in GDP. As implicated by any standard theory of consumption smoothing, the consumption share shows remarkable stability in both countries. However, the consumption share is slightly lower in the crisis period.

Panel B in Figure V.1 shows that investment was indeed most devastatingly affected by the crisis. In both countries the investment share drastically decreased during the recession and did not recover fully until 2001. An interesting point to note is that while Malaysia's investment share before the crisis was higher than Korea's, it becomes slightly lower after the crisis. We believe that this is closely related to the fact that Malaysia was heavily dependent on FDI in the formation of investment before the crisis, but FDI inflows did not fully recover after the crisis. We will return to this issue later.

Figure V.2 shows the growth rate of components of GDP for both countries from 1996 Q1 to 2002 Q1. Again we can confirm from Panels A (consumption) and B (investment) that the consumption growth rate fluctuates much less than the investment growth rate in both countries. Panels C and D show the growth rates of exports and imports. Interestingly, the growth rate of imports fluctuates more than that of exports in both countries. Further, the fact that growth of imports at

A. Consumption

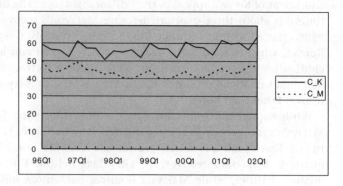

B. Investment

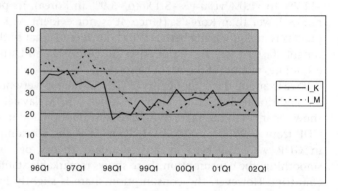

Figure V.1   Changes in GDP shares of expenditure components, 1996 Q1–2002 Q1 (%)
Source: IMF, *International Financial Statistics*.

the beginning of the recovery remained negative in both countries, accompanied by a positive growth rate of exports, seems to have contributed to the recovery process.

Another important factor in the recovery process was monetary policy.[18] While Korea initially imposed high interest rates as recommended by the IMF, its subsequent lowering seems to have helped the recovery. Figure V.3 shows monetary policy stances of both countries in terms of the three-month inter-bank lending rate. It confirms the discussion in section 2. By June 1998 Korea had brought down interest rates below the pre-crisis level. In Malaysia, also after the sharp rise by

[18] In general, Park and Lee (2001) find that monetary policy is less important than fiscal policy for post-crisis recovery in 95 episodes of crises during the period from 1970 to 1995.

A. Consumption

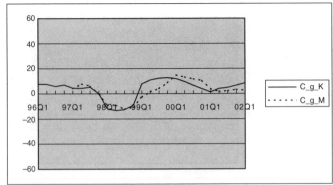

B. Investment

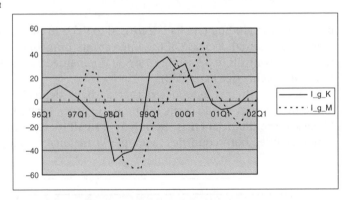

C. Exports

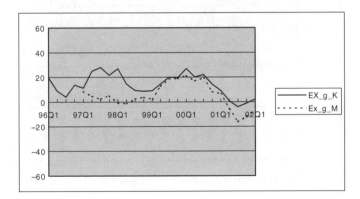

Figure V.2   Growth rates of expenditure components, 1996 Q1–2002 Q1
Note: Due to the lack of quarterly data, all the series start from 1997 Q1 for Malaysia.

D. Imports

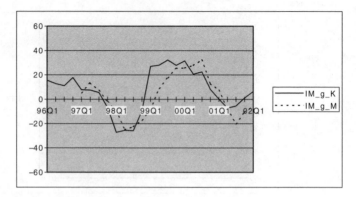

Figure V.2   (continued)

mid-1998, the lending rate had decreased to 9.5% in August 1998, but a more substantial decrease of the interest rate immediately followed the capital controls in September 1998 and remained below the rate in Korea afterwards (see figure V.3).

In general, there was concern that a sharp depreciation of the domestic currency would create inflation. However, for both Korea and Malaysia, the financial crisis led only to a small increase in inflation, which enabled both countries to adopt expansionary policies. Figure

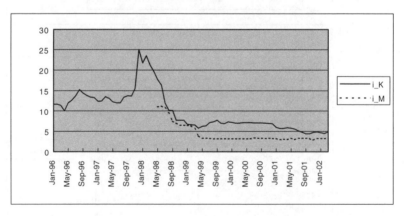

Figure V.3   Monetary variables, Jan 1996–Jan 2002 (three month inter-bank lending rate)
Note: The available quarterly interest rate series for Malaysia starts from 1998 Q2.

V.4.A shows the inflation rates for both countries. During the crisis, it was over 7% in Korea and around 5% in Malaysia. Subsequently, both returned to lower ratio; in particular, Malaysia's inflation rate fell further. The main factor that prevented the inflation rate from jumping during the crisis was the drastic fall in domestic demand, particularly investment. Even during the recovery, both countries' strong manufacturing sectors with excess capacity were able to meet the higher demand without generating further inflation.

Panel B in Figure V.4 shows the change in the unemployment rate. The unemployment rate in Malaysia was not particularly high even during the crisis, partly because the large group of immigrant workers in Malaysia at the time absorbed the severe impact of the economic

A. Inflation rate

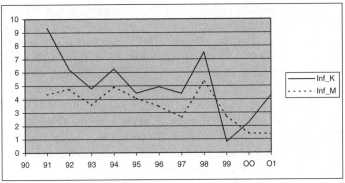

B. Unemployment rate

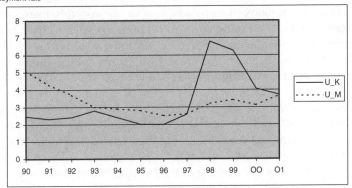

Figure V.4   Inflation and unemployment rates, 1990–2001
Source: IMF.

recession, causing many of them to leave Malaysia for their home countries.

In Korea, the financial crisis took a heavy toll on the labor market, but this market showed significant flexibility in response to the crisis, both in terms of prices and quantity. Faced with the collapse in demand in the wake of the crisis, firms slashed both wages and employment. Nominal wages fell by an average of 9% in real terms in 1998. A 2.5% decline in nominal wages was the first since 1970. Layoffs were concentrated in SMEs where the highest rate of bankruptcies was recorded, as well as in the financial sector. By contrast, with few exceptions, chaebols did not undertake large-scale layoffs, although many reduced their workforces through voluntary separation and early retirement packages.

Unemployment in Korea, which averaged about 2.5% during 1990–97, rose sharply following the crisis to peak at 8.7% in February 1999. The unemployment problem was moderated by a significant decline in the labor force participation rate, mainly as a result of the postponement of job search by younger workers and a substantial withdrawal from the labor force by discouraged female workers. As dramatic as the recovery of GDP was the drop in the unemployment rate to almost the pre-crisis level in 2002 (3.1%; see table V.4). The fact that the crisis was relatively short-lived, along with the existence of a newly and rapidly developed information technology sector, in particular in the small and medium-sized business sector, contributed to the rapid restoration of the unemployment rate.

Despite some differences in details, Korea and Malaysia were similarly successful in their economic recovery. While Malaysia chose to take the heterodox route by adopting capital controls, its recovery was remarkable. The capital controls on outflows seem to have been successful. Further, as emphasized by "second-generation" models of currency crises, even an economy with strong fundamentals can face credit panic and a run on reserves due to a loss of market confidence. In such cases, a temporary suspension of capital outflows can stop the run and eliminate the bad equilibrium. In the case of Malaysia, the existence of an active offshore securities and ringgit market provided an important and critical aspect of the usefulness of capital controls in managing a "second-generation" type of crisis. As shown by evidence of pressures on the exchange rate, the ringgit continued to face severe pressure from January 1998 up to the time when the selective capital controls were introduced. On the other hand, the currencies of the other crisis-hit economies had already stabilized by then.

For capital controls to be successful, it is crucial for the crisis country to be fundamentally strong. If the crisis is due to fundamental problems, then the second-generation models are not applicable and the crisis can end only when the fundamental problems are eliminated. Then, why did Korea, which was as fundamentally strong as Malaysia, not choose to follow the same route? We believe that, while capital controls were a tempting choice for Korea, Korea may have worried about the possible side effects. Furthermore, Korea was not free from the IMF's advice under the IMF program.

As regards capital account liberalization, the Korean government opted for a "big bang" approach by substantially accelerating its ongoing liberalization plan. In reference to the IMF program, one can say that the IMF is a veiled agent of a Wall Street-Treasury complex that is expanding its domain of influence. Under the IMF program, the Korean government pursued a far more extensive capital market opening than what had been agreed upon with the IMF. The goal was simply to stabilize the exchange market by attracting more foreign capital. Korea was facing an increased demand for the liquidation of foreign currency claims. On the other hand, there was little risk of domestic capital flight, because of restrictions on domestic residents to take capital abroad.

4. Policy implications

The recovery has been far greater in Korea and Malaysia than in other crisis-hit countries. In this section we summarized some policy implications of the experiences of the two countries.

First, the standard solutions are not the only effective ways of dealing with a crisis. In deciding on the appropriate response measures, it is critical for policy-makers to be fully cognizant of the real causes of the crisis and the initial domestic conditions and capacity to respond. Under some circumstances, capital controls with an expansionary policy can be as effective as the standard solutions, at least in the short run. However, strong economic fundamentals are essential in enabling a country to choose different response measures. These fundamentals not only include all macroeconomic factors but industry-level factors as well. For example, manufacturing industries must also be able take advantage of the recovery, the financial system must be well capitalized and supervised, and there must be sufficient domestic sources of funding. Under such circumstances, a country will be freer to choose the measures that best suit domestic conditions since it will not be dependent on external financing.

Second, the swift change toward an expansionary macroeconomic policy stance helped the two economies recover quickly. The positive role of counter-cyclical macroeconomic policies in the post-crisis recovery, including fiscal and monetary policies, raises the question of whether the initial monetary and fiscal tightening was kept high for too long, and as a consequence deepened the crisis. In Malaysia, the expansionary monetary policy was essentially possible due to the capital controls. A policy of a high interest rate to stabilize the exchange rate would have had severe implications because of Malaysia's large domestic banking debt. Although Malaysia was less vulnerable to external shocks mainly due to a more stable pattern of capital movements (smaller share of short-term external debt), an expansionary monetary policy could not have been effectively implemented without the capital controls.

Third, in both countries, a favorable external environment and more export-oriented economic structure helped the quick recoveries. Achieving a current account surplus helped injecting liquidity into the economy and to boost domestic demand and stabilize the exchange rate. Robust export growth propelled the strong recovery in the manufacturing sector, which, given its large share of GDP in both countries, became the engine of output recovery.

Fourth, the crisis was induced by the private sector, the domestic private sector was not a likely candidate to lead the recovery. As a consequence, an expansionary fiscal policy played a leading role in the recovery of economic activity.

References

Agosin, M. R. (2001), "Korea and Taiwan in the financial crisis", in R. Ffrench-Davis (ed.), *Financial Crises in Successful Emerging Economies*, ECLAC/Brookings Institution Press, Washington, DC.

Athukorala, P. (2001), *Crisis and Recovery in Malaysia: The Role of Capital Controls*, Edward Elgar Publishing, Cheltenham.

Borensztein, E. and J. Lee (2000), "Financial crisis and credit crunch in Korea: Evidence from firm-level data", *IMF Working Paper* 00–25, International Monetary Fund, Washington, DC.

Cerra, V. and S. C. Saxena (2003), "Did output recover from the Asian crisis?", *IMF Working Paper* No. 03–48, International Monetary Fund.

Chopra, A., K. Kang, M. Karasulu, H. Liang, H. Ma, and A. Richards (2002), "From crisis to recovery in Korea: Strategy, achievements, and lessons", in D. T. Coe and S. Kim (eds.), *Korean Crisis and Recovery*, International Monetary Fund and Korea Institute for International Economic Policy, Seoul.

Danaharta, *Annual Report*, Kuala Lumpur, various issues.

Edison, H. and C. Reinhart (1999), "Stopping hot money", *Working Paper*, University of Maryland.

Feldstein, M. (1998), "Refocusing the IMF", *Foreign Affairs*, 77.

Furman, J. and J. E. Stiglitz (1998), "Economic crises: Evidence and insights from East Asia", *Brookings Papers on Economic Activity*, 2.

IMF (2000), *Republic of Korea: Economic and Policy Development*, International Monetary Fund Staff Country Report No. 00/11, February.

Jomo, K. S. (2001) (ed.), *Malaysian Eclipse: Economic Crisis and Recovery*, Zed Books Ltd., London.

Kaminsky, G. and S. Schmukler (2000), "Short-lived or long-lasting? A new look at the effects of capital controls", in S. Collins and D. Rodrik (eds.), *Brookings Trade Forum 2000*, The Brookings Institution, Washington, DC.

Kaplan, E. and D. Rodrik (2001), "Did the Malaysian capital controls work?", *NBER Working Paper*, No. 8142, Cambridge, Mass.

Kim, S., S. H. Kim, and Y. Wang (2001), *Capital Account Liberalization and Macroeconomic Performance: The Case of Korea*, Policy Analysis 01–01, Korea Institute for International Economic Policy, Seoul.

Krugman, P. (1999), "Capital control freaks – How Malaysia got away with economic heresy", *Slate*, September 12.

——— (1998), "Saving Asia: It's time to get radical," *Fortune*, issue date September 7.

Mahani, Z. A. (2002), *Rewriting the Rules: The Malaysian Crisis Management Model*, Prentice Hall, Kuala Lumpur.

Malaysia, *Treasury Economic Report*, Ministry of Finance, Kuala Lumpur, various issues.

OECD (2001), *OECD Economic Outlook*, No. 68, Organization for Economic Cooperation and Development, June, Paris.

Park, Y. (2001), "The East Asian dilemma: Restructuring out or growing out?", *Essays in International Economics*, No. 223, Department of Economics, Princeton University, Princeton, New Jersey.

——— and J. Lee (2001), "Recovery and sustainability in East Asia", *NBER Working Paper*, 8373, Cambridge, Mass.

———, C. Chung, and Y. Wang (2001), "Fear of floating: Korea's exchange rate policy after the crisis", *Journal of the Japanese and International Economies*, 15.

——— and Y. Wang (2002), "What kind of international financial architecture for an integrated world economy?", *Asian Economic Papers*, 1: 1.

Radelet, S. and J. D. Sachs (1998), "The East Asian financial crisis: Diagnosis, remedies, prospects", *Brookings Papers on Economic Activity*, 1.

Rodrik, D. and A. Velasco (2000), "Short-term capital flows", *Annual World Bank Conference on Development Economics 1999*, World Bank, Washington, DC.

VI

Macroeconomics in Post-Apartheid South Africa: Real Growth versus Financial Stability

*Stephen Gelb**

Introduction

At the time of South Africa's transition to democracy, marked by the election of the African National Congress led by Nelson Mandela in April 1994, the new government was faced with formidable challenges. Apartheid's legacy was extremely high levels of poverty and income inequality, as well as an economic power totally concentrated within the white population. The economy had been in long-term decline for over twenty years, and had experienced more than a decade of substantial economic isolation, resulting from politically-linked sanctions on trade and investment and exclusion from global capital markets. But democratization made global reintegration possible.

A decade later, only limited progress has been made in improving growth and distribution. GDP growth between 1994 and 2003 has been disappointing, averaging only 2.8% per annum: with a population growth rate of 2.0%, *per capita* growth was only 0.8% per annum. Ten years after apartheid ended, poverty and inequality remain very high: 32% of the population were living on less than $2 per day in 1995, and this *rose* to 34% in the subsequent five years. The Gini coefficient was 0.56 in 1995 and it *increased* to 0.58 in 2000 (Hoogeveen and Ozler,

* I would like to thank comments from participants in seminars at ECLAC in Santiago and in Buenos Aires, in the Department of Economics at Wits University, Johannesburg, and the Wits Institute for Social & Economic Research. For his comments and his support, I am particularly grateful to Ricardo Ffrench-Davis at ECLAC. Some of the material in this chapter also appears in S. Gelb, "The South African economy: an overview", in J. Daniel, *et al.* (eds.), *State of the Nation: South Africa, 2004–2005*, HSRC Press, Cape Town, 2004.

2004). By 2000, the share of the higher income decile was 45.2%, while the lowest decile's share was merely 0.4%. In September 2003, the official unemployment rate was 28.2%, and on the "broad" definition of unemployment, it was as much as 41.8%.[1] Unemployment rates differed markedly amongst racial groups, 48.8% of Africans being unemployed on the broad definition compared with only 7.6% of whites (Statistics SA, 2004).

To be sure, internal financial stability has been established: consumer price inflation has been held below 8% almost permanently since 1996 compared with 15.3% in 1991 and 9% in 1994, and the fiscal deficit reduced from 7.3% of GDP in 1993 to below 3% since 1999. Yet it is fair to ask, first, whether this represents macroeconomic success, since the *external* financial position has been extremely volatile, and second, even if it is regarded as successful, whether the price has been too high, given the poor performance of output and employment growth.

This chapter examines macroeconomic policy and performance during the 1990s, to answer these questions. Section 1 starts with a discussion of the political economy of the transition period which shaped the policy choices of the democratic government. Section 2 describes the processes of external liberalization and macroeconomic reform between 1990 and 1994, which provided the context for macroeconomic policy since 1994, which is then discussed in section 3, starting with fiscal policies and then turning to monetary and exchange rate policies. Section 4 examines macroeconomic performance, looking at investment, savings and the balance of payments. Section 5 discusses briefly sectoral issues, and section 6 concludes.[2]

1. The political economy of transition

Poverty and inequality in South Africa are rooted in colonial military conquest and the exclusion of people of color from the political system when the country became independent from Britain in the early 20th century. Racial inequality was deepened by the pattern of economic growth after mineral discoveries in the late 19th century. The forced labor regime in mining extended into a system of migrant labor and

---

[1] The official rate reflects only economically active people who had actively sought work during the previous four weeks, while the broad rate includes those who want to work but have become discouraged from actively seeking jobs.

[2] The appendix presents basic economic and social data for South Africa.

racial discrimination in the labor market when secondary and tertiary sectors developed behind tariff protection after the First World War. The end of the "easy" phase of import-substitution in labor-intensive consumer goods was followed after 1945 by a shift to capital-intensive production for the domestic market of both consumer durables (autos, electrodomestics) and heavy intermediate goods.[3] This helped to build political support for apartheid amongst urban whites who benefited from discrimination in the upper skill levels of the labor market. Growing mineral export earnings (stabilized by the fixed international gold price) financed imports of investment goods, making strong long-run growth possible in the 1950s and 1960s with a widening racial gap in living standards. Increasing capital-intensity limited labor absorption of low-skilled workers and open black unemployment rose from the late 1960s, when long-run manufacturing profitability began to falter. With low labor productivity, because of the apartheid labor and education systems, the manufacturing sector was not internationally competitive, and import dependence was high because low effective protection on machinery and assembled intermediates had restricted backward integration. The breakdown of the Bretton Woods system followed by the 1970s oil shocks led to pressures on South Africa's trade account, while renewed domestic opposition to apartheid resulted in capital flight and growing momentum for international trade and investment sanctions against apartheid. These pressures led to some liberalization of apartheid restrictions, combined with severe repression as the regime struggled to maintain its hold on power.

GDP growth dropped from about 5.5% in the 1960s to 3.3% in the 1970s to 1.2% in the 1980s; fixed investment was reduced from more than 25% of GDP in the 1970s to about 18% in the mid-1980s and TFP growth in manufacturing dropped from 2.3% per annum in the 1960s to 0.5% in the 1970s and –2.9% during the first half of the 1980s. Adding to pressures on the balance of payments, international creditors recalled public sector debt in 1985, as government intransigence over political liberalization led to fears of endemic political unrest. The necessity to finance debt repayment imposed a current account surplus and import restrictions, severely tightening the external constraint on growth given the dependence on imported capital and intermediate goods.

---

[3] This was a pattern similar to that of many Latin American economies, but different from East Asia which followed import-substitution with labor-intensive export-promotion resulting in higher employment rates and greater equity.

The distributional impact of economic decline in the context of political liberalization was very uneven. White business groups based in mining and in finance did well, while medium-sized firms in manufacturing and services (also white-owned) became vulnerable. Ownership concentration increased: in 1990, six conglomerates based on mining and finance controlled companies with 86% of the market capitalization on the Johannesburg Stock Exchange. As late as 1986/7, big business had given explicit support to the continuation of martial law and political repression, but by 1989 these economic groups supported constitutional negotiations with the hitherto-banned nationalist political movement, eventually recognizing that their long-run interests were tied to democratization as the only route to relaxing the binding external constraint and restoring economic growth.

The black urban middle class also made gains during the period of economic decline. There were substantial job losses primarily amongst unskilled workers, in manufacturing and construction as well as the public sector and services, but blacks with education and skills benefited: technical and white-collar occupations increased as a proportion of the labor force in all sectors. The number of Africans in "middle class" occupations grew 6% per annum, nearly trebling between 1970 and 1987 when 19% of employed Africans were in middle class jobs and comprised nearly a quarter of the middle class (Coloreds and Indians another 18 %) (Crankshaw and Hindson, 1990). Despite the rise of a middle class, black control over resources, especially in the corporate sector, was almost non-existent: it is estimated that black management in white firms was 4% in 1990, and blacks owned only 0.1% of the capitalization of the Johannesburg Stock Exchange in 1994.

From the mid-1970s a diverse urban black civil society grew: in addition to an effective black trade union movement, community organizations, professional and business bodies, media and cultural organizations and women's and youth organizations were established. This became a significant factor driving the society to negotiated democratic transition, together with strategic focus from the exiled nationalist movement, the African National Congress (ANC). In early 1990, the ANC was unbanned and Nelson Mandela released from prison. The form of the transition – not the overthrow of the apartheid state but constitutional negotiations which lead ultimately to a *de facto* coalition government with the previous (apartheid) ruling party for over two years until June 1996 – reflected the prevailing balance of class power. It implied blacks' recognition of whites' role in society and

of their property rights, though the latter were qualified by the impera-
tive of "capital reform" to open the ownership and management of the
private sector to blacks (together with state institutions and public
corporations).

The ANC leadership recognized that sustainability of future growth
would depend not just upon the immediate benefits from relaxing the
external constraint represented by sanctions and the debt moratorium,
but on increased exports and capital inflows, as well as on improving
investment ratios and industrial productivity. In prioritizing the revival
of growth, the ANC recognized its interdependence with (white) big
business, reaching an "implicit bargain" with the latter, combining on
the one hand the latter's support for deracializing (private) economic
power and the state, with the new government's acceptance of reintegration into international goods and capital markets on the other,
involving trade and financial liberalization and supposedly "investor-
friendly" macro policies.[4]

Although a "basic needs" program was articulated within ANC circles
during the course of the constitutional negotiation phase of the transition, spelling out a "growth through redistribution" process premised
on the expansion of labor-intensive sectors producing consumer goods
and services for the poor, it too would require relaxing the external
constraint (to finance capital equipment imports), as well as a considerable increase in deficit financing. The basic needs approach thus
failed to win much support from either domestic business groups or
foreign financial institutions, while within the ANC its support was
limited by the weakness of the two constituencies who would be its
major beneficiaries: small black business and the unemployed poor.
More influential in the ANC alliance were organized black labor with
members in established industry and the black intelligentsia and professional middle classes looking to move into government and the
public sector, neither of whom would benefit greatly from a basic
needs focus.

---

[4] ANC views on fiscal policy were strongly influenced by the political consequences in Chile and Nicaragua of rapid fiscal expansion to address popular
needs by the Unidad Popular and Sandinista governments, respectively.

2. External liberalization and macroeconomic reform, 1990–94[5]

Policy formulation and implementation to liberalize international trade and finance began well before the first democratic election in 1994. Some reforms were driven by private institutions such as the Johannesburg Stock Exchange (JSE), while individual state agencies pursued their own agendas. ANC policy-makers were incorporated into most discussions, but before 1994 were not in a position to direct policy reforms. The context of an ongoing political transition and a weakened state meant that the reform process was highly fragmented and lacking a coherent framework. Between 1990 and 1994, the debate over economic policy for "the new South Africa" took place in hundreds of workshops, conferences, seminars and publications, convened by dozens of different organizations inside South Africa and abroad. The contemporary version of the Washington consensus provided an "off the shelf" set of prescriptions which were aired on all these occasions, often by representatives of the Bretton Woods institutions. Consequently, these ideas inevitably influenced resulting policy specifics. But little attention was paid to issues being debated internationally at the time, such as the pace and (especially) sequencing of capital account and current account liberalization, or the interaction between policy reform and social safety net issues.

Processes begun in 1992 led to legislation in 1994 and 1995 allowing foreign banks to establish branches, deregulating the JSE via a "Big Bang" opening to foreign security dealers, and abolishing the two-tier exchange rate together with all capital controls on foreign investors.[6] The removal of the financial rand discount re-established the link between international and domestic interest rates. Re-entry to international borrowing had been facilitated by the signing of an IMF standby credit facility of US$750 million in November 1993 by the Transitional Executive Council (a joint ANC-National Party authority which ran for six months prior to the election). By the end of 1994, both Moody's

---

[5] More extensive discussion of these issues is developed in Gelb (1998; 2003) and Gelb and Black (2004a).
[6] Restrictions on outward investment by domestic investors were relaxed through gradual raising of investments ceilings, though some restrictions remain; for example, domestic corporations are allowed to invest from their domestic sources up to ZAR2 billion per project elsewhere in Africa, and ZAR1 billion per project outside Africa. The South African currency is the Rand, abbreviated here to ZAR.

and Standard and Poor's had included South Africa in their ratings and the government had floated a US$750 million international bond issue.

South Africa has long had very sophisticated financial markets by emerging country standards, and following liberalization, foreign entry into both banking and securities trading was rapid and portfolio inflows rose quickly from their sanctions-era levels (figure VI.1). This helped to fuel strong growth in the financial sector (table VI.2) and to transmit capital flow volatility to the macroeconomy. In 1996, the JSE ranked 14th globally by market capitalization. Trading volumes rose from 2.2 billion shares in 1992 to 5.2 billion in 1995 (and over 55 billion by 2002), and liquidity (value of shares traded as a proportion of market capitalization) from 5% in 1992 to 43% by 2002. Non-residents accounted for 52% of share transactions by value in 2002. Foreign bank presence also grew rapidly, from 40 representative offices to over 80 banks present in 2000.

Trade policy shifted from import protection to export promotion in the late 1980s, but the new instruments mainly benefited capital-intensive sectors dominated by the big business groups. In 1990, the General Export Incentive Scheme (GEIS), a tax-free cash subsidy to exporters based on domestic value-added, was introduced "to encourage the production and export of processed raw materials, [which] overlooked ... labor-intensive exports" (Jenkins and Siwisa, 1997, p. 12; Levy, 1992, p. vii). Generous tax incentives for investment were introduced in 1991, also aimed at encouraging natural resource "beneficiation" to promote exports of processed materials. In 1990, the state-owned Industrial Development Corporation formulated a tariff reform program, which became the basis of South Africa's offer to GATT in 1992, when the ongoing political transition opened Uruguay Round negotiations to the government's participation. Domestic political pressure led to organized labor (and business associations) becoming directly involved in the GATT discussions in 1993. South Africa acceded to the WTO in 1995, but in September 1994, the ANC government announced tariff reductions in the auto industry ahead of the GATT deadline, and in March 1995, it scrapped proposed adjustment subsidies to the textile sector while accelerating tariff reductions. The 1996 depreciation of the currency offering implicit protection led to further acceleration of tariff reductions.

Trade liberalization has simplified the tariff structure and lowered protection levels: from 1990 to 1999, the number of tariff lines was reduced from 12500 to 2463 with positive tariffs, the number of bands from 200 to 45, and the (unweighted) mean rate from 27.5% to 16.5%.

But the structure of protection remains biased against both upstream development of the machinery and equipment sector, and also against exports, especially after the elimination of GEIS and other export subsidies in 1997 (Lewis, 2001, p. 43). Sectoral duty drawback programs replaced GEIS for exporters in two sectors, autos and apparel. Tariff reform was intended in part to reinforce anti-inflation policy through more vigorous product market competition, reinforced by scrapping the 22 single-channel marketing boards in agriculture.

Macroeconomic policy reforms were also introduced before 1994, and these set the tone for subsequent policy. Inflation had cycled around 15% since 1973, but from 1989, the central bank used fiercely contractionary interest rate policy to lower it into single digits by 1993. The Bank also proposed to enshrine its own independence in the constitution using the German Bundesbank as a model in its arguments for lower inflation. This was accepted by ANC negotiators, anxious to "build credibility" amongst international and domestic investors. As a result, the central bank governor appointed in 1989 was retained in 1994 and only in 1999 was replaced by an ANC politician.

Fiscal policy during the transitional period did not support the monetary policy stance. The deficit rose from 1.4% of GDP in 1991 to 7.3% in 1993 (and government debt from 29% of GDP in 1990/1 to 48% in 1994/5) as the old regime increased politically-related expenditure, raising salaries and pension payouts amongst its white public service support base while it still had the power to do so, raising welfare expenditure for blacks in an effort to buy votes in the forthcoming democratic election, and raising police spending in response to growing political violence. In a break from tradition, the outgoing government appointed a leading private sector industrialist rather than a party politician as Minister of Finance in 1993, who introduced fiscal deficit targeting which like independent central banks had become standard fare in the international consensus. Like the central bank governor, he was retained by the ANC when it established the Government of National Unity in 1994. An ANC politician was appointed as Finance Minister for the first time in 1996.

Despite the ANC's formal alliance with black trade union and community organization federations, fiscal decisions were increasingly "insulated" from popular political pressures, as the "Washington consensus" recommended, to build the credibility of economic reforms. The ANC's election platform had included an economic program labelled the Reconstruction and Development Program (RDP). An RDP

Ministry was established in the President's Office but its influence over fiscal decisions was tightly circumscribed.[7] ANC ministers, including the former trade union leader appointed RDP Minister, publicly committed to fiscal stringency as reflected in the 1993 targets, and the overall deficit was maintained even though the budgetary share of social spending rose significantly from 1995. In 1996, the labor movement was explicitly excluded from the process leading to the *Growth, Employment and Redistribution* (GEAR) policy, discussed below.

3. Macroeconomic policy post-apartheid

After embracing financial openness, capital inflows to South Africa expanded many-fold. But flows have been dominated by portfolio investment rather than direct investment. As in emerging economies in Latin America and Asia, efforts to "build credibility" by adopting and sticking to the "right" policies – tight monetary and fiscal policies favored by portfolio investors, and aggregate demand restrictions even when domestic cyclical conditions support a more relaxed approach – have not enabled South Africa to avoid the volatility and destabilization associated with external capital flows. During the decade, there were three foreign exchange crises involving capital inflows reversals and exchange rate collapses. Interestingly, flows to South Africa are not closely tied to those to Latin and Asian economies: only the second crisis was linked to other emerging economy capital out-surges, the first and the last of these being purely South African affairs.[8]

Macroeconomic conditions and policy shifts during the past decade have been dominated by these crises. The first started in February 1996, triggered by domestic *political* uncertainty and consensus that the Rand was overvalued. The policy response was a major re-statement of policy in the form of GEAR, which "repackaged" the government's commitment to investor-friendly fiscal and monetary policy, tariff reduction and privatization in the expectation that the "announcement effect" would restore calm to the capital account. The second forex crisis in 1998, in the wake of the Asian crisis, resulted in the abandonment of exchange rate stability as a policy goal and the introduction of

---

[7] An "RDP Fund" of 5% of government expenditure was set up from which line departments could apply for funds for special projects.

[8] Nor have the rise in capital inflows since 2002 and the associated overvaluation of the ZA rand been linked with parallel flows into Latin economies – the ZAR's value is more closely correlated with currencies of other mineral-exporters such as the Australian dollar.

inflation-targeting. The third crisis occurred in late 2001, with causes that remain unclear despite an official inquiry. Currency depreciation during the third crisis was rapidly reversed, partly as a result of rising global commodity prices in the wake of September 11 and the dollar's weakening globally, and in fact the ZAR has probably been substantially *overvalued* since late 2002. Thus, interest rate and exchange rate fluctuations through the decade have provided "unfriendly" signals to the real sector, notwithstanding the success in achieving fiscal stability and low inflation rate. The rest of this section looks in more detail at fiscal policy, monetary policy and exchange rate policy.

a) Fiscal policy – the success story

Fiscal policy has largely met its immediate objectives during the post-apartheid era. The National Treasury has completely reconstructed the budgetary and expenditure processes, a task both imposed and facilitated by the fundamental changes in provincial and local government jurisdictions in the new constitution, which naturally scrapped the apartheid "bantustans". But the Treasury has gone well beyond this aspect, introducing new systems of financial planning, expenditure management, reporting and accountability. Since 1997/98, budgeting has taken place within a Medium Term Expenditure Framework (MTEF), a three-year rolling framework intended to provide greater certainty to line departments to plan and implement policy programs, which are budgeted and evaluated on the basis of output-linked performance indicators, rather than on inputs. For the Treasury it enables a combination of aggregate fiscal restraint with strategic reprioritization for allocative efficiency. The MTEF is supported by the Public Finance Management Act (PFMA) passed in 1999, which imposes strong controls over financial management in all public sector institutions, with stiff penalties for transgressions. The PFMA requires departments to set measurable objectives for their spending, including details of outputs and service delivery indicators. The Treasury has imposed stringent discipline on provincial governments which have overspent budgets, though at the same time, many departmental budgets, at both national and provincial levels, have been underspent due to capacity constraints in the public sector.

These reforms have contributed to a steady decline in the fiscal deficit since 1994, when deficit targets were first made explicit. The Treasury met its own fiscal target set in the 1996 GEAR statement – to reduce the deficit to 3% of GDP by 1999. However, the primary surplus (revenue less non-interest expenditure) has experienced erratic shifts between pro- and anti-cyclical stances, underlining that in a context of sudden capital flow reversals and exchange rate declines, fiscal policy cannot easily be used to stabilize activity levels in the real economy. Since 2001 "a more expansionary fiscal stance has been adopted" (National Treasury, 2004, p. 56): the primary surplus declined, with real non-interest expenditure rising 7.8% per annum on average, after real cuts of almost 2% per annum the previous three years (table VI.1).

Table VI.1 also shows that since 1999/2000, public debt levels have been substantially reduced from close to 50% of GDP to below 40%, where there need be little concern about sustainability or a "debt trap". With lower nominal interest rates, reduced debt levels have helped to bring down interest expenditure. Van der Berg (2001) shows that between 1993 and 1997, overall per capita social spending increased by 23.8% in real terms, with significant redistribution across income and racial categories: per capita spending on the lowest income quintile increased 28%, and on the next two quintiles 56% and 31%, respectively. Allocations to social security and welfare increased dramatically, but at the expense of housing. Capital expenditure by government was severely cut during the mid-1990s to make room for the increased share of social spending, dropping to very low levels. Investment spending for the overall public sector fell below 5% of GDP from 1992, compared with an average of 10% during the 1980s (see figure VI.5, below). It can be argued that Treasury's successful institutional reforms have privileged the financial dimension of public expenditure over its substantive contribution to sustained economic development.

There has been a substantial improvement in revenue collection, which has been an essential aspect of the success in managing the fiscal stance. The SA Revenue Service, given organizational autonomy from the Treasury in 1997, re-organized and modernized itself, resulting in increased efficiency in revenue collection, greater compliance by taxpayers and a significant widening of the tax base. Efficiency improvements are reflected in the smaller backlog of unassessed returns at the end of the tax-year: in March 1998, the backlog was 49% of the 4.7 million (individual and corporate) returns, but by March 2003, it was only 5.4% (South African Revenue Service, 1998, 2003). Compliance measures include risk-profiling of taxpayers, more extensive and integrated taxpayer auditing, improved enforcement and debt collection. The number of taxpayers in the tax base has been widened substantially: over the four years from 1998/99 to 2002/3, the number of individual and company income taxpayers each grew an average of 12% per annum.

Table VI.1 Government budget: size and distribution, 1990–2004

	1990/1	1995/6	1998/9	2001/2	2002/3	2003/4[1]	2004/5[2]
1 Growth rate, real non-interest expenditure (%)	n.a.	n.a.	−5.1	7.1	6.7	9.5	5.0
2 Current non-interest expenditure	23.2*	23.6	22.5	22.2	22.9	24.9	25.0
3 Interest expenditure	4.3*	5.9	5.7	4.7	4.1	3.9	3.8
4 Budget deficit	1.4	4.5	2.3	1.4	1.1	2.3	2.3
5 Capital expenditure	1.7*	1.6	0.8	1.1	1.2	1.3	1.3
6 Net government debt	29.0	48.0	47.6	42.1	36.3	36.8	38.0
7 Education	18	21	22	20	20	20	20
8 Health	9	10	11	11	11	11	11
9 Social security, welfare	6	10	12	12	14	15	16
10 Housing, other soc services	13	5	3	4	4	5	5
11 Social services (total)	46	46	48	48	49	50	51
12 Protection services	20	17	16	17	17	17	16
13 Economic services	14	11	9	11	12	13	13
14 Interest	12	19	20	17	15	13	13
15 Other	8	7	8	7	6	7	6
16 Total	100	100	100	100	100	100	100
17 Company income tax	21.5	13.9	16.4	23.6	26.1	25.6	n.a.
18 Personal income tax	33.6	40.2	42.1	35.8	33.4	32.4	n.a.
19 VAT	25.4	25.7	23.8	24.2	24.9	26.7	n.a.
20 Other	19.4	20.2	17.7	16.3	15.6	15.2	n.a.
21 Total	100	100	100	100	100	100	100

Source: Calculated from National Treasury, Budget Review (several years).
Notes: Fiscal years, ending March 31. [1] estimated; [2] budgeted; n.a. = not available; * 1991/2 data.
Rows 2–6: % of GDP; Rows 7–16: % of expenditure; Rows 17–21: % of tax revenue.

Tax revenue declined as a share of GDP during the early 1990s, reaching a low of 22.6% in 1995/96 before increasing. Since 2001/2 it has been maintained just below the GEAR-specified ceiling of 25%. Government has had a formal commitment to promote growth and employment through private investment, and officials have often expressed the view that tax cuts on company profit (income) are the most effective mechanism to increase investment. Surprisingly then, the strong performance on the revenue side of the budget has been directed to tax cuts for the middle and formally-employed working classes, enabling these groups to increase their consumption spending, rather than to possible alternatives which might directly or indirectly – via provision of public goods and services, or increased private investment to create jobs – have benefited the informally employed and unemployed. According to the Treasury, R73 billion in tax relief has been given since 1994/95, of which 86% has gone to individuals (National Treasury 2004, p. 79). Table VI.1 shows that the relative contribution of company income tax first fell and then rose during the 1990s, while the share of personal income tax increased substantially to a peak of 43% in 1999/2000, before falling as a result of tax relief. Over the six years to 2003/4, the income tax burden – the share of aggregate personal income paid in tax – fell from almost 15% to below 12%, despite the improvement in tax collection efficiency. At the same time, revenue from company income tax grew 12% per annum in real terms.

b) Monetary and exchange rate policy – moving goalposts

Monetary and exchange rate policies are considered together, because capital account liberalization restricts choices in both. Policy-makers would choose, if they could, to have all three of the following features in the macroeconomic policy regime: an open capital market to enable access to external finance; a stable nominal exchange rate to underpin international trade; and control over domestic interest rates to support objectives such as output growth or price stability. The problem is that these three goals constitute a "trilemma": achieving all three simultaneously is not possible, at least not in a sustainable manner, so that policy authorities must decide which two to prioritize and which one to abandon (Obstfeld, 1998).

Up until 1995, policy in South Africa opted for the latter two goals – exchange rate stability and independent monetary policy. But capital account liberalization in March 1995 re-posed this choice, and subsequent monetary and exchange rate policy can be divided into two phases. Initially policy-makers tried to pursue all three objectives, but by September 1998 the costs of trying to avoid the trilemma had become too high, and exchange rate stability was abandoned in favor of monetary policy autonomy, with the introduction of inflation targeting.

From the early 1990s until 1999, the Reserve Bank set formal targets for money supply (M3) growth, though in practice monetary policy was "eclectic" (its term) with the nominal exchange rate sometimes also implicitly targeted. High interest rates were used to lower inflation, together with a slowly depreciating nominal exchange rate to stabilize the real exchange rate for export competitiveness (figure VI.3 below). Prior to the 1994 elections, South Africa's capital account had been closed. Exchange controls restricting capital outflows were in place on and off from 1961, and were re-imposed during the debt standstill in 1985, together with the dual exchange rate (separate rates for commercial and financial transactions) which discouraged disinvestment by foreigners. The removal of restrictions on South Africans' investing abroad was a priority concern for domestic business in the context of their support for democratization to enable re-integration with global financial and goods markets. In his keynote Annual Address in August 1994, the Reserve Bank Governor responded to the pressure for the early and total removal of controls by re-affirming the Bank's commitment to their removal but in an orderly and gradual process of financial re-integration (Stals, 1994).

Even with the capital account closed, South Africa experienced massive capital inflows in the wake of the 1994 election, fulfilling the expectation that democratization would relieve the external constraint. Between July 1994 and June 1995, *net* inflows amounted to 3.8% of GDP (Stals, 1995). These inflows were undoubtedly driven in part by supply factors in global financial markets, specifically the search for profitable outlets for funds. During 1994 there was a rise in global flows to "emerging markets", and in the wake of the Mexican crisis from late 1994, a further increase in the flows to EEs outside Latin America (Ros, 2001). The Reserve Bank became alarmed by the size, speed and composition of inflows, which went mainly into short-term assets, worried that its efforts to lower inflation and enhance international competitiveness would be undone by excessive money supply growth and pressure for currency appreciation.

The Bank began to emphasise these *disadvantages* of capital inflows. But though it referred approvingly to controls on capital inflows adopted in other emerging markets,[9] it opted instead for capital account liberalization in March 1995, as a strategy to reduce the size of *net* short-term inflows, by offsetting large *gross* inflows with capital outflows. The dual exchange rate was unified to remove restrictions on non-residents' transactions, and a series of steps begun towards the relaxation of restrictions on residents' foreign investment. For the Reserve Bank, the unified exchange rate carried the additional substantial advantage that capital inflows would now occur on the same basis as commercial transactions, adding to forex reserves and enabling the reduction of its "forward book" and uncovered foreign currency position, which the policy authorities saw as major risks.[10] In the next 12 months, the Net Open Forward Position (NOFP) was reduced by about two-thirds from US$25.8 billion to US$8.5 billion (Mboweni, 2004).

The strategy was based on an assumption of large capital inflows with a longer-term maturity profile, to avoid the risk of net outflows. This was remarkably optimistic, more so in light of the "tequila" crisis in Mexico from December 1994, the first big emerging market financial crisis of the 1990s globalization. Although South Africa's capital liberalization strategy has been praised for being gradual (IMF, 1997),[11] the freeing of foreigners' transactions in a one-off "Big Bang" has produced a substantial increase in capital flow volatility.

Figure VI.1 illustrates the instability of inflows after 1994, which have been dominated by portfolio flows, which are more volatile than direct or "other" investment (mainly bank loans). Substantial direct investment into South Africa was expected, but as things have turned out, South Africa has not been a major destination for FDI since 1994 (Gelb and Black, 2004b). Portfolio flows by contrast have been very large: between 1994 and 2002 portfolio flows to South Africa were about three times as large (as a percentage of GDP) as flows to a group of 16 emerg-

---

[9] See the discussion on Chile and Colombia in Ffrench-Davis and Villar (2005).

[10] These were contingent liabilities reflecting the "insurance" against Rand depreciation, which the Bank provided after the debt standstill in 1985, in order to maximize foreign inflows by encouraging international borrowing. If the exchange rate depreciated, the Bank would compensate public and private sector borrowers for the additional debt service burden, with taxpayers bearing the cost. The dual exchange rate system required non-residents to trade ZAR assets only with each other, not with residents, and non-residents' financial flows were not recorded in the BOP capital account. After the exchange rate was unified in 1995, non-residents' financial transactions went through the capital account, were available to the central bank and affected forex reserves.

[11] Gradualism is now part of the orthodoxy, but it was not at that time.

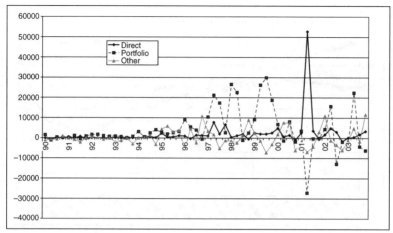

Figure VI.1 Gross capital inflows, 1990–2003
Source: South African Reserve Bank Quarterly Bulletin (various issues). Unless otherwise noted, data for all figures are from this source.

ing markets with similar sovereign credit ratings, while FDI flows were less than half as big as for the comparator group[12] (IMF, 2004b). Portfolio investment into South Africa is dominated by unregulated equity flows into the Johannesburg Stock Exchange, about 70% of the total. Between 1995 and 2002, South Africa received 22% of net total portfolio equity flows to developing countries (World Bank, 2003). The composition of inflows is partly a consequence of the sequencing of liberalization: direct investment, the banking system and equity and bond markets were all liberalized at roughly the same time in line with the contemporary international consensus. By the late 1990s, after the tequila and East Asian crises, the conventional argument had shifted to recommend first liberalizing direct investment, the "least footloose" flow, well before any financial flows (Eichengreen, 2000).

Notwithstanding capital account liberalization in March 1995, the Reserve Bank continued to pursue its existing policy goals of cutting inflation together with nominal exchange rate stability (or at most slow depreciation) to maintain a competitive real exchange rate. This implied a combination of high real interest rates and some "sterilization" of the monetary effects of net capital inflows to limit money

[12] Portfolio flows to the group of emerging markets comprised only 28% of inflows, but for South Africa, the share was 70%. Mexico, Colombia, Costa Rica, Guatemala and Uruguay were included, but not Argentina, Brazil and Chile.

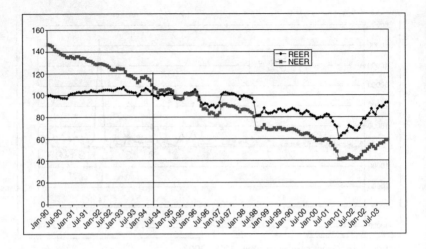

Figure VI.2 Effective exchange rates indices, 1990–2003 (monthly data, 1995 = 100)
REER = real effective exchange rate
NEER = nominal effective exchange rate

supply growth. In other words, the Bank continued to pursue both monetary policy and exchange rate goals despite having shifted to an open capital account. Such evasion of the "trilemma" was possible as long as net capital inflows were large enough to finance current account deficits and to reduce the NOFP, the Reserve Bank's exposure in the forward foreign exchange market.[13] Net inflows were sufficient in this sense between March 1995 and January 1996 and again from September 1996 through April 1998. But given foreign portfolio investors' herd-like behavior, net inflows were subject to abrupt drops, as in February 1996 and May 1998. On both occasions, the Reserve Bank tried to stem the outflow by absorbing exchange rate risk from both importers and foreign investors, selling dollars into the spot market and increasing its NOFP (Stals 1996; 1998). In 1996, it sold about US$ 14 billion and in 1998, about US$ 10 billion, which pushed the NOFP back up close to its March 1995 level. In other words, foreign exchange purchased to reduce the NOFP during 1995 and again during 1997 through April 1998, had in effect been wasted. In a somewhat contradictory move, given the support via the exchange rate to

[13] The Reserve Bank reduced the NOFP by purchases of dollars in the forward market, funded by spot market sales.

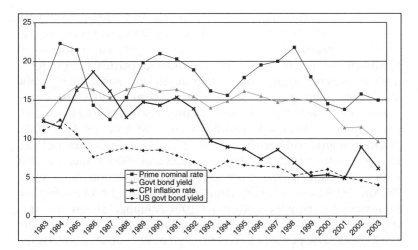

Figure VI.3   Interest rates and inflation, 1983–2003 (%)

importers, real interest rates were pushed up substantially – about 2.5 percentage points in 1996 and a full 7 percentage points in 1998 – to attract foreign portfolio flows back. In both crises, the rand eventually re-stabilised at levels about 20% below the pre-crisis level, and net inflows surged again, so that financial recovery was at the expense of domestic equilibrium (figures VI.1 and VI.2).

Late in the 1996 crisis, the GEAR policy statement was issued to restore (portfolio) investor credibility. It explicitly re-stated commitments to all three "trilemma" objectives: "consistent monetary policy to prevent a resurgence of inflation, ... [a nominal] exchange rate policy to keep the real effective rate stable at a competitive level, ... [and] a further step in the gradual relaxation of exchange controls", that is, an open capital account (Department of Finance 1996). After the 1998 crisis, in contrast, the costs of trying to maintain all three objectives and ignore the "trilemma" had become clear, and monetary and exchange rate policy shifted to a new phase. Capital account liberalization was not reconsidered, so that the choice lay between targeting the nominal exchange rate and maintaining monetary autonomy. Given the already heavy investment in low inflation and the perceived constraint of a large NOFP, the authorities unsurprisingly opted for the latter, abandoning efforts to target the nominal exchange rate, taking "a decisive decision ... to reduce the NOFP to zero" and establishing an inflation targeting regime, the "best practice" monetary policy according to the late-90s international consensus (Mboweni, 2004).

Inflation targeting was formally instituted in February 2000, with interest rate adjustments being the Reserve Bank's main policy instrument to meet the Minister of Finance's target. The institutional arrangements include mechanisms for broader participation (a semi-annual Monetary Policy Forum) and improved transparency (public statements after each meeting of the Bank's Monetary Policy Committee). The initial target was to bring inflation (the CPIX, excluding mortgage interest rates) within a range of 3–6% by April 2002. Inflation inertia had been broken by the mid-1990s and the CPI had dropped steadily from 10% between 1993 and 2000, helped by tariff liberalization and increased product market competition (figure VI.3). But the ZAR's nominal depreciation of 25% in late 2001 pushed price increases (especially for food) above 10%. Nominal interest rates had dropped from 1998 until 2000, before rising slightly during 2001, and the Reserve Bank pushed rates up through most of 2002 to address the uptick in inflation from late 2001. The absence of inflationary expectations meant the increase was a temporary blip, and by the second half of 2003, inflation was within the target band and interest rates were dropping.

Although the 2002 interest rate increase was the appropriate response within the inflation targeting regime, it was pro-cyclical rather than anti-cyclical; in other words, monetary policy destabilized the real economy. The rate hike coincided with the start of the strong ZAR appreciation, reinforcing the impact on output of the extreme exchange rate volatility from the last quarter of 2001. This underlines the rigidity of inflation targeting, which allows for monetary policy autonomy but focuses on a single objective, ignoring output and the need from time to time for rapid reflation to counter a cyclical downturn. Figure VI.2 illustrates the fluctuations of the real trade-weighted exchange rate: a gradual depreciation of 25% from late 1998 to August 2001 was followed by a sharp 25% depreciation until December 2001, and was itself followed by a 45% *appreciation* in the next 18 months up to mid-2003. Over the three years since mid-2001, the ZAR was one of the most volatile currencies in international markets.

According to the Finance Minister, "government has chosen to follow a flexible exchange rate to act as a shock absorber against global developments. Exchange rate adjustments help cushion the economy from external trade and capital shocks and mitigate the impact of economic contraction, especially for the poor" (Manuel, 2002). One problem is that any mitigating effect may be asymmetric – true for depreciations, but not appreciations – and also require that monetary policy act in concert. Further, the argument may hold only for adjustment from one "long-run equilibrium" position to another, in which the direction of capital flows remain stable allowing time for the offsetting effects of exchange rate adjustment to work themselves through. The situation since early 2001 cannot be described as a "shift between equilibria". The international financial markets have experienced increased turbulence since the dotcom bubble burst in April 2001, which was followed by "9/11", rising commodity prices, the war in Iraq, and the weakening of the US dollar. During this period, capital flow volatility has increased for South Africa, with five abrupt and large reversals between quarters during the subsequent two years: for example, an outflow of 0.4% of GDP in Q1:2003 was followed in Q2 by an inflow of 2.4% of GDP (South African Reserve Bank, 2003).

Capital inflows since 1994, including foreign borrowing by government, have allowed the rebuilding of the economy's "balance sheet": in February 2004, the NOFP was "closed out" and the Reserve Bank was no longer exposed to the risk of exchange rate depreciation. Foreign exchange reserves had reached secure levels by late 2002, with the help of capital inflows. This has certainly removed a "structural" constraint from macroeconomic policy and has contributed to the further upgrading of South Africa's credit rating by international agencies. The stronger financial basis is also reflected in the declining long-term bond yield and the narrowing of the differential between US and South African yields (figure VI.3). As a consequence, as in several Latin American countries in the early 1990s and again after the tequila crisis,[14] there have been repeated claims by the monetary and fiscal authorities that "overall macroeconomic stability has now been achieved" and economic policy should in future focus on "microeconomic reforms".

But it is hard not to conclude that macro policy has, intentionally or not, privileged financial concerns over output growth, and portfolio investment over fixed investment. Capital account openness has produced exchange rate volatility, which worsened after the explicit float since 1998, but throughout the decade has meant inconsistent signals from interest rates and exchange rates to producers of tradables, increasing uncertainty and encouraging "waiting" in production and investment decisions. Stability of domestic prices and in the fiscal accounts has been achieved only at the expense of external instability, and fluctuating aggregate demand.

[14] See Ffrench-Davis (2005) and ECLAC (2002).

4. Macroeconomic performance post-apartheid

Figure VI.4 illustrates the disappointing performance of GDP which, as noted earlier, averaged only 2.8% per annum between 1994 and 2003. The chart underlines that the economy is firmly trapped on a "low growth" path, with GDP growth reaching a peak of 4.3% during the period though still positive, in contrast to the experience during the 1980s and early 1990s when growth was negative during recessions. Reinforcing the impression of a shift in macroeconomic behavior, the chart also shows that the output gap – the difference between actual and potential output – has fluctuated within a narrow range since 1995 compared with the period since 1983. [15] Declines in output growth have not been associated with large drops in utilization, while stronger growth has not created pressure for higher utilization rates – the growth elasticity of utilization is low and the economy has not been operating close to full capacity notwithstanding the apparently small output gap. The underlying problem, reflecting a low growth "trap", is that the accelerator is weak: capital formation has not been strong enough to raise the growth rate of the capital stock above a paltry 1.25% *per annum* between 1994 and 2003, so that growth of potential output averaged a mere 2.1% per annum, which in turn has fed back into low rates of capital formation.[16]

The three foreign exchange shocks – in 1996, 1998 and 2001 – have not been reflected in a consistent manner in lower GDP growth or rising output gaps. In 1996, GDP growth rose, though the business cycle shifted into downswing late in the year and the growth rate dropped in 1997. In contrast, the 1998 crisis lowered growth for the year and widened the output gap, but there was a recovery the following year in GDP growth.[17] In 2001, growth declined notwithstanding a higher domestic activity level, but the currency appreciation in 2002 enabled a growth improvement. What is noteworthy is that different components of aggregate demand have "led" growth at different stages

---

[15] The output gap is based on the residual between the actual capital-output ratio and its polynomial trend line for 1967 to 2003. The depth of fluctuations in the curve is more important than the absolute size of the gap indicated on the scale.

[16] The marginal productivity of capital (incremental output-capital ratio) averaged 0.74 and the capital-output ratio 2.3.

[17] Though domestic utilization actually declined in 1999 as indicated by the small increase in the output gap, the GDP growth being driven by a strong increase in net exports.

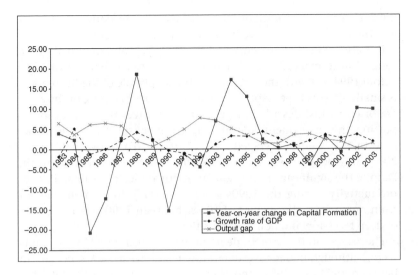

Figure VI.4 Growth in GDP, year-on-year change in real capital formation, average output gap, 1983–2003 (%)

of the cyclical fluctuations since 1994 – there has not been a stable "adjustment mechanism" to shocks.

We turn now to examine the behavior of key macroeconomic variables, looking in turn at fixed capital formation, national savings and the balance of payments.

a) Fixed capital formation

There was a brief spurt in fixed investment between 1993 and 1995 associated with the shift to democracy and the opening of the economy, but since 1996, capital formation has performed poorly. Figure VI.4 suggests that investment behavior has responded to volatile macroeconomic "prices" – exchange rates and interest rates – in the context of the foreign exchange shocks and policies used to address them.[18] In 1996 and 1997 and again in 1999, investment growth dropped following large depreciations and interest rate hikes exchange. In 2001, there was again a drop in investment, which was reversed in

[18] For discussion in the Latin American and Chilean context of the negative impact on fixed capital formation of an overemphasis on low inflation and fiscal discipline as the two macro policy goals, see Ffrench-Davis (2005, chs. II and IX).

2002 as currency appreciation lowered costs for imported equipment and the real interest rate declined due to higher inflation.

It is also evident from figure VI.4 that the cyclical response of capital formation to macroeconomic conditions is weaker than was the case before 1994 – as with the output gap, the amplitude of the fluctuations is smaller.[19] This is perhaps a consequence of a weakening of the accelerator effect just described. Figure VI.5 reinforces this impression by putting the investment *rate* in longer-run perspective. The private investment rate has averaged only 12.1% of GDP between 1994 and 2003, still below the rate in 1988 *after* the foreign debt standstill. Despite the significant improvement of private sector profitability and productivity during the 1990s (Nattrass, 2003), investment has not risen much from the average of 10.6% between 1990 and 1993, years of deep recession and political transition.

The "slack" in investment demand has not been filled by the public sector, although public investment rose in real terms by 9% per annum between 1994 and 1997, and from 3.7% to 4.7% of GDP. But when private fixed investment and GDP growth were slowing by 1998, the broad fiscal stance led to a slowdown of public investment. With several ups and downs, it remains well below its 1980s levels both in real terms and as a share of GDP. Additionally, since 1994 growth in investment in social infrastructure has been stronger than in economic infrastructure.

Beyond the impact on macroeconomic prices of policies oriented to financial concerns, the "muting" of the investment function seems to be related to low "animal spirits", a lack of "fundamental" investor confidence related to socio-political factors and the democratic transition. In recent surveys, firms operating in South Africa have cited problems of poverty and inequality like crime and disease (such as HIV/AIDS) as central discouragements to investment. They also report that investment is constrained by issues such as labor regulations or the tax regime. Together with the socio-economic factors, this suggests underlying anxiety about the security of property rights and about government commitment to a business-friendly operating environment (Gelb, 2001). Such uncertainty about the stability and predictability of the operating environment can severely retard fixed investment decisions, which involve longer time horizons and less reversible commitments than portfolio investments. Government has

---

[19] The figure shows total investment but a similar conclusion holds for private investment.

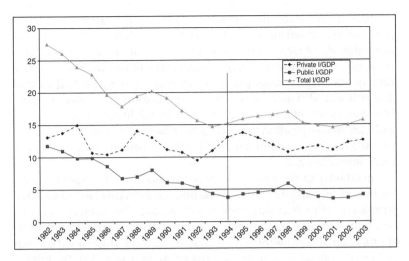

Figure VI.5   Fixed investment as share of GDP, 1982–2003 (%)

repeatedly dismissed these sentiments as reflecting racist bias towards the new black government on the part of white corporate decision-makers, but it remains the case that "credibility" of the policy framework in broad terms was not yet established, even a decade after the end of apartheid.

The broad-based nature of the ANC's political constituency and government's own actions – for example, the poor management of the GEAR policy statement – have made it difficult to rule out the prospect of a shift in the political balance within the ruling party leading to far-reaching policy changes. As noted earlier, GEAR's primary aim was to build investor credibility, though the emphasis on fiscal and domestic price stability was more likely to appeal to portfolio investors than productive investors. But government leaders actively excluded the ANC's labor allies from policy discussions both before and after the policy's publication, notwithstanding the crucial nature of the "announcement effect". When the statement was released in June 1996, senior government officials made a crude attempt to establish *bona fides* with international portfolio investors by describing the policy as a "home-grown version" of the Washington consensus and as "non-negotiable" with the trade unions. They also refused to discuss GEAR at the statutory tripartite National Economic Development and Labor Council (NEDLAC), notwithstanding that the labor movement was at the time deeply involved in policy consultations as such key areas as labor market regulation and trade liberalization. These tactics merely served to provoke the unions into hostile public opposition to GEAR. Political infighting about GEAR persisted within the alliance for over five years, irreparably damaging the image of unity within the alliance and reinforcing uncertainty about policy stability, particularly given the social and political "distance" between black politicians and white business. Whereas a show of union support for GEAR might have contributed to a picture of co-operation amongst government, business and labor and promoted investor confidence, GEAR's investment objectives were undermined instead.

Uncertainty in the broad investment environment has reinforced a "wait and see" attitude amongst individual investors, and obstructed firm-level policy strategies to raise investment. One strategy has been to try to overcome "co-ordination failure" amongst investors by communication and mobilization for collective action. Investment accords or social contracts have been debated at two national "economic summits", but these have not resulted in *binding* commitments on the "social partners"; that is, organized business and labor. Government has tried to unify business associations across racial, linguistic, regional and sectoral lines, and established high-level "presidential working groups" for domestic and foreign business. Regional corridors were identified as targets of focused public planning and financial resources, to overcome co-ordination failure by a "big push" effect,[20] identifying anchor projects (usually large capital-intensive materials processing plants) and attempting to "lock in" other investments through public-private dialogues.

Several investment incentives schemes have come and gone during the 1990s, though it is debatable whether these alter firms' decisions even in the absence of such inconsistency of instruments and targets. Early 1990s incentives focused on natural resource-based industrialization and cheap energy, supporting large capital- and energy-intensive plants. They were scrapped in 1993 but the focus continued through the Spatial Development Initiatives. A Tax Holiday Scheme was introduced in 1996 in the GEAR statement to provide incentives for employment creation and investment in specific regions, but withdrawn in 1999 due to low take-up rates. A general export incentive scheme (GEIS) was established in 1990 and halted in 1998, to be

---

[20] As advocated by Rosenstein-Rodan in his classic article "Problems of industrialisation in Eastern and South-eastern Europe" (1943) and adapted by Albert Hirschman in his *Strategy of Economic Development* (1958).

replaced by duty drawback programs for exporters, but only in two sectors: autos and apparel. Investment promotion agencies have been established to actively pursue potential projects, especially FDI. But as noted, new FDI since 1994 has disappointed, with gross inflows averaging $1.9 billion per annum between 1994 and 2002, while net inflows were 1.5% of the developing country total (UNCTAD, 2003). On a dollar per capita basis, FDI inflow was close to developing countries' average, though South Africa's per capita income is about 2.5 times the developing country average (Gelb and Black, 2004b).

b) Savings

South Africa's national savings averaged 15.8% of GDP since 1994, well below the average level of 20.8% between 1984 and 1993. South African policy since 1994 has been premised on a neo-classical view of the savings-investment relation. A key justification for the tight fiscal stance from 1993 was to raise government savings, which had become negative during the early 1990s spending spree, but have been above 2.5% since 1999. But household savings have averaged a mere 0.5% of GDP since 1994, compared with 3.5% between 1984 and 1993, and corporate savings have also dropped from 15.2% to 13.5%. However, it is doubtful that investment has been held back by lack of savings, since overall domestic savings have been sufficient to finance fixed capital formation (excluding changes in inventories) in all but two years since 1990. In addition, corporate savings have been adequate to finance corporate investment: the corporate sector (the major contributor to domestic savings) has had a financial surplus – an excess of sector savings over its own investment – between 1994 and 2000 and near-balance (tiny surpluses or deficits) since 2001.

It does not automatically follow that an investment increase would be unconstrained by lack of savings, however, since the savings propensity has not been stable, but appears to have dropped for both corporations and households over the past decade, so that income growth yields a smaller rise in the volume of savings than before. The corporate sector's savings has declined as a share of GDP since 1996, notwithstanding a rise in net profit as a share of GDP from 24.7% in the 1980s to 31.1% since 1994. This suggests that firms have increased dividend payouts to equity-owning households relative to retained earnings to fund investment. At the same time, households have been increasing consumption rather than savings. Household savings, which averaged 2.8% of GDP during the 1980s, were already very low in 1995 at just 1% of GDP, and have fallen to near zero since 1999. During the 1980s, falling household savings were linked to rising debt levels, as households borrowed to maintain both consumption levels and contractual savings (insurance and pension funds). But the links between household wealth, debt and savings shifted after 1993, as household wealth rose as a result of lower inflation and rising asset values, especially for housing. At the same time, trade liberalization encouraged higher consumption of imports. This led to a consumption spurt in the mid-1990s and further declines in household savings. Consumption growth continued to be strong during the late 1990s with the decline in interest rates from 1998, which meant household debt-to-assets ratios dropped further (Prinsloo, 2002).

c) The balance of payments

Since 1994, South Africa has returned to the "normal" developing economy situation with a current account deficit and net capital inflows, compared with the debt standstill period between 1985 and 1993, when foreign savings were negative. Figure VI.6 shows that the current account deficit (the contribution of foreign savings to overall savings) has remained very small since 1994, never rising above 2% of GDP, and since 1999, more or less in balance. The figure supports the "Keynesian" view that investment is constrained not by lack of savings, but by the issues of confidence and macroeconomic instability: had investment levels warranted it, a larger current account deficit could have been financed by net capital inflows notwithstanding their volatility. Instead, capital inflows in excess of the external deficit have been used to build foreign reserves.

Both non-gold exports and imports have risen by around 50% since 1993. The volume of imports grew very rapidly until 1997 in the wake of trade liberalization but levelled off thereafter, as slower output growth limited imports of investment goods. Non-gold exports have risen more steadily, and the improvement in export performance – partly driven by currency depreciation – reflects a major post-1994 shift, particularly given the increased share of manufacturing exports compared with primary commodities. Gold exports and output have undergone long-term decline (IMF, 2004a). Including the small non-factor services deficit, the trade balance has been in surplus, averaging just over 1% of GDP between 1995 and 1998 but then rising to 3% since 1999. The factor services deficit has been a persistent failure in the balance of payments for decades, and rose from 1.9% of GDP in

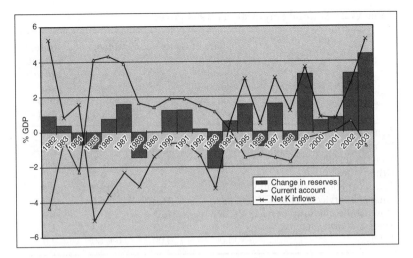

Figure VI.6   Balance of payments, 1982–2003 (% of GDP)

1995 to 2.6% in 2000, driven by profit and dividend outflows in part due to the relocation to the UK and US of the head offices of several major South African corporations.

5. Employment and the composition of growth

As noted in the introduction, South Africa's (broad) rate of unemployment was 41.8% in 2003, and the prospects for lowering the similarly high level of poverty depend to a large extent on the creation of jobs. Performance in this respect has been as dismal as growth. A careful assessment of the increase in employment between 1995 and 2003 suggests that about 1.4 million jobs were created in a labor force that was estimated to be 13.6 million people in 1995, of whom 4 million (29.4%) were unemployed (Casale, *et al.*, 2004). But the size of the labor force was certainly undercounted in 1995, as in 2003 it was estimated at 20.3 million people. Of the new jobs, more than half represent work in subsistence agriculture, informal sector self-employment or domestic service.

The low growth of overall employment has been exacerbated by changes in the sectoral composition of output and of trade, which have resulted in a "skills twist" within the labor force. In every sector except construction, employment of highly-skilled workers has grown since 1985 while employment of unskilled workers has declined. Table VI.2

Table VI.2   Sectoral output shares, 1995 prices

	Share of Gross Value Added, percent			Annual output growth rate, 1990–
	1990	1994	2003	2003
Agriculture	5.0	5.0	4.0	0.3
Mining	7.3	7.4	5.5	–0.2
Manufacturing	22.0	20.5	19.8	1.2
Other industry	6.9	6.7	6.7	1.7
Transport and communication	7.9	8.3	12.2	5.5
Financial services	15.6	16.3	19.6	3.8
Govt. and community services	16.0	16.5	13.7	1.0
Trade and other services	19.4	19.3	19.3	1.7
Total	100.00	100.00	100.00	2.0

Source: South African Reserve Bank (2004).

shows that the shares in output of both mining and manufacturing declined, together with "other industry" (construction and utilities), while transport and communications and financial services grew strongly. Within manufacturing, there were also output composition shifts. Labour-intensive sectors (food and beverages, textiles and clothing and footwear) grew slowly at around 0.2% per annum, declining from 23% of manufacturing value-added in 1990 to 20% in 2000. Capital-intensive materials-processing industries – basic metals, wood products and chemicals – were the fastest-growing sectors: basic metals and wood products each grew by more than 4% per annum and increasing their shares of manufacturing value-added to 16% and 3.9% respectively (Kaplan, 2003).

The shift to more capital-intensive sectors was linked to trade and trade policy. Import penetration in labour-intensive sectors rose from 55.5% to 67.5% between 1993 and 1997, squeezing domestic output and employment (Edwards, 1999). A significant change took place in the sectoral composition of exports between 1990 and 2003; in particular, there was a shift from minerals to basic processed goods (chemicals and plastics, wood products and basic metals) and to machinery and equipment, though the latter has been dominated by basic vehicle components, comprised of processed natural resources (Black, 2002).

Before the shift to a more export-oriented trade policy, the manufacturing capital stock was dominated by capital-intensive materials-processing: in 1988, chemicals comprised 29.8% of the total stock, iron and steel and non-ferrous metals 19.2%, and paper and non-metallic minerals each more than 6%, together nearly 62%. Thus a World Bank analysis concluded in 1992 that "the industrial policy of the past four decades ... [has] helped create competitive capability in relatively capital-intensive activities, so these activities would disproportionately be the beneficiaries [of a package of outward-oriented policies]. ... South African manufacturing might be an engine of growth, but not of (direct) employment creation" (Levy, 1992). Although most studies of South Africa's trade liberalization have concluded that employment losses have been due to technological change to enhance export competitiveness, rather than trade liberalization and increased import penetration (Edwards, 1999; International Labour Organisation, 1999), it remains true that "South Africa has a low and declining share of exports that use unskilled labour, and a high share using more skilled labour" (Lewis, 2001).

6. Conclusion

This chapter asked at the outset whether the reduction in the fiscal deficit and the rate of price inflation which have been achieved in South Africa during the past decade can be taken to represent macroeconomic "success", given the volatility in the external accounts over the same period, and asked also whether this "success", if it be so judged, came at too high a price in the form of low growth of output and employment.

The chapter has answered the first question in the negative and the second in the affirmative. But it is fair to ask, in conclusion, whether it is too early to define answers, and whether in any event there were alternatives to the approach adopted. The first question is particularly pressing, since by the end of 2004 many believed the South African economy had "turned the corner" and established itself on a higher growth path. Between 1999 and 2003, growth averaged 2.9% per annum, but it rose to 3.7% in 2004. Macro prices have also "recovered" as the ZAR has steadily but slowly appreciated in nominal terms since early 2002, the effective and the US dollar rates both returning to their levels of late 1999/early 2000. The currency risk premium on South African bonds declined by over 100 basis points during 2004, and domestic nominal interest rates dropped from 17% at end-2002 to 11% two years later.

These favorable shifts in macroeconomic prices have boosted domestic expenditure, including household consumption, over 2003–04. Two additional factors have been significant in contributing to the growth upturn and more optimistic perceptions. The first is the global commodity price boom, which resulted in earnings from metals and minerals exports rising 12.5% in 2004 notwithstanding the strong ZAR, and these products' share of total exports to 58% (2002: 47%). The second is the rapid growth of the black middle class, in large part as a consequence of "Black Economic Empowerment" (BEE), affirmative action policies which have been increasingly assertive since 1999. This group's presence in managerial and professional positions has increased rapidly during the decade since the end of apartheid, and the share of black people in the middle class is now estimated to be about 55%, compared with a quarter at the start of the 1990s. The incomes of this group have increased rapidly, linked to their access to both higher salaries than in a competitive market as well as to equity in corporations (their own employers and others) which are increasingly required to diversify their ownership. There is also considerable pent-up demand within this group for housing and consumer durables, given their exclusion from the suburbs under apartheid and the rapid upward mobility in their social status. This has contributed to substantial increases in nominal housing prices during 2004 – a rise of 35% in some South African cities – resulting in a wealth effect further fuelling demand, so that household consumption expenditure grew 5.9% during 2004 (notwithstanding the poverty and unemployment numbers). But this consumption-led growth has sucked in imports, which grew nearly 10% in 2003, and 15% in 2004.

With memories of the tequila crisis in Mexico in 1994 and the Argentinean crisis of 2001, Latin American analysts will immediately question the sustainability of the growth process described here. As discussed earlier, there has been a significant drop in private savings, and the downward shift in corporate and household savings propensities is linked to long-term increases in import and tax propensities, rather than reflecting a temporary adjustment to the opening of the economy and the establishment of democracy. This points to the limits of consumption-led growth, since private savings may not respond strongly to rising income if investment were to increase, which would augment reliance on foreign savings, and result in "stop-go" cycles associated with capital flows volatility. Raising investment is of course a separate problem, and the discussion above has shown that capital formation stayed flat even while export demand increased from 1999. Whether investment will respond to the growth in consumption is similarly moot, but the BEE policies which are driving the latter are also producing a progressive "blackening" of business which over time should help resolve the democratization dilemma facing investment by building government's policy credibility in the corporate sector.

None of this addresses capital flow volatility and its monetary and exchange rate consequences. There is a disturbing lack of public debate about this aspect of macroeconomic policy. In early 2004, a short-lived outburst of opposition to the growth and employment impact of high interest rates and ZAR overvaluation elicited little reaction and soon died out, notwithstanding that the voices raised included once-powerful mining and manufacturing interests. Real interest rates have since declined, but remain very high comparatively, and there is widespread consensus – amongst observers concerned with real growth rates – that an exchange rate around ZAR6.00 per dollar is overvalued by as much as 50%. A more enduring solution to the problem is required. The central bank has recently expressed the view that volatility is "a fact of life beyond its control", emphasising its unwillingness to reintroduce capital flow regulations. This leaves government on the one hand desperately looking for larger direct investment inflows, and on the other seeking global responses to capital flow volatility, and neither route is very promising in the short to medium term.

Appendix

Table A. Population

	1991	2001
Total population (millions)	36.2	44.5
Population groups (% of total):		
African	70	79
White	16.5	9.5
Colored	10.5	9
Indian	3	2.5

Sources: Statistics SA, *South African Statistics 2002; 2001 Census in Brief.*
Note: Population growth rate was 2.0% *per annum* between 1991 and 2001.

Table B.   South Africa: Indicators of millennium development goals

	Early 1990s	Post-2000
a. GDP, current US$ bn	112.0[90]	159.9[03]
b. GDP per capita 1995 US$	4082[90]	4013[02]
c. GDP per capita, current PPP US$	8282[90]	9401[00]
d. Human Development Index	0.69[96]	0.695[00]
e. Life expectancy at birth (years)	62[90]	47[02]
f. Under 5 mortality rate (per 1000 live births)	73[90]	65[02]
g. Adult literacy rate (% of people 15 and over)	81.2[90]	86.0[02]
h. Net primary enrolment rate (% of age group)	103[91]	89[01]
i. Urbanization (% of population)	53.7[96]	56.1[00]

Sources:
a, c, e, f, g, i: World Bank, *World Development Indicators*;
b: SA Reserve Bank, www.sarb.co.za;
d: Statistics SA *Human Development Index* (2001);
h: Development Bank of Southern Africa, *South Africa: Inter-Provincial Comparative Report* (2000).
Note: The superscript indicates the year to which the data applies.

References

Black, A. (2002), "The export 'success' of the Motor Industry Development Programme and the implications for trade and industrial policy", paper presented at TIPS Annual Forum. www.tips.org.za

Casale, D., C. Muller and D. Posel (2004), "'Two million net new jobs': A reconsideration of the rise in employment in South Africa, 1995–2003", paper presented at TIPS/DPRU Conference. www.tips.org.za

Crankshaw, O. and D. Hindson (1990), "Class differentiation under apartheid", in *South African Labour Bulletin*, 15(1).

Department of Finance, South Africa (1996), *Growth Employment and Redistribution (GEAR)*, Pretoria.

ECLAC (2002), *Growth with Stability*, CEPAL books, Santiago.

Edwards, L. (1999), "Trade Liberalisation, Structural Change and Occupational Employment in South Africa", paper presented at TIPS Annual Forum. www.tips.org.za

Eichengreen, B. (2000), "Taming capital flows", *World Development*, 28 (6).

Ffrench-Davis, R. (2005), *Reforming Latin Americas' Economies: After Market Fundamentalism*, Palgrave Macmillan, London.

Ffrench-Davis, R. and L. Villar (2005), "Real macroeconomic stability and the capital account in Chile and Colombia", in this volume.

Gelb, S. (1998), "The Political Economy of Macroeconomic Reform in South Africa", Conference on *The Political Economy of Reform in South Africa*, University of Cape Town. www.tips.org.za

Gelb, S. (2001), "Socio-political risk, confidence and firm investment in South Africa", paper for CSAE/UNIDO Workshop on *New Industrial Realities and Firm Behaviour in Africa*, Oxford.

Gelb, S. (2003), "Addressing Inequality in South Africa: Nature, Causes and Responses", Seminar on *Addressing Inequality in Middle Income Countries*, UK Development for International Development, London.

Gelb, S. and A. Black (2004a), "South African case studies", in S. Estrin and K. Meyer (eds.), *Investment Strategies in Emerging Markets*, Edward Elgar, Cheltenham, UK.

Gelb, S. and A. Black (2004b), "Globalisation in a middle-income economy: FDI, production and the labour market in South Africa", in W. Milberg (ed.), *Labor and the Globalization of Production*, Macmillan, London.

Hoogeveen, J. and B. Ozler (2004), "Not separate, not equal: Poverty and inequality in post-apartheid South Africa", mimeo, World Bank.

International Labour Organisation (ILO) (1999), *Studies on the social dimensions of globalization: South Africa*, Geneva.

IMF (1997), *South Africa: Selected Issues*, Staff Country Report 97/82.

IMF (2004a), *International Financial Statistics* http://www.imf.org, accessed March 20.

IMF (2004b), *South Africa: Selected Issues*, Staff Country Report 04/379.

Jenkins, C. and N. Siwisa (1997), "Overview of trade policy in South Africa", paper presented at TIPS Annual Forum. www.tips.org.za

Kaplan, D. (2003), "Manufacturing Performance and Policy in South Africa: A Review", paper presented at TIPS Annual Forum. www.tips.org.za

Levy, B. (1992), "How can South African manufacturing efficiently create employment? An analysis of the impact of trade and industrial policy", World Bank informal discussion papers on aspects of the South African economy, 1.

Lewis, J. D. (2001), "Policies to promote growth and employment in South Africa", World Bank informal discussion papers on aspects of the South African economy, 16.

Manuel, T. (2002), "Closing remarks to the Commission of Inquiry into the Rapid Depreciation of the Exchange Rate of the Rand", May 24, National Treasury http://www.finance.gov.za.

Mboweni, T. (2004), "Announcement regarding the Foreign Forward Exchange Book", South African Reserve Bank media release 2004-03-01 http://www.reservebank.co.za.

National Treasury, South Africa (2004), *Budget Review*, Pretoria.

Nattrass, N. (2003), "The state of the economy: A crisis of employment", in J. Daniel, A. Habib and R. Southall (eds.), *The State of the Nation: South Africa, 2003–2004*, HSRC Press, Cape Town.

Obstfeld, M. (1998), "The global capital market: benefactor or menace?", *Journal of Economic Perspectives*, 12(4).

Presidency, South Africa (2003), *Towards a Ten Year Review: Synthesis Report on Implementation of Government Programmes*, Discussion Document, Pretoria.

Prinsloo, J. W. (2002), "Household debt, wealth and saving", *Quarterly Bulletin*, 226, South African Reserve Bank.

Ros, J. (2001), "From the capital surge to the financial crisis and beyond: The Mexican economy in the 1990s", in R. Ffrench-Davis (ed.), *Financial Crises in "Successful" Emerging Economies*, Brookings Institution/ECLAC, Washington, DC.

South African Reserve Bank (2003), *Quarterly Bulletin* 229, Pretoria.
South African Reserve Bank (2004), *Online Statistical and Economic Time Series* http://www.reservebank.co.za.
South African Revenue Service (1998), *Annual Report,* Pretoria.
South African Revenue Service (2003), *Annual Report,* Pretoria.
Stals, C. (1994), "Governor's address at the ordinary general meeting of shareholders", SA Reserve Bank, Pretoria.
Stals, C. (1995), "Governor's address at the ordinary general meeting of shareholders", SA Reserve Bank, Pretoria.
Stals, C. (1996), "Governor's address at the ordinary general meeting of shareholders", SA Reserve Bank, Pretoria.
Stals, C. (1998), "Governor's address at the ordinary general meeting of shareholders", SA Reserve Bank, Pretoria.
Statistics SA (2004), *Labour Force Survey,* Statistical release P0210, March.
UNCTAD (2003), *World Investment Report,* Geneva.
Van der Berg, S. (2001), "Trends in Racial Fiscal Incidence in South Africa", *South African Journal of Economics,* 69: 2.
World Bank (2003), *Global Development Finance 2003: Striving for Stability in Development Finance,* Washington, DC.

Index

absorptive capacity 4, 19, 119
actual growth performance 9–11
adjustment process 11–12, 19
  Chile 91, 92–3
  Korea 173–81
  Malaysia 173–81
AFP (Private Pension Funds in Chile)
  61, 67–76, 79–80, 82–93
African National Congress 184,
  187–92, 207
aggregate demand 18–19, 21–4, 55, 160
  Chile 86, 96, 114–15, 123
  Colombia 96, 114–15, 123
  South Africa 192, 203, 204
American depository receipts (ADRs)
  8, 116, 130
animal spirits 206
announcement effect 192, 207
apartheid (South Africa) 184–216
arbitrage 74, 78, 92, 107, 110
Argentina 3, 21, 25, 28, 36, 40, 48, 65,
  214
Asian crisis 12, 23–4, 34, 37, 192
  Chile 72, 74, 81, 86, 92, 97, 106,
    109, 117, 118, 125, 131–2,
    134
  Colombia 97, 106, 111, 118, 131–2,
    134
  Korea 139–40, 143, 150, 159, 173–5
  Malaysia 139–40, 153–5, 159, 173–5
Asian Development Bank 3, 14, 26,
  136, 149, 165
asset management 166, 171
automatic destabilizers 35
automatic stabilizers 161

balance of payments 61, 62
  Chile 67, 78, 84
  Malaysia 167–8
  South Africa 186, 210–11
Banco de la República (Colombia)
  105, 110–13, 117, 121, 129, 131
Bank of England 166

Bank for International Settlements
  124
Bank of Korea 142, 145, 147, 149–50,
  163, 164, 166
Bank Negara Malaysia 153, 154, 156,
  167
banking sector 62
  Chile 68–9, 78–9, 85
  Korea 141–2, 164–5
  Malaysia 152, 159, 169–72, 182
  South Africa 190, 199
bantustans 193
base lending rate 169
basic needs approach 188
big bang approach 181, 189, 198
"big push" effect 208
Black Economic Empowerment
  214–15
Bolivia 48
bonds 63, 165, 199
  Chile 65–6, 72, 74–5, 80–2, 85–6,
    88, 90, 91–2
  corporate 64, 66, 90
  indexed 65–6, 72, 80, 90
  long-term 65–6, 74–5, 90
boom-bust cycles 2, 8–9, 11–15, 38–9
  see also counter-cyclical behavior;
    procyclical behavior
Brazil 3, 10, 36, 42–3, 48, 65, 112–13
Bretton Woods system 186, 189
Britain 9
budget deficit 22, 33, 34, 161–2
Bundesbank 191
business cycles 2, 8–9, 11, 35, 39, 204

call options 112
capital
  accumulation 38, 55
  flight 163, 181, 186
  -output ratios 36, 37
  physical 24, 33
  -rich economies 3–5
  -scarce economies 3–5